Covering China

Covering China

*The Story of an American Reporter
from Revolutionary Days to the Deng Era*

John Roderick

Imprint Publications
Chicago
1993

For Yochan

Library of Congress Catalog Card Number 93-061153
ISBN 1-879176-18-1 (Cloth)
ISBN 1-879176-17-3 (Paper)

Printed in the United States of America

"Mr. Roderick, you opened the door"—Premier Zhou Enlai, the Great Hall of the People, Beijing, April 12, 1971

Contents

Preface

In the late fall of 1945 a very young and very new Associated Press correspondent named John Roderick got off a U.S. military plane at the bleak airport of Yan'an, to start reporting on the then virtually unknown Chinese Communists. An AP reporter before the war, he rejoined the American news agency in West China, in the closing months of the conflict, where he had served with the OSS, the wartime predecessor of the CIA. In his first month as a foreign correspondent, based in Chongqing, he met Chiang Kai-shek and Zhou Enlai, the Nationalist and Communist leaders. Later, he spent seven months in Yan'an, the Communist capital. As the only American reporter there, he lived with and interviewed the Chinese leadership, from Mao Zedong on down. His reminiscences of that time are extraordinarily clear-sighted and valuable. Probably no American had the chance to meet and appraise Communist China's future leadership over such a long period of time.

If Roderick were doing nothing but relating his reminiscences about the beginnings of China's still continuing postwar revolution, his recollections would be of intrinsic value. But this book goes far beyond old correspondents' reminiscences. For Roderick, unlike most of the American observers at that time, stuck with the job. From his wartime reporting in Chongqing, through years of China-watching in Hong Kong and Tokyo, then reporting the first American and Japanese visits to China in early 1970s—until the time he reopened the old AP Bureau in Deng Xiaoping's Beijing in 1979, Roderick lived the history he is writing. A man whose shrewd insights belie his relaxed Down-East manner—he still keeps a vestigial Maine accent—Roderick is a walking ad for fair and thoughtful reporting. His book offers a fascinating vision, from the perspective of almost half a century, at how China's leaders rose and fell and, variously, grew or diminished in stature. Roderick is an equally good analyst of Japan, from his years as a reporter and Special Correspondent, one of only seven in AP, in Tokyo—and he has had his share of reporting in the United States and Europe—but China has remained the object of his concentration.

When I first went to China in 1979, and met Deng and other members of the Party hierarchy, I was overwhelmed at the suddenness of the post-Mao changes and concerned for yardsticks to evaluate it. John Roderick's apartment in Beijing was one place where you could clear out both the cobwebs of reminiscences and the immediacy of first impressions, to reach a good evaluation of what was going on. I was not the only reporter who gained from John's insights. Through the years he has been characteristically generous in sharing his knowledge with others—an attribute not frequently found among prominent American newsmen.

Covering China is a very special book. It is written by a man who carries his authority gently, but has no compunction about evaluating people and their times. The unique value of the book is his ability to come back at his subjects and see them from the perspective of changing times. The writing of many veteran China watchers has been dominated by their fixed points of view. Many were taken in by the Communists' propaganda—the servile description of China's Great Proletarian Cultural Revolution (1966-1976) by sympathetic American visitors is a case in point. Others let their appraisals of people and events be influenced by a kind of automatic anti-communism. Roderick has never fallen into either of these extremes. He writes his history fairly. In addition, he leavens his reports with an unfailing sense of humor—another commodity generally not found in American authorities on China.

The wire service reporter traditionally suffers from deadline trauma. Because of the desperate need to get all the news as quickly as possible—and get ahead of the competition—his literary conventions often suffer. Roderick himself amusingly recounts his disappointment, when his hope for an interview with Franklin D. Roosevelt turned into the need to monopolize the telephone, talking to the AP office—preempting the line for a senior reporter who would take over and telephone in the story. Nonetheless, the virtue of the wire service reporter is that he builds up an extraordinary fund of information and an insatiable appetite for facts. When this is combined with a capacity to write interestingly and evaluate events fairly, you have a very happy result—which you can see in the pages of Roderick's book.

Anyone who reads this book will come out more knowledgeable and wiser about the Chinese Revolution—the great and still exploding cultural, political, and economic phenomenon of our times. The reader will also learn to appreciate Roderick's firm grip on his subject and the historical perspective that can come from almost a half century of straight, honest reporting.

Frank Gibney
August 1993

1

China Discovered

I was 13 when I discovered, in a brutal way, the existence of China. Of course, I knew it was there—a vaguely perceived, densely populated country where human life was cheap. But it meant nothing to me, nothing that I could relate to. If you had told me that forty-four years later Zhou Enlai, its Communist premier, would announce that "Mr. Roderick, you opened the door," I would have laughed in your face. My overweening interest at that age was candy bars and milk shakes earned from caddying at the country club in Waterville, the central Maine town where I was born.

The moment of revelation came in 1927 when one of the golfers, an engineer just back from a visit to Shanghai, proudly showed us the snapshots he had taken there. I looked at them and felt sick. They showed, in black and white, death by beheading. The victims looked like students or young workers, some not much older than myself. Their hair close-cropped, their clothes baggy, they neither struggled nor grimaced but stared straight ahead as the heavy swords fell on their necks. The eyes of the severed heads were closed, the mouths twisted in the rictus of death. A faint, astonished smile hovered on the lips of one of them.

The memory of these starkly realistic pictures remains like a scar on my subconscious. I think of them almost always when the subject of China comes up in my reading, my thoughts, and my conversations. They recur, like a haunting leitmotif, at strange and unpredictable moments in my life. From 1945, when I began reporting on the unfolding revolution there, these photos have symbolized for me the pain, the drama, and the tragedy of China. I suppose that despite many intensely happy years among the Chinese, I will carry this dark memory to my grave.

China was not otherwise much on my mind as I grew up in Waterville, a mill and college city of 15,000 on the Kennebec River. The only Chinese in this elm-shaded community of Yankees and

French immigrants were two families, one running a hand laundry, the other a Chinese restaurant whose chicken chow mein and chop suey were prized by the after-the-movie-crowd as the definitive Chinese cuisine.

At 15 I became a reporter on the *Sentinel*, the local daily, and at 16 an orphan when first my mother then my father died. From my father—tall, handsome, and feckless—I inherited a pair of new brown shoes, which fitted perfectly, and a love of travel and adventure. I was barely a year old when he left his wife and five small boys to disappear into the wilds of Alaska. No one knew where he had been until he returned in his coffin fifteen years later.

I did the city hall beat, attended the green peas and rubber-chicken luncheons of the Lions, Rotary, and Kiwanis Clubs, and covered high school and college sports and other social events during my first years on the *Sentinel*. Murders were my specialty, described in a prose beside which purple paled. My first big interview was with the boxer, Jack Dempsey, a gentle giant who I will always remember as the soul of kindness; he abandoned a cocktail party to spend an hour with me in his hotel room while *le tout* Waterville waited.

Colby College, from which I with difficulty graduated—studying interfered with what I regarded as my infinitely more valuable experience as a reporter—had no courses either in journalism or in Chinese. If they had had (they do now) I might have been better prepared to cope with the Chinese Revolution years later.

I joined the Associated Press (AP) in Portland a few months later and, in August 1941, helped report the story of the Atlantic Charter Conference, an event which rudely reminded me of the imminence of war. The Charter, the stepping stone for the postwar United Nations, spelled out the principles in which the United States and Great Britain believed. Hammered out in a secret meeting between President Franklin D. Roosevelt and British Prime Minister Winston Churchill, it was part of the psychological preparation for the conflict just ahead.

AP assigned me, Douglas Cornell of the White House staff, and Alex Singleton of Boston to cover FDR's arrival from Halifax, Nova Scotia, in Rockland on the Maine coast. As it turned out, I did little but learned the true meaning of humility.

It is unfashionable these days to have heroes, but in 1941 Roosevelt was mine. Besides having taken up arms against a sea of personal and economic troubles he had led the Democratic Party, in which I believed, out of the wilderness into the promised lands in the state and national capitals. No Moses could have been more popular with me and my friends.

Arriving in Rockland early, I eagerly looked forward to meeting the great man during his press conference aboard the presidential yacht. Minutes before it began, Cornell took me aside.

"John," he said, "I hate to ask you, but would you mind hanging onto the phone during the press conference? I don't want anyone else to get it."

It was more a command than a question but, despite my all-too-evident disappointment I saw its logic. A wire agency man without a telephone is naked. Worse. He is dead.

While everyone else basked in the glow of FDR's wit and the knowledge that they had a story of paramount importance, I talked drivel to the Boston bureau which was standing by to take Cornell's report.

A tall, handsome fellow with years of experience covering American presidents, Cornell emerged from the historic press conference at a run, seized the phone and, reading from notes in a small notebook, dictated flawlessly for an hour.

While he talked, I leaned out the window and saw an extraordinary sight. Unseen by the thousands milling outside—a high wooden fence concealed the pier area—the stricken president walked, or rather inched, down the yacht's ramp on the arms of his son Elliot and an aide. By common consent, American newspapers never referred to the polio which had crippled him years before. Photographers refrained from taking photos of the leg braces which allowed him, with help, to hobble short distances.

Reaching his specially built automobile, after what seemed to me an agonizing age, he shook off his helpers and flung himself onto the floor at its rear. It shocked me to see the most powerful man on earth on his hands and knees, scrambling like a child to reach the solid security of the rear seat. Reaching up, he grasped the metal bars installed for that purpose inside, and with a lunge of his powerful arms and shoulders pulled himself up. No one in the presidential party paid any attention. They had seen this many times before. Once in place, FDR pulled out his long cigarette holder, inserted a cigarette into it, clamped his old fedora on his head and signaled he was ready. The doors of the walled pier area swung open and the vast crowd, aware of none of this, cheered as the beaming president, his holder at a jaunty angle, a broad smile on his face, waved and nodded. He was the perfect showman.

Afterwards, I rode with the others for several miles on the presidential train but I never did meet my idol.

Singleton, later a correspondent in Yugoslavia, did the overnight story. I did nothing except hold the phone.

Gathered around the hotel bar that night the subject of journalism schools came up. They were new then and not popular with some editors. I said emphatically they were no substitute for experience. The silence which followed was ominous.

"Where," I asked Cornell, "did you study?"

"The Missouri School of Journalism," he replied.

"And you?" I asked Singleton, already sure of the reply.

"Boston College Journalism School," he said. "And you?"

"Colby College," I replied lamely. "We didn't believe in journalism schools."

I tell this story because four years later, months after Roosevelt's death, these events recurred to me in a dream as I debated whether to return to Washington from West China or to stay and become a foreign correspondent. In the dream, repeated obsessively for a week, I drank dry martinis with an urbane FDR aboard his presidential train while he gave me an exclusive interview. I remembered none of what he said and the pencil with which I took notes had no lead. Freudian or otherwise, it persuaded me to stay, perhaps to demonstrate to myself that I could do something more than hold the phone. It was a preoccupation which lasted for forty years overseas.

Back in Portland, I stood over the AP teletype machine on December 7 of that year as it clacked out the news of the Japanese attack on Pearl Harbor. Reading it, I thought with a pang that my life, in some not yet decipherable way, had changed.

In 1942, AP sent me to Washington, a wartime capital more preoccupied with the European battlefield than that of China and the rest of Asia. Six months later, the Army claimed me and, because the sight of my left eye was impaired, stuck me out of harm's way—theirs and mine—in an old Civil War fortress in Virginia called Fort Monroe. A year later it pulled me out of there on the mysterious ground that I could speak French and moved me to Yale University. It turned out that the War Department, already planning the defeat of Japan and Germany, wanted to build up a pool of engineers, language officers, and others with skills needed for the military occupation of those enemy countries. It reasoned, dubiously, that if anyone already spoke a language, he could master Japanese or German. A flush-faced Irish captain from Boston formed us into a company on the famous Quadrangle and told us we had been chosen to study either Chinese or Japanese.

"Alright men!" he bellowed. "First three ranks move two paces left, next three two paces right. All those on my left will study Japanese, those on my right Chinese. Com-pa-ny dismissed!"

Well fed and luxuriously installed in an apartment in Trumbull College, I studied Japanese with the help of some very distinguished Japanese interned for the duration and only too glad to avoid imprisonment. The nationwide training program, called the Army Specialized Training Program (ASTP), halted suddenly without any explanation eight months later. Those in the top third of their class were allowed to continue their studies but, though I qualified, my failing eyesight ruled me out.

I had picked up only a smattering of spoken Japanese and no reading or writing at all, but one of the benefits from those eight months was that I learned a good deal about modern Chinese and Japanese history. During the history course I finally discovered who the young Chinese victims were in the execution photographs shown to me in 1927. It turned out that they were Communist students and leftist workers rounded up after Nationalist Generalissimo Chiang Kai-shek, strapped for money and already resentful of their growing power, brutally broke relations with his Communist allies. Besides being beheaded, shot, and bayonetted, the unlucky victims were crammed into the red hot boilers of steam locomotives. This additional knowledge did not convince me that China was a pleasant place in which to live.

Back in army ranks, this time at Camp Edwards, Mass., I learned that a visiting major was looking for French speakers. Persuaded that the ASTP was about to reopen its doors, I presented myself to him. After a half hour of close questioning, he leaned forward and asked:

"Sergeant, are you interested in a dangerous and hazardous mission overseas?"

I protested weakly that I might not be in the best shape for anything so rigorous but he smiled and handed me a set of official forms to fill out.

Nine months later, after having forgotten about it, I got a telegram ordering me, without explanation, to report to a "temporary" office building in Washington, D.C. Arriving at night, I found it dark. In a barracks at the rear a score of tough, old first sergeants and master sergeants were playing poker. After checking in I asked one of them where I was.

"You'll find out," he grunted and turned back to his game.

Next day, reporting in the now alive office building, I was directed to a room where a full-bird colonel smiled up at me. He seized my hand as I attempted a smart military salute, shook it vigorously, beckoned me to a chair, and offered me a cigarette.

"Welcome aboard, John," he said heartily. "You may have been wondering what it was all about but you are now a member of the OSS. With any luck, you should be in West China within three months."

Created in the early days of World War II, the OSS, or Office of Strategic Services, carried out espionage, black propaganda, and sabotage activities usually behind enemy lines. Headed by General "Wild Bill" Donovan, a New York lawyer and two-time Medal of Honor winner, it parachuted agents and saboteurs into France before D-Day, tying down five German divisions.

"Do you recall your interview eight months ago with the major who was looking for French speakers?" he asked.

I nodded.

"Well, we were looking for agents to drop into France before the invasion. You missed out on that little show. But we thought your Japanese might prove useful in our China operation, and so here you are."

He smiled and I wondered to myself how I might have managed in occupied France with a loaf of bread, a jug of wine, and a radio transmitter. Though the operation had been a success, the OSS casualties were high.

In the Washington of 1943, little was known of the genuinely significant achievements of the OSS. Because its agents often could be met at posh cocktail parties it earned the derisive nickname, "Oh So Social." Donovan's reputation and the exploits of its men in the field inspired another. It was, "Oh So Suicidal."

After more than two years of being treated by the Army as a potential enemy not to be told the least bit of confidential information, the OSS struck me as recklessly easy-going and careless. For one thing, it entertained the highly unmilitary idea that we were adults and could be trusted. Troop movements were known in the Army only to a handful of top officers. But the affable OSS colonel did not hesitate to tell me, a mere sergeant, that I soon would be in faraway West China. I like to think that no ships were torpedoed or planes shot down because I was privy to this secret but I am not really sure.

After volunteering this bit of news to me, the colonel added:

"While you're waiting, would you mind checking out a funny little school we have here. You might find it amusing. Let me know what you think."

"Amusing" was a word the colonel used a good deal.

The "school" in question turned out to be more than a little so. Situated in an estate in Virginia, donated for the duration by a wealthy Washington hotelier, its objective was to weed out any of us it found emotionally or psychologically unfit to spy, lie, or kill for the United States of America. It determined this through an intensive four days and nights of testing by a team of thirteen psychiatrists, one of them a woman. I arrived there dressed in battle fatigue in the back of a military truck along with eleven other "candidates." They included a foreign service officer, a Marine general, an Army major, and a number of civilians. We were outnumbered.

At the outset we were told to forget our names. We were assigned new ones. Mine, unimaginatively, was "John." The others were more creative. The marine general, a peppery, white-haired, tough-looking number, became "Mary." This done, we were instructed to forget what we had done in real life and assume new identities. Betraying a secret longing, I chose that of novelist. These preliminaries out of the way, we were ordered to stick by the new names and false occupations under all circumstances during our stay or risk being thrown out of the OSS. There was one exception. If one of the psychiatrists told you "these are X conditions," you could safely reveal them.

We were told that the tests we were to undergo could determine what roles we would play in the OSS.

The organization, it was explained, carried out three missions: the first espionage, the second demolition of enemy installations and of the enemy himself, and the third "black" propaganda, deceiving the enemy through fake radio broadcasts, newspapers, or other means.

The object of the various games and situations to which we were exposed was, it soon became apparent, to determine whether we had the physical and mental stamina to operate behind enemy lines and, if captured, to keep one's mouth shut.

During a very busy four days we walked tightropes, clambered up trees and swung into third-story windows, threw makeshift bridges across streams, and otherwise demonstrated our manliness or cowardice. To my astonishment, I came out of those ordeals much better than I had expected.

In the midst of these labors, our mentors decided we had worked hard enough and threw a party to which they invited a dozen lissome young ladies from, they said, the neighborhood. We were sternly warned, however, not to reveal to these lovely things that we were in the OSS, who we were, or what we were doing. The whisky and dry martinis flowed and the dancing became torrid. A dog could have sensed that "les girls" had been brought in to see whether, while pleasurably tiddly, we would give away our little secrets. No one, except the major, did. His face flushed from too many vodka tonics, he fell heavily for one of the young ladies. Literally, I mean. While dancing, he collapsed in her arms. But not before he had blurrily blurted out everything. Next morning he was whisked away and out of the OSS.

There were ways to see how well one could control one's temper. Assembling the frame of a makeshift house with interlocking rods was one. Easy enough. But there was a hitch. One could not do it by oneself. It had to be done by giving verbal instructions to a staff "assistant." One soon saw he was there to hinder rather than help. Ordered to do one thing he did the opposite. This merely amused me. But it infuriated the Marine general.

"Goddam it, obey orders!" he thundered.

The "assistant" responded by becoming even clumsier and more uncooperative.

"Grandpa," he shouted derisively at the general, "you're too ancient and too weak for this sort of thing. Give up!"

That did it. Seizing his tormentor by one arm, the general threw him neatly and cleanly over his shoulder and to the ground.

"Too old, am I?" he said with a grunt, looking down at the dazed and shaken young man. "How do you like that?"

The most elaborate of the trials we underwent was, in a way, a trial.

Arriving at the head of the cellar stairs there was a clock and a note.

"This is a hypothetical situation," it said. "You have been caught red-handed in a government office with secret papers in your possession. You are to give a plausible explanation to the night watchman of what you are doing there. Check the clock. You have ten minutes in which to make up an alibi. You will then be cross-examined. Whether or not you remain in the OSS will depend on how convincing you are."

Trying to find out how well we could lie in a crisis? That was what it seemed like. But nothing was that simple during those four "amusing" days.

I was among the last to be questioned. Those ahead of me said they had invented a number of stories, none of which appeared to have been very persuasive. One ingenious fellow pretended he was dead drunk and collapsed on the floor. Not good enough.

When it came my turn, I descended the stairs into the pitch black cellar. The only visible thing was a straight back chair in a halo of light from a spotlight.

"John," a voice said from the darkness. "Sit down!"

I sat.

"And what," it continued, "is your explanation?"

"Well," I said, "it was this way. I had been out drinking with friends and made a bet that I could break into a government office and get into the safe. I had had too many drinks."

This was so weak, even I was not impressed. But it was all I could think of under such short notice.

Several persons seemed to be on the invisible panel in front of me. Nervously, I crossed my legs.

"Uncross your legs!" the voice, stentorian and threatening, shouted.

I uncrossed my legs and crossed my arms in front of me.

"Uncross your arms!" it thundered.

Feeling a little foolish and reflecting that all this had the earmarks of a B-grade spy movie, I complied.

There was a murmur among the interrogators.

"Well, John. Our verdict is that you have failed," said the voice. "Report to Room 32 for further instructions."

"Thank you," I mumbled and left.

In Room 32 I found one of the psychiatrists, an affable, pipe-smoking fellow dressed in a tweed jacket and radiating *bonhomie.* Clearly someone one could trust.

"Hello, John," he said with a smile. "Do sit down. Have a cigarette. And how did you make out?"

"I'm afraid I failed," I said.

"That's a shame," he clucked. "But perhaps we can still find a place for you in the organization. What did you do in civilian life?"

I hesitated. He seemed so obviously sympathetic, what could be the harm in telling him? On the other hand, I had no particular desire to remain in the OSS. Killing and maiming, even black lies, were not my cup of tea.

"Before telling you," I said, remembering that this kind of information was supposed to be secret, "are these X conditions?"

"Suit yourself," he replied, annoyed.

"But we were told not to say anything unless they were," I persisted.

"Okay, okay. Have it your way," he said. "These are X conditions."

After I had told him about my journalistic career, he smiled, leaned over, and said, "John, you are the only one so far not to have taken the bait. The purpose of this little exercise was not to see how well you explained yourself but whether, after going through stress, and then relaxation with me, you would disclose your identity."

I smiled.

"To tell you the truth," I said, "I am not enthusiastic about staying with the OSS. I don't relish the idea of spying or getting rid of someone I don't even know."

"Well, maybe black propaganda would suit you better," he said, "I'll see what I can do."

A few days later I moved out of intelligence into black propaganda.

The OSS had gone to considerable trouble to make the cross-examination realistic. The interrogator, a famous New York trial lawyer, strove to make us uncomfortable and anxious before we met the urbane gentleman upstairs. It did not work with me because I would have been happy to be bounced out of so secretive and disturbingly lethal an organization.

Our four days wound up with a one-on-one, four-hour interview with one of the psychiatrists. The fiesty Marine general drew the lady psychiatrist.

"When," she asked, "was your last homosexual experience?"

The general flushed a deep red.

"What kind of a question is that?" he shouted.

The lady shrink persisted.

"Then when did you last masturbate?" she asked.

"See here," he said. "I'm old enough to be your father. And I didn't expose my ass in the South Pacific to answer damfool questions like this. Certainly not from a girl who could be my daughter."

Rising from his chair and throwing back his shoulders, he stomped out of the room and out of the OSS.

My interviewer was the tweedy chap upstairs, a Harvard man devoted to Maine lobsters and intrigued by reporters. After we had gotten through the book questions and answers on sex, we settled down to a nice, chatty talk. He was amused by my downstairs performance.

Back in F Building, the colonel asked: "Well, John, how did you like it?"

"Amusing," I said, and he smiled.

"That's good. I don't put much stock by these things," he continued. "But somebody dreamt them up and I guess we have to play along. Ready for another one?"

The next morning a trans-continental train hurtled me from the winter chill of Washington to the soft breezes of Los Angeles. Sworn once more to secrecy, a handful of us reported to our "cover," a lawyer's office in a high- rise building.

On the way up, the elevator man leaned over and said, confidentially, "Guess you boys are the new OSS people."

So much for "cover."

Next day we boarded a fast boat at Long Beach to Catalina, a vacation island then owned by the Wrigley chewing gum company. We bedded down in what had been an elite boy's school, over the hill from Avalon, a city we were prohibited from visiting.

A place of beauty set among fields and giant eucalyptus trees, the school taught us the gentle art of killing enemy spies and sometimes those of our own discovered to be double agents. The preferred method for the latter: an accident—getting run over by a street car, for example.

The course, based on commando lines, was not for the weak or the squeamish. I was astonished that I survived it. There were landings from the sea at night to plant mock bombs in the mess hall, exercises in jungle fighting, the use of plastic explosives, and the niceties of fighting with a knife.

The weapon in use was the Fairburne knife, a nasty frog-sticker invented by the former chief of the International Concession in Shanghai. Heavy in the handle and stiletto sharp, its weight alone was enough to penetrate the skin. It was effective and efficient for silently slitting the throat of an unsuspecting guard.

A nervous, slightly effeminate captain demonstrated its virtues.

"Slash up! Slash down! Slash across!" he cried, his voice wavering as he went through the motions.

He paused, hugely pleased with himself.

"And now," he exclaimed, "the family jewels!"

He gave an upward thrust clearly aimed at man's most sensitive and treasured private parts.

He giggled. We winced.

Among other things, I succeeded in climbing up the sheer face of a 200-foot cliff, using only ropes. But the most daunting challenge came last: a five-day survival hike.

Equipped with only half a tent, a knife, and a flask of water, we were sent out in pairs to live off the land while picking up messages hidden at specified points on the island. We were to cover eighty-five miles in the process.

No Southern Californian will admit that it rains during the winter. A mist perhaps. A slight fog. Maybe a drizzle. But never rain. From the day we set out until we dragged ourselves back, it did not merely rain, it poured. In buckets. Gusty, driving, cold rain penetrating to the bone.

My partner, a rosy-cheeked, strappingly robust young man—he later became a distinguished professor—and I searched in vain the first night out for a tree, a pole, or a branch on which to erect our tent. Soaked to the skin and chilled, we settled for a bush which drooped. Removing our clothes, we climbed naked into our respective sleeping bags and fell into an exhausted sleep. In the middle of the night the tent collapsed, pouring rivulets of water trickling onto our faces and into the sleeping bags. Tired and sleepy, we took turns scrambling out in the downpour to prop up the sagging bushes. The next morning, my companion, suffering from pneumonia, had to be evacuated to a hospital, leaving me alone to face the California dew.

Hungry and sleepy-eyed I saw little chance of catching the fish or collecting the berries which were supposed to keep me alive. Fortune intervened in the form of "survivors" more imaginative than I. They had discovered an abandoned farmhouse in whose fireplace they had built a roaring fire. Stripped to the buff, we hung our clothes in front of it to dry.

Meanwhile, teams were organized to forage for food. One captured and killed a goat whose meat, roasted, provided a feast. Others gathered abalone from the rocks on the coast. Badly cooked and prepared, they were tough and rubbery, but edible. Old oranges and potatoes washed up from the sea were gourmet fare. Bedded down in our cozy shelter, we worked as a team. Some of the more adventurous set out to collect the messages which proved we had hiked around the island. Coast guardsmen, bribed with small contributions of cash, took us by boat to some of the more remote points. The hot soup they whipped up for us made life seem worth living once more. Returning to the farmhouse, laden with food, we settled in for the duration, playing cards and munching on chocolate bars.

On the day of our scheduled return, we smeared our clothes and bodies with mud and staggered in to the cheers of our friends.

Not everyone was so deceitful. Some actually survived in the endless rain and hiked the distance required. Made of sterner stuff, they were not more appreciated than we craven few.

Expecting to be severely reprimanded after someone leaked the truth of our misadventure, we were relieved to hear one of the senior instructors say:

"Not bad, Not bad. You demonstrated initiative, imagination and teamwork. We like that. As for bribing the coast guard, all's fair in love and war. Bribery is the least of our sins. We have others."

Returning to Washington, I found the genial colonel cleaning out his desk.

"I'm off to our base in West China," he said, then added:

"Oh, yes. Before you go, please drop over to Georgetown University. We have a real school and real professors there. You'll probably learn something about China and Japan. See you in Kunming!"

Georgetown lasted two weeks and was stiff with Old China and Old Japan hands, some of them scholars, others journalists or missionaries. They told us what they knew but war had already begun to change these countries they had known and loved so long.

After Georgetown, I returned to the West Coast to board a troopship sailing for Calcutta. My final destination: Kunming.

A few days before we left, Roosevelt, the cripple who had become such a giant of American politics, died. Remembering Rockland and the jaunty way he had carried himself, I wept.

The passage to India by way of Australia took a month in serene Pacific waters and three days of tumultuous storms in the Great Australian Bight. The three thousand troops aboard became ugly and muttered words like mutiny when they were fed slops in ten-minute meal times eaten like animals while standing at high tables. Filing past portholes of the officer's mess in the brutal tropical heat, they were further enraged by glimpses of the military brass and officer nurses consuming grapefruit in chilled bowls at tables covered with spotless white cloth. The situation became so bad, the army troop officers met to see what could be done. They resolved it with military logic by rerouting the "chow line" to another part of the ship away from the officer's mess, adding another hour of waiting to the two hours already needed to reach the soldier's mess. The food remained repellant.

There was another crisis when the ship tied up at the docks in Melbourne and Perth after twenty days at sea. Only the officers, nurses, and crew were allowed ashore.

The ship's speed of twenty knots an hour saved it from possible destruction by Japanese submarines, two of which were sighted but outdistanced in the Pacific. Alone, and innocent of protection by navy escorts, we were dangerously vulnerable to attack.

The European war ended while we were in mid-Pacific, touching off a muted celebration (we continued to be blacked out) and the sober knowledge that though the centipede of aggression had been cut in half, the surviving portion had a deadly sting in its tail.

The bilious green seas of the Great Australian Bight knocked the stuffing out of us, standing the ship on end, smashing hatchways and lifeboats. For a seasick four days no one complained about the food; few showed up at meal time. I survived by pacing the decks vigorously and gulping down huge quantities of sea air.

As we sailed into the Bay of Bengal and up the ninety miles of the Hooghly River enroute to Calcutta, the violent colors of man and ancient India replaced the wonders of the sea. Standing on the hot metal deck, we stared at the bodies floating by in the muddy water and the Indian bearers dressed in white flowing robes striding purposefully on shore, large bundles balanced on their heads.

I walked through Calcutta with Ben Brannon, my closest OSS friend, in a daze, suffocated by the intense heat, repelled by the filth, and annoyed by the swarms of beggars. It was May and the temperature was over 100 degrees Fahrenheit. The only relief was to get out of the blazing sun and under cover. There was no air conditioning. With a little more than a million inhabitants Calcutta was the largest city in India and, had we seen it solely as tourists, might have been impressed by its large, European-style public buildings and extensive parks. But, thanks to Brannon, who had been in India as a foreign service officer several years before, I saw not only its run down splendor but also its seamy aspect. Threading our way through streets piled high with rubbish and the ordure of sacred cows we stumbled on humans so gaunt, diseased, and poor they seemed to occupy a class lower than that of animals.

The beggars, their faces crawling with flies, extended stumps of hands and legs and cried for alms. Though Ben told me many of them were professionals with self-inflicted wounds, it was impossible not to feel a surge of pity.

Of the hundreds who barred our way, one remains stuck in my memory all these years later. Looking down at him, the first thing I saw was his head, youthful and well formed; he could not have been older than thirty. The features of his face were fine and well drawn, the mouth full, the eyebrows arched, and the forehead high and intelligent. He said nothing, but like a Spaniel his eyes looked up at me pleadingly. It was then that I saw that his body was tiny, like that of a spider's, and that the hands were long and tapering. As he continued to stare at me with those intense, pleading eyes, deep and coal black, a shudder ran through me as though, in the oppressive heat, I had suddenly contracted a chill. Recognizing in him a symbol of all the unnecessary poverty in the world, I felt embarrassed at being free, well, and comparatively wealthy. I fumbled in my pocket and handed him a rupee which he took gravely, as though it were an offering. He had seen and recognized my guilt.

At the end of these verminous streets, with their scabrous humans living in structures which looked like enlarged pigeon holes, Ben took me to Firpo's, then Calcutta's most famous restaurant. Sitting under lazily moving fans in its cool interior and waited on by "boys" in turbans and long gowns gliding over the floor in their bare feet, it was easy to forget the tragedy outside. We ordered tea but rejected "biscuits" until we discovered that they were the English for what we knew as little cakes or petit fours.

At four in the afternoon, the gaily uniformed band played Elgar's "Pomp and Circumstance."

We remained in Calcutta a month then took a five-day journey in a train pulled by a steam locomotive to Assam. Our dilapidated car contained only hard wooden benches on which we slept but the first-class dining car, to which we escaped, had all the luxury and fine food associated with the British raj, India's colonial rulers.

A baby tiger played in our tent in Assam, and the Red Cross gave us piping hot coffee and doughnuts. To break up the monotony we volunteered to drive huge trucks down the Burma Road to the OSS base in Bhamo, a project which took ten days. Flown back to Assam, we arrived in time to board a C-46 propeller-driven U.S. Army transport plane for the flight over the Himalayas to Kunming. Told that the great mountain range had claimed more planes than Japanese bullets, we did not care. We were young and optimistic. It could not, we reasoned, happen to us.

I would have missed the greatest show on earth if I had obeyed orders to sit still, strapped to my seat like the other forty "dog faces" aboard as the transport labored into the air and headed into the Himalayas. But, after ten minutes, my curiosity having taken over, I carefully unhooked myself from the life supports, knelt on the bench and peered out at a choppy sea of snow and ice glinting in the blinding sunlight. Among the peaks I saw one, higher than the rest, which I took to be Everest. This was opera on a grand scale; you could almost hear the trumpets blaring, the drums throbbing. It was nature resembling art on a heroic-sized canvas. In the short time that it passed before my eyes, I was exhilarated then, for some inexplicable reason, desolated by this uncompromisingly pure snowscape. As the snowy panorama gave way to the warm earth tones of upper Burma and Yunnan, I looked uncertainly into the future. The European war had ended with Hitler's suicide in his Berlin bunker. Now the last act of a great drama was being played out in China and the Pacific. In some obscure way I felt, as I had on Pearl Harbor day nearly four years earlier, that when it ended things would never again be the same for me.

Was I, at last, to meet the men and women—the Shanghai survivors—whose fate had so often darkened and quickened my thoughts since childhood? While I was absorbed in these thoughts, our plane landed, light as a feather, at the Kunming Military Airport.

Kunming, the capital of Yunnan province, had a population at this time of about 500,000 and was the terminus of the U.S. Himalayan airlift from Assam as well as of the Burma Road, both of which intermittently carried military supplies for the Chinese forces and the 50,000 American airmen who constituted the bulk of the wartime U.S. forces in China. There were almost no ground troops and, being so far inland, offered no gainful employment to navy types. Gen. Douglas MacArthur had nothing but contempt for the OSS—he and its commander, General Donovan, wasted no time in mutual admiration— so it was banned from Mac's island-hopping Pacific Command. China was the best it could do and Kunming was its China headquarters, a motley collection of mud-and-wattle buildings thrown up by Chinese contractors at astronomical prices whose walls tended, during the floods which marked the rainy season, to dissolve into the water. I moved into a tent along with half a dozen other new arrivals and set out to examine my new environment.

In contrast to the heat and squalor of Calcutta and Assam, Kunming was cool and green, an emerald on the index finger of the Yunnan Plateau. It sat beside a large sparkling lake and was surrounded by picturesque hills dotted with Buddhist shrines. Its people were desperately poor—I stumbled almost daily on corpses beside the road, their bodies emaciated, the skin parchment brown—but the gentle climate, the dry air, and the sun made life seem less tragic than it was. There were fewer beggars than those of Calcutta whose running sores and self-mutilated limbs inspired more revulsion than sympathy. India with its fatalistic religions, its tortured holy men, and its apparent inability to pull itself out of the gutter of poverty reeked of pessimism and defeat.

There were few large buildings and most of these were occupied by military or government offices. The Red Cross maintained one of them in the center of town as a recreation center for allied officers and soldiers—there were a few Brits and a handful of Frenchmen who had escaped from the Japanese in Indochina. Once over the border they rode in style to Kunming over the rickety, French-built Haiphong to Kunming Railway, one of the marvels of railway engineering built in 1910. During my Kunming stay I got to ride down its 530-mile length, through its countless smoke-choked tunnels and across towering bridges whose height and flimsiness defied both logic and gravity. It took me to the border where French and American forces lived companionably with the Japanese across the way. The war, to all intents, was over and a brisk trade kept both sides happy. The French keeper of the inn where I stayed—my assignment was to interpret lectures to French paratroopers being sent back into Vietnam—groused when there was a shortage of lemons for the *limonade*. He blamed the Japanese suppliers.

In Kunming, even the poorest Chinese looked you straight in the eye, cockily, and never passed up a chance to put something over on you. Americans were fair game and theft a daily problem. Why not? American K-rations, radios, pistols, chocolate bars, and cigarettes in inflation-ridden West China represented wealth. The rewards of theft were great. OSS security men said they shot and killed several thieves a week fleeing with their booty.

I spent six months in Kunming, three before the war ended and three afterward. During that time the only Chinese I knew were coolies, ricksha pullers, interpreters, junior officers, bartenders and bar madams. The Chinese have never had much respect for military men of any rank and this attitude applied to Americans as well. It was only later, after becoming a civilian and a correspondent, that the doors of "higher" society opened to me. Given this social situation, we peons in the OSS tended to patronize the few existing bars on a regular basis. One of our favorites was Madame Schaeffer's across the street from the wholesome salons of the Red Cross where American nurses dated American officers and pretended enlisted men did not exist. Madame Schaeffer was a mixture of French, Cambodian, maybe German, no one quite knew the exact ingredients. The mystery of her origins was matched by the equally mysterious interior with its beaded curtains, soft lights and low music. We spent many happy nights there feeling that at last we had torn aside the veil of the inscrutable East. Madame Schaeffer's specialty was the "B et B," logically benedictine and brandy. Though it tasted like kerosene and beer, we drank it happily, ignorant of the real thing.

Another bar, on a dirt lane not far from the OSS compound, was run by a Japanese woman whose husband, we assumed, either was Chinese or Indochinese, we never learned which or whether. The bar was tiny and its main attraction a record player from which wheezed music of the thirties. It was there that I heard the nostalgic Japanese song, "Sakura, Sakura," redolent of cherry blossoms, Mt. Fuji, and all those things we had committed our sacred lives and honor to exterminate. Or had we? When we wanted to drink on our own, we made deals with shady-looking Chinese down a dark alley. Hard liqour was not illegal but it was expensive and the dealer generally did not want you to see the rotgut he was peddling. Once, we heard of the existence of a genuine bottle of White Horse whisky, a rarity in those days. Four of us chipped in to pay the then exorbitant price of $35 for it. Back in the compound, mouths watering at the thought of its smoky flavor, we opened it ceremoniously only to find that it was tea.

There were Chinese whores too but my appetite vanished when

one of my more experienced colleagues insisted on spreading their legs and examining them by the light of smouldering matches.

"You can't be too careful," he explained. "These girls have a variety of clap nothing can cure."

My job with OSS was called Morale Operations, or MO. The idea was to demoralize the Japanese enemy through false newspaper and radio reports. In the closing months of the war several hundred surrendered on the strength of some of these blandishments. I demoralized no one except myself.

The OSS liked people with imagination. If they had a flair, no matter how outrageous, this was even better. A fresh-faced young lieutenant from Boston parachuted into a base a thousand miles behind the Japanese lines with a record player and his favorite Bach records strapped to him. When he returned from this obviously dangerous mission I asked him how it had gone.

"Oh, simply splendid," he said. "I broke only one record on the jump."

If he had encountered anything more adventurous he did not say so.

There was an uglier side to the operation. One day I met an agent just in from the field.

"Be careful," I was told, "he's a little flaky. He likes to torture prisoners. Skinned one of them alive when he refused to talk."

We celebrated the end of the war prematurely, draining all the many-colored liquors and liqueurs in the OSS bar on the strength of an erroneous United Press report. When Emperor Hirohito did surrender a few days later, on August 15, 1945, it was anticlimax. We went to bed with cocked pistols under our pillows because of an expected military coup by Chiang Kai-shek.

It came soon after and was intended to teach the warlord governor of Yunnan, Long Yun, 57, who was boss. A small man with an enormous appetite for money, power, and women, Long controlled everything and profited immensely from the presence of the American airmen in his province. As soon as it became apparent that the war was about to end, he set off at the head of his troops for Vietnam to take the surrender of the Japanese and indulge in a little pleasurable plunder. This example of defiance and cupidity infuriated the Generalissimo in Chongqing. In Long's absence, Chiang attacked. The OSS was in the crossfire, machine-gun bullets and mortars flying crazily overhead, some burying themselves with a thud in the mud walls of the compound. It was my first experience under fire. I felt neither exhilarated nor alarmed, just curious about what would happen next. With two friends, I took up a comfortable position under a desk in the OSS classroom. Stuck there for three hours, we grew hungry. One of our threesome, a Harvard man of gourmet bent, produced a can of *pâté de foie gras* and we lunched luxuriously while the hostilities, such as they were, continued. It was my first exposure to this French delicacy. It has never since, not even in Paris, seemed better.

Kunming provided me with my first taste of Chinese cuisine; its variety and imagination have never ceased to delight me. The pleasure of the initial experience may have been that the restaurant where it took place had been declared off limits by the military, presumably because of its deplorable sanitation. A four-story building hollow in the center, the cooking was done on the ground floor from whence heavenly aromas rose to the olfactory organs of the diners positioned on the balconies above. We solved the problem of noncommunication by halting the waiters as they ascended the stairs loaded down with succulent dishes, indicating to them the ones we would like to sample.

At war's end the Americans in West China began streaming home. The OSS invited me to move with it to Shanghai but I was a reporter, not an intelligence agent. I recognized that spying was necessary in a dangerous world but the idea of working under cover, of hurting anyone no matter how deserving—let alone skinning someone alive—repelled me. I thanked them and said no. For a week I anguished over whether to return to Washington, where my old job awaited me, or to stay in China. The old urge, handed down from father, prevailed. I wanted the kind of adventure Washington could not supply, to explore new places, to see Beiping and Shanghai, Nanjing and Guangzhou. And somewhere in my subconscious, something told me to hang on, to follow up the trail of those in Chongqing, others in Yan'an, the Communist capital. Perhaps I would meet them at last. I messaged Kent Cooper, head of AP in New York, and within two weeks was assigned to Chongqing.

Spencer Moosa, AP's Chongqing bureau chief, phoned to congratulate me. Much influenced by the British and the cult of the gentleman, he assured me he could arrange to have me separated from the OSS within days.

"I'll just have a spot of tea with the American colonel here," he said. "He's a decent sort. He'll understand."

It was not that easy. The OSS was blissfully ignorant of procedures for discharging someone in China; no one in his right mind had attempted it. And there was also the problem of the coup. I had attempted without success to get the story to Moosa while it was going on. The OSS was not amused. It threatened to hold up the discharge process indefinitely if I did not promise to behave. It did not want to get involved, publicly, in the Chiang-Long Yun mess. To make sure I kept my word, it monitored my phone calls and kept me confined to the compound. I struck out on my first big China story.

It took six weeks to get me out of the OSS and the U.S. Army. The colonel to whom I handed my papers for signature placed them on his desk. Before he could put ink to paper, a crew picked the desk up and loaded it on a plane for Shanghai. He signed them on the floor.

Now a civilian, I moved into officer quarters and was treated like a human being rather than a mere soldier. Four days later an army air force plane flew me to Chongqing where I became a foreign correspondent.

Returning to Kunming thirty-seven years later, I found that the 50,000 American military people stationed there during the war had been all but forgotten.

After so many years, and a couple of others wars in Korea and Vietnam, it was little wonder. A new generation of Chinese had other things to think about.

Like ancient Troy, wartime Kunming had disappeared under the turned earth, new buildings, bric-a-brac and infrastructure of a modern Chinese city. Once a quiet, back country town it had become a lively market center of a million.

Yunnan Province in my day had a population of 13 million. Three decades later it had been expanded into a huge area of 390,000 square kilometers and 31 million people. It touched on three countries, Vietnam, Laos, and Burma. A third of its population was composed of thirteen distinct national minorities. They made for a rich and colorful racial mix but also added to its political problems.

. I met a few aging American veterans of that long-ago time. Like me, they had difficulty recognizing the Kunming of the 1940s. The filth, squalor, and poverty had disappeared. Wide streets and avenues had eliminated the narrow, winding lanes once clogged with donkeys, heavily laden camels, horse-drawn carts, jeeps, and a never-ending stream of people of many colors and origins. Huge traffic circles set off by trees, a stately museum, scores of apartment houses, and a sprinkling of theaters and schools altered the look of the city beyond recall. It was plain and dull in a well-ordered, sanitized way. I yearned for the aromas, noises, and street chaos of the past but they were nowhere to be found. The picturesque had given way to the predictable and prosaic. I was grateful for my memories but sad that this, my first gateway to China, no longer existed as I had known it.

Age, I thought, had not improved it even though its standard of living was higher. It had character and a touch of Eastern mystery when I lived there. Thirty-seven years later it was about as mysterious as a door knob or a lamp post, both useful but hardly exciting. Materialism, Marxist style, had triumphed but it had taken the adventure out of living.

Few buildings of the 1940s remained standing. Those that did had been converted to other uses. The Fourteenth Airforce chapel and its recreation center had survived but other signs of the American military presence had been washed away by the high tide of modernization.

After years of neglect, the chapel was being restored, its interior walls and ceiling repainted an azure blue. Thanks to the government's new policy of religious tolerance it had reopened to the city's few Christians, their number unknown.

Though Americans in 1982 were welcomed, even lionized, some Chinese memories of the past were not agreeable.

"At that time," said 57-year-old Mrs. Shui Xulan, a bank clerk, "we were afraid of the Americans. We were quite young and I recall an American soldier chased me down the street. I fled to my home but he followed after me, hammering on the door. He was drunk."

I met Mrs. Shui during a day-long search for my old OSS compound. Neither she nor the elderly ladies of the neighborhood committee could recall any Americans in the area. I found it the next day, 200 yards across the tiny Panlong River. The tents we had slept in were long gone and the headquarters building had become a local cooperative office.

The old U.S. consulate general, where Ben Brannon and I had sipped Chinese wine together with the vice consul, now housed a middle school. But the handsome ornamental gate and the carved stone lions outside were still there, mute witnesses to the evanescence of life.

At the turbulent confluence of the Yangzi and Jialing Rivers, Chongqing in 1945 seemed like the end of the earth. It rained without letup, the streets winding down steep hills were an inch deep in mud most of the time and one slithered rather than walked. The ramshackle buildings, gray or mud-colored, did nothing to alleviate the somber mood. More than 1,400 miles from the sea and connected to it only by the Yangzi, it was the principal city of Sichuan Province. Sitting on a rocky peninsula high above the angry, roiling rivers, it had been the site, over the centuries, of numerous rebellions and independent kingdoms. The Japanese Imperial Army had driven Chiang Kai-shek and his armies to this remote, last-ditch redoubt in 1938. These were its days of anguish as Japanese bombers, flying almost unhindered, laid waste to large areas of the city. Once Chinese and American fighters gained control, however, the danger from the air passed while the Imperial Army, stretched thin and preoccupied with its troubles in the conquered areas, ran out of steam.

The city had a population of about 500,000 before Chiang's arrival but it reached close to a million as the fleeing government bureaucracy, refugees, and students eager to join the war effort poured in. A small army of foreign correspondents and diplomats gave it an international flavor but it must have been one of the grimmest capitals of the war. It was far from everywhere, unattractive, boring. When the Japanese surrendered it felt, as one American put it, "as though the gates of prison had been opened." Seven years of confinement to this West China backwater had ended and the prospect of freedom to go wherever one liked gave its inhabitants, a feeling of elation.

One of the happiest of Chongqing's temporary residents was Chiang Kai-shek. Now he could get on with the high-priority business which the war had disrupted—the destruction of the Chinese Communist Party.

A small, erect man, his head close-shaved, always dressed in the sharpest of military uniforms, Chiang combined in his wiry person all the elements which influenced modern China: Confucianism, Marxism, and Christianity. He studied under the Bolsheviks in Moscow and, thanks to his American-educated wife, Soong Mei-ling, had become a Protestant Christian. Deep in his heart, though, he was a disciple of Confucius, the sage who had given China tradition, social classes, and centuries of do-nothing-to-upset-the-existing-order stability.

My contacts with him over the years were fleeting, at press conferences, in the summer resort of Kuling where he and Mei-ling holidayed, and later, in 1969, with U.S. Secretary of State William Rogers in Taipei. Since Rogers was on an Asian swing cultivating better relations with Beijing, the encounter was frosty.

I last saw Chiang in death in 1975 in Taipei where I reported on the great outpouring of grief on the island to which he had fled in defeat in 1949. To millions of Chinese he was a national hero, to other millions a reactionary, small-minded militarist standing in the way of (Communist/Socialist) progress. He was neither saint nor devil. It is interesting to speculate what would have happened had he won rather than lost. On Taiwan he carried out land reform without killing any landlords and put the island on the road to astonishing economic achievement. But his was a small playing field. Could he have done the same on the mainland? Even the Communists conceded, in the 1930s, he was the only possible national leader. In 1945 they were prepared to accept him as head of a national coalition government. He could not have been all bad. The Kuomintang bedevilled him. It contained too many warring factions, too many stand patters and crooks. Besides fighting the Communists he had to do a dazzling balancing act just to keep his party and government together.

It was cold and wet in Chongqing when I arrived in October. My Chongqing home for a month was the Press Hostel, a two-story affair looking inward to a courtyard of battered banana trees up which tiddly correspondents would shinny on liquid nights out.

Correspondents of many countries, including those of the Soviet Union, a wartime ally, had spent many dangerous and uncomfortable years within its walls. But despite unreliable plumbing and spartan accommodations, it was a bright oasis in a depressing landscape.

A widely circulated book written by a Chinese reporter gave it something of a scarlet reputation. He was scandalized when a male correspondent kissed a female colleague, pictured the banana tree climbing as an orgy, told how one of the younger lady correspondents had shared a "bed" with five others. The bed was a raised clay platform, heated underneath, on which most Chinese slept, fully clothed, in winter. Though it was known as a *kang,* he chose for his purposes to call it a bed.

The war had ended but the relationship between the resident correspondents and K. C. "Casey" Wu, the information minister, remained an adversarial one. They suspected him of lying about the Yan'an Communists. Wu accused them of sympathizing unduly with the charismatic Zhou Enlai, then representing Yan'an in Chongqing.

Graduate of an American university, his hair slicked straight back, a frozen smile on his face, Casey spoke fluent English and could be charming. But he was obsessed with the belief that the press corps conspired against the Nationalists and he searched tirelessly for evidence of this.

He appeared, one day, to have found it. Storming into the press room, his eyes glowing behind horn-rimmed glasses, he accused Henry "Hank" Lieberman, feisty correspondent of the *New York Times,* of having written an unfair and erroneous article about the government.

"But Casey," Hank retorted with a crooked grin. "How on earth did you know that? After writing it, I had second thoughts and threw it into the waste paper basket."

My boss, Spencer Moosa, turned out to be as British as he had sounded on the phone, quiet, mild-mannered, much given to pipe smoking and a wry kind of humor. In an often rowdy business, he was the quintessential gentleman, never raising his voice, always polite. He had begun work with AP in the 1930s and remained loyal to his distant employer in New York despite periodic and senseless economy drives which kept his salary low and his allowances meager. He had once had a chief who insisted on locking up the pencils at night and grudgingly allowed him $75 expenses for a two week trip to Tokyo.

Spencer had the most famous apartment in the press hostel. To it came cabinet ministers, military officers, diplomats, and correspondents. His hostess was his Russian-born wife, Nina, a woman of considerable beauty but formidably near-sighted. Unwilling to wear glasses, she intimidated the uninitiated on introduction by making nose-to-nose contact in an effort to get their hazy faces into focus. It was an unnerving experience.

The favorite drink dispensed by the Moosas was tomato juice mixed with vodka, a concoction subsequently famous as a Bloody Mary.

Bloody Marys were the refuge and the consolation during the war of the press corps. The only other available drinks were *shaoxing*, a warm, brown rice wine, a deadly *eau de vie* called *baigar*, and a French-style, locally produced wine with an odious taste. The wine's age was pretentiously printed on each bottle, not by year but by day. A week-old wine was one of distinction. Demand outstripped production.

An incident during my stay there demonstrated the healing properties of Bloody Marys as well as the notorious geographical ignorance of foreign editors.

Anticipating the move of the capital from Chongqing to Nanjing, the foreign editor of *Life* magazine dispatched a telegram to his correspondent in Chongqing:

NEED FULLEST COVERAGE OF NANKING MOVE STOP GIVE US PHOTOS OF GENERALISSIMO AND MADAME CHIANG LEADING THOUSANDS OF THEIR FOLLOWERS DOWN LONG DUSTY ROAD TO NANKING STOP BE SURE HAVE DUST RISING IN FOREGROUND FULLSTOP

The editor in New York ignored the fact that it was 800 miles from Chongqing to Nanjing over steep mountains and raging rivers. The idea that the president of the Republic of China would cover this distance on foot rather than, as happened, in his plush private plane, was romantic nonsense.

The correspondent showed me the telegram then retired to the bar to consume an impressive quantity of Bloody Marys. Thus fortified, he sent his reply:

YOU DON'T WANT ME STOP YOU WANT CECIL BBB DEMILLE FULLSTOP

Four decades later, Chongqing had leaped from the Middle Ages into the twentieth century. Immense new bridges across the two great rivers allowed it to expand from a million to six million people. Many of the hilltops had been cut away, new roads laid out intersected by great squares and hundreds of new buildings thrown up. As modern Chinese cities went, it was one of the best and most functional. Though much improved, it had an air of proletarian grayness and utility.

A newly built hotel-conference center glittered, by contrast, like an umbilical jewel at the city's center. It was a garish copy of the graceful, blue-tiled Hall of Agriculture in Beijing's Temple of Heaven, a swirling riot of fierce dragons, violent reds, venomous greens, and gold gilt.

"Though you are not dear ones, we treat your better," said the poster in the medical lab of the No. 1 Worker's Hospital, what once had been the U.S. embassy. The round spot on the wall where the great seal of the United States once hung was covered with green paint.

A noisy middle school stood where the Press Hostel once existed. There were no banana trees in sight.

There are people one loves to hate. They become the heroic-sized villains of history. Zhou Enlai was one of those one loved to love.

When I met him in Chongqing one sunny day, he had been a Communist revolutionary for twenty-four years and was involved to the hilt in all the battles, conspiracies, lies, and murders of the Chinese Communist Party. Yet he somehow seemed different from the general run. Son of a mandarin of the lower rank, there was something in his manner, his origins, and his undoubted integrity which cried out for admiration and respect. His given name, Enlai, meant "advent of grace." Few historical figures have had personal grace to such an extraordinary degree.

By 1945 he had lived more lives than one. As a university student he was active in the massive 1919 street protests against foreign imperialism known as the May 4th Movement. In France, he and other Chinese students, including Deng Xiaoping, formed the first Chinese Communist party overseas. Back in China, he flung himself into the joint Communist-Kuomintang expedition to overthrow the corrupt Northern warlords and unify the country under the republic the old revolutionary, Sun Yat-sen, had so long dreamed of creating. When Sun died suddenly and Chiang Kai-shek succeeded him, the Communist-Kuomintang collaboration, which Sun favored, began quickly to unravel. It fell apart in 1927 after Zhou set up leftist governing bodies in Shanghai which he and a handful of Communists had captured. He barely escaped with his life from the wave of terror Chiang initiated. The youths whose execution I had seen in photos that year were not so lucky.

Undaunted, Zhou and his comrades went underground, tried unsuccessfully to seize power by storming key Chinese cities. Abandoning this tactic, he moved to the secure Chinese soviets Mao had established in the East Coast mountains.

Driven out of this safe haven by five sledgehammer Nationalist assaults known as the "Bandit Extermination Campaigns," he embarked, along with Mao and a motley army of 250,000 men, women, and children, on an epic retreat to a new base in Shaanxi Province. They fought a battle a day, crossed a dozen mountain ranges, struggled over deserts and through forests, jungles, and swamps. To keep alive, they ate the bark of trees and drank their own urine. Thousands gave up from illness or exhaustion. Many surrendered or died. Only 10,000 survived. Called euphemistically the Long March, it was a saga of endurance, tenacity, and faith seldom equalled in human history.

In 1936, a year after they had reached Shaanxi, Zhou played a key role in a drama which helped recoup the fortunes of the faltering Long March survivors and put them on the road to the victory of 1949. He arranged the release of the Generalissimo, kidnapped in Xian by his own Manchurian army chief, Zhang Xueliang. For this, the Gimo reluctantly abandoned plans to finally destroy the weakened Reds and form a united front with them against the invading Imperial Japanese Army. This gave the Communists national prestige and time to rebuild their shattered military forces.

The uneasy truce lasted a couple of years, and though sporadic fighting still occurred, both sides observed the fiction of the United Front. The Red Eighth Route Army, which Zhou represented in Chongqing, had grown to 800,000 when I reached there and was taking in new recruits daily. Because of this, Zhou, the youth Chiang had marked for death in 1927, talked to him as an equal.

He was 47 when I met him, urbane, confident, and witty. Lively dark eyes peered out from under heavy eyebrows which seemed to have been painted by an artist with quick strokes of the brush. When he laughed, which was often, long vertical creases appeared on his cheeks. A fountain pen stuck out of the left pocket of his gray, high-collared Mao jacket.

The scene was the grassy terrace of the Press Hostel where he delivered a luncheon talk and answered questions. The day, unusually, was sunny and warm.

I met him again at a small lunch he hosted in a well-known Sichuan restaurant. Speaking through an interpreter whose English he occasionally corrected, he ranged over the outstanding issues of the day, spoke of the possibility of a Nationalist-Communist coalition government and said he hoped the United States would help bring the feuding parties together.

He took particular pains to explain Yan'an's position to me and followed this with a brief history of the Chinese Communist Party. He said he would be available any time of the day or night if I needed Yan'an's comment on a breaking story.

His headquarters, which I soon began visiting once or twice a day, occupied the basement and ground floor of a three-story, white stucco building down a lane littered with garbage. Kong Peng, daughter of a warlord, served as full-time liaison officer. Her husband, Qiao Guanhua, was a journalist who later became foreign minister. A recent mother, she received us over a cup of fragrant tea while giving suck to her infant child. A string of safety pins cascaded down one side of her blouse, looking like a proletarian decoration for motherhood.

Over the years she rose to become a department head in the Communist Ministry of Foreign Affairs. I never saw her again. She died in 1970.

Zhou had a restless, searching mind eager to explore every aspect of human behavior. Mao Zedong could not have chosen a more effective ambassador/foreign minister. He gave Yan'an an aura of respectability it might not have otherwise enjoyed. General Carton de Wiart, Winston Churchill's personal representative in Chongqing, met both Mao and Zhou during later talks with Chiang Kai-shek. He looked down on Mao as an uncouth country bumpkin, but thought Zhou a gentleman one could deal with.

2

Yan'an

I had been a foreign correspondent little more than a month, and still had difficulty spelling some of the names of the principals in the Chinese drama, when it was announced that Chongqing-based correspondents would be allowed a two-week visit to Yan'an, the little-known and seldom-visited Communist capital next to the Gobi Desert in Shaanxi Province.

Though the Pacific War had ended three months earlier, Yan'an continued to be cut off by a Nationalist military blockade from the rest of China. The barriers had been lowered a year earlier to let in a group of foreign reporters whose dispatches gave the world the first glimpse into life there since the American journalist Edgar Snow's visit in 1936. Now, the situation had changed drastically. The old enemies talked of peace, not war. Negotiations raised hopes that Chiang Kai-shek and Mao Zedong might, once again, enter on a new stage of cooperation rather than mutual hostility. The impending Yan'an visit promised to yield a clearer understanding of what Mao and his colleagues wanted in exchange and how far they were prepared to go in helping bring about a coalition of all Chinese parties. My interest in the Shanghai Massacre survivors had been sharpened by reading Snow's *Red Star over China* and meeting Zhou Enlai in Chongqing. The prospect of getting to know Mao and the rest of them excited me, even though I had to admit to myself that there was little likelihood I would be chosen to go.

Logically, Moosa should have represented AP on this long-sought-after visit to Yan'an. He had the seniority and the experience I lacked. But, conservative in his thinking, he was not comfortable with the Communists. He had not allowed his personal feelings to color his writing but as an individual he disliked them. They were not his kind of people.

"You go Rod," he said, biting down on his pipe stem. "New York would want an American to go." I was elated.

My companions were Tillman Durdin, the respected and veteran correspondent of the *New York Times,* George Weller, a comparative newcomer, for the *Chicago Daily News,* and Jules Joelson, the cerebral chief of the French News Agency.

We made the two-and-a-half-hour flight in a U.S. Army transport plane, the same type in which I had overflown the Himalayas. The landscape below could not have been more different. As we neared Yan'an the mountains gave way to enormous plateaus criss-crossed by deep fissures. A giant hand with immensely long fingernails seemed to have scratched deep into the brown earth. Then came the loess hills, created by wind-blown sands from the Gobi Desert over a period of thousands of years. Much later, I was reminded of the bleak landscape of the moon. Approaching the tiny Yan'an airfield, the plane threaded through deep valleys, its wing tips threatening to scrape the mountains on either side. We landed heavily, like a fighter plane hitting the deck of an aircraft carrier.

We were met by Huang Hua, Yan'an's foreign liaison chief later (1976–82) to become foreign minister, and Ling Qing, 22, an interpreter, the bespectacled descendant of an imperial viceroy, who was to become in the 1980s ambassador to the United Nations.

Leaving the airfield we stared up from our jeeps at Yan'an's trademark, a Tang dynasty pagoda, symbol of Chinese communism's days of youth and comparative innocence.

Twenty minutes later, after fording the Yen River, we entered Yan'an, the most bizarre capital city I have ever seen.

Yan'an had once been a walled city, an ancient county capital next to the Gobi Desert. In 1938, Japanese bombers leveled it, leaving the broken walls and a forlorn old tree to mark where it had stood. An army of workers digging into the loess hills carved out a new city, one of 10,000 caves. The spectacle of this honeycomb of caves all around us made me gasp in astonishment. Thousands of humans lived and worked in these primitive habitations so reminiscent of man's earlier shelters. There were hospitals divided into many wards, a university, a party school, newspaper plants, government offices, the headquarters of the Xinhua (New China) News Agency and many homes. Smoke pouring from a chimney poking its nose up from the middle of a millet field came from a live-in cave underneath.

Driving through the city we reached the Yan'an Guest House, a spartan, white-washed, spotlessly clean building atop a hill with a commanding view of the network of caves and ruins below. It was November 28, the sun had set and our teeth chattered in the dry, cold air. Seated in the dining room, warmth and good humor returned along with a meal unusual in its country simplicity washed down by tea, *shaoxing,* and *baigar.* I was unfamiliar with some of the dishes, such as soybean cakes, soybean milk, and pig's intestines. But along with the fried, many-layered wheat rolls, the spicy chicken, boiled Tianjin cabbage, goat cheese, honey, and Shaanxi pears they made a feast to be remembered.

Lying on my hard bed in an unheated room, the stars outside seemed brighter and bigger than any I had seen before. The silence and the dark sky gave me a feeling of loneliness. Marvelling at the chance which had brought me to this remote cave city, I thought back, with a start, to that distant day in 1927 when China seemed so terrifying and unknowable.

Early the next morning a 1935 Oldsmobile, the most luxurious car in Yan'an, trundled us in style to a meeting with Zhu De, the Eighth Route Army commander and the second of my Shanghai Massacre survivors. Zhu represented Mao, who, he explained, was recovering from talks with the Generalissimo in Chongqing. We were joined by Zhou Enlai, dressed in a long black cloth coat and fur collar, a soft felt hat on his head. Grinning widely, he said he had flown in ahead of us.

Zhou introduced us to Ye Jianying, the third of our survivors, and Bo Gu, a high-ranking party member.

Sitting around a long table mounted on saw horses in the weak November sun we downed endless cups of hot tea, smoked Great Wall cigarettes and munched peanuts while being briefed on the political and military situation.

It somehow seemed absurd to hear these doll-like figures in their padded clothes, in such a remote and primitive part of the country, talking about the future of China. But when one reflected on the distance they had traveled, the hardships they had endured, and the courage they had shown in a thousand battles, it did not appear so strange. They spoke with the assurance and quiet authority of men who had commanded thousands and they apparently expected to be taken seriously.

Afterwards, we sat down to an enormous lunch to which came Col. Ivan D. Yeaton, chief of the small U.S. Observer Group, better known as the Dixie Mission, which the Americans had succeeded in establishing in 1944. With Yeaton were his deputy Maj. Kenneth Lau, and Maj. Harold Gelwicks, representing the American command in Chongqing.

Lunch finished, we strolled an hour through the city which we had only glimpsed on arrival. Small one- and two-story buildings lined the narrow main street displaying pots and pans, cloth, furs, salt, and an assortment of other goods for sale. There was a laundry and a bank, more solid than the rest, which issued Communist currency.

There were no street lights, no telephones, no sewage or water systems, and almost no automobiles moving up or down its brief length. There were horses and mules and man-drawn carts as well as camel caravans padding silently in from the Gobi. Situated below the Great Wall, it had once been an imperial prefectural capital and had seen the heavily laden caravans moving along the Silk Road from Central China to Persia.

In 1945 it was a city of about 50,000 north central Chinese, Inner Mongolians, and Tibetans. The latter had the shiny blue-tan faces of people living at high altitudes. They wore delicately chased silver receptacles around their necks containing tiny Buddhist prayer scrolls and rough but colorful woolens topped by frilled red hats.

The 20,000 or so Yan'an Communists lived in their own cave complexes and were distinguished from the rest by their "uniforms" of padded cotton trousers and jackets worn thin by much use, blue cotton caps with ear-lappers tied with string, and black cloth shoes.

The focal point of their activity was the Wangjiaping military compound next to the Yen River where permanent-looking buildings housed the various military commissions and meeting halls of the Communist party. There was no electricity but a complete hand-cranked military telephone network captured from the Japanese provided instant communication.

Our hosts talked about peace during those first few days in Yan'an, but with little real optimism. It would, they said, take something dramatic to avert civil war.

Harry S. Truman in faraway Washington D.C. supplied the drama. He announced that he had named Gen. George C. Marshall, the U.S. Army Chief of Staff, his personal envoy with the specific mission of bringing the hostile parties together in a coalition government.

Truman's motives were simple: He distrusted the Russians and wanted military bases in China to deter any plans they had for expansion in Asia. Chiang would have given his approval. But Truman saw his weaknesses and feared that in a showdown fight he would lose to the Communists. A coalition which might take a neutral position between the Soviet Union and the United States was preferable to that.

Durdin, Weller, and Joelson cut their visit short and returned to Chongqing to cover Marshall's arrival. They were disappointed not to interview the ailing Mao but this was a bigger story. I remained behind to cover Yan'an's side of the negotiations and moved from the guest house to my own cave in the Dixie Mission. AP was the only foreign news organization to supply daily coverage from Yan'an during the critical months of the Marshall mediation mission.

My new landlord, Colonel Yeaton, was a fellow New Englander. White-haired, ruddy-cheeked, and ramrod straight, he was a cavalryman from New Hampshire and ran a tight ship. He was not particularly pleased to have a civilian on board. Tight-lipped, humorless, and suspicious, he worried that someone in the mission might "leak" something to me. The first mission chief, Col. David Barrett, knew China, the Chinese, and the language. A jovial man, he reacted with wry humor when passed over for promotion because he ired the then U.S. ambassador, Gen. Patrick Hurley. Yeaton became embittered when he suffered a similar setback. Assistant military attache in Moscow, he made the mistake of criticizing Harry Hopkins, Roosevelt's confidant, for recommending generous lend-lease aid to the embattled Russians.

Hopkins got him out of Moscow and blocked his promotion to brigadier general.

"I didn't see any objection to helping the Russians during the war," Yeaton told me. "But when Harry proposed giving them oil-cracking plants and other big projects you knew couldn't be used until after the war, I blew the whistle. No one talked back to Harry. Instead of becoming military attaché I got sent here." He looked around him with distaste.

The trouble with Yeaton was that he considered Yan'an a come down. If he had had more imagination, he would have seen that the men he dealt with might one day rule China.

The major survivors of the Shanghai Massacre and the Long March except Lin Biao and Deng Xiaoping, who were away on secret missions, were concentrated in this primitive cave city. Many of them because of their wartime exploits, such as Zhu De and Peng Dehuai, already were heroes in the Communist pantheon, others like Liu Shaoqi and Zhou Enlai, famous for their work in the underground.

But one figure in this motley collection of shabbily dressed revolutionaries stood out from the rest. It was Mao, a peasant's son fired by the romance and derring-do of the Chinese past, earthy yet well read, a teacher turned activist, co-founder with Zhu De of the Red Army, classical poet and lover of the Peking opera, writer of a stream of homilies on what to do and how to do it, a lonely man counting few close friends among those surrounding him, hungry for power and suspicious of rivals, quick to recognize flattery but too weak to resist it.

In 1945 he had been chairman of the Party for ten years and would retain this post until his death thirty-one years later. His younger colleagues treated him with condescension, even contempt, before the Shanghai Massacre but he had come into his own during the Long March when they had finally bowed to his superior wisdom, both in guerrilla warfare and the discovery that the peasants—eighty percent of the population—were reliable leaders and defenders of the Communist Revolution. This flew in the face of Marxist wisdom as interpreted by Moscow and earned the hatred and derision of Stalin, kindling the flames of doctrinaire disagreement with the older Soviet comrades which would persist well into the 1980s. The Russians subscribed to the Leninist idea that the workers, the proletariat, were the natural leaders of the anticapitalist revolution, the only ones to be trusted.

Mao and I met a number of times at social occasions after my colleagues had left but his Soviet doctors told him he was not yet strong enough for an extended interview. Prodded by the then American ambassador, Patrick Hurley, Mao had spent an exhausting month in Chongqing in fruitless negotiations with Chiang Kai-shek which left him physically and mentally exhausted. But by the first of February, 1946, he had recovered enough to see me. I was the first reporter to talk at length with him in the aftermath of his illness.

Photographs of him as a youth in 1924, three years after he had joined eleven others in forming the Chinese Communist Party, show him with the eyes of a dreamer, the mouth of a sensualist. He is wearing the traditional Chinese long gown, the kind preferred by poor scholars. A year later, in another photograph, the face is leaner, the look in the eyes resolute, the mouth a thin line of determination. He wears a red star on his military cap even though the Red Army will not come into existence for another two years.

He met me at the door of the one-story mud-and-wattle house which had become home after so many wartime years of cave dwelling. The man who vigorously shook my hand now was 51, at the peak of his mental and physical form. There was nothing in his face or his physique which suggested that he had undergone the terrible rigors of the Long March. Zhu De and others of his comrades on that epic retreat reflected the ordeal in their lined faces and gaunt bodies. But Mao's face was round as a Buddha's, his body flabby. The naturally high forehead had receded, the ears were large and heavy-lobed, the mouth though firm was sensual, poised for laughter. Whatever labors he had indulged in seemed, outwardly at least, more cerebral than mental. The hands were smooth, innocent of callouses. Stooped shoulders suggested long years of hunched-over reading and writing under candlelight. But this exterior softness concealed a mind alive and alert.

Dressed in faded blue cottons and carelessly tied sneakers, he carried himself with an air of self-confidence and authority, just short of arrogance. Courteous and attentive throughout our talk and the dinner which followed, he dominated his surroundings. Even his old friends, Zhou Enlai, Zhu De, and Liu Shaoqi deferred to him. None addressed him by his first name, Zedong. To them he always was *zhuxi,* the Chairman. In a crowded room anywhere in the world, I thought, he would stand out, recognized as a leader of men, a general used to giving orders and being obeyed. A similar aura must have emanated from men as diverse as Alexander the Great, Napoleon, and Lenin.

This first meeting lasted two and a half hours, in his sparsely furnished living room—straight-back chairs, a wooden table, and a clock mounted on glass pillars which he particularly admired—then afterwards at the dinner in the military headquarters nearby. Over scalding cups of tea he talked through Huang Hua, his interpreter, inquiring into the state of my health and expressing concern over my living and working facilities. He asked me to let him know directly if I needed anything.

Mao opened our conversation with praise for Truman. He said he had made a major contribution to Sino-American friendship. The prospects for Chinese democracy were bright. To show its good will, Yan'an would hold its own socialist program in abeyance until the country clambered to its feet as a multiparty democracy. He was ready to cooperate with the Kuomintang in forming a coalition government. He warned, however, that the United States should not put too much of its trust in Chiang Kai-shek.

"He has often broken his promises," he said.

While we talked, he leaned forward and peered into my eyes as though searching for a clue to my personality, something to insert in the pigeon-hole of his mind. His gaze was level, not unfriendly, but it was an unsettling experience. I felt, in a way, as though I were on trial.

He went on to say that China must have a long period of peace in which to rebuild its war-torn economy. During that time there could be controlled capitalism and socialist democracy in order to create the economic and financial base for socialism. Less than twenty years later, he would denounce Liu Shaoqi and Deng Xiaoping for proposing the same thing.

The notion, originally advanced by Stalin, that the Yan'an comrades were not Communists, merely land reformers, had got around internationally. I received a number of queries on this subject during my Yan'an stay.

Mao's reaction was emphatic. Communism might be a long way off but it was a shining ideal, one neither he nor his friends would abandon.

He said that he was deeply influenced by the American Revolution, by Washington and Jefferson, and insisted socialism had to be preceded by a bourgeois revolution such as they had carried out.

Mao had admired American democracy before he had ever heard of Marxism. And he told me repeatedly that China would indeed have to go through a capitalist/democratic stage. General Marshall's appearance on the scene as a friendly arbiter between the two antagonists contributed significantly to the mood of pro-Americanism in Yan'an.

(During the first four months of my stay, when the goodwill was at its peak, both Ling Qing and Tian Jiang, my young interpreters, repeatedly lectured me on the virtues of Jefferson, Washington, and Lincoln and Yan'an's devotion to them. They had done their homework and knew more about their subject than I did. I had not heard from Tian since his departure in April 1946 for the civil war front in Sichuan as secretary to Gen. He Long, carrying with him the inflatable rubber mattress I had pressed on him as a parting gift. I thought him dead until I got a letter from West Virginia in 1989, breaking a forty-three-year silence. His son was taking a doctorate there and he still possessed, he told me, the rubber mattress. He was a retired diplomat having served in London and Bonn.)

Near the end of the interview, Mao asked me a question which struck me, at first, as rather unusual.

"We have a huge rural population," he said, "and they need a great variety of consumer goods. We do not possess a distribution system able to reach all of them. It has occurred to me that the answer might be in mail order houses. Do you think that Sears Roebuck or Montgomery Ward would be interested in doing business in China?"

After thinking a bit the question did not seem so unusual. He was right. Distribution had always been a major problem in China. When it broke down or simply did not exist, whole provinces suffered from famine. I thought, too, of the age-old American dream of doing business with China's millions, of supplying oil for the lamps of China and replied:

"Yes, I rather think they would."

At dinner that night the mood was festive and the food excellent. The fish, Mao told me, had been brought from a stream fifty miles away.

"I didn't know," I said with tongue in cheek "that Communists lived so well." Mao smiled.

"You are a guest," he replied, "and nothing is too good for a guest."

He paused then went on.

"It is true we are Communists, but we also are Chinese and we love good food."

There was laughter and he added: "Besides, we don't eat like this every day."

Of all the Communists I met in Yan'an, and later, Mao struck me as the coldest and most calculating. There was warmth in Zhu De, wit and great intelligence in Zhou Enlai, an undoubted honesty in Liu Shaoqi, and an elfish humor in Deng Xiaoping. I felt comfortable with them even though I did not always believe the propaganda they fed me. I understood their need to lie, or to distort the truth, in order to advance their revolutionary cause. But I got the impression, perhaps wrongly, that they did not believe everything they told me and might, in a different time and circumstance, admit it. They were, I thought, fallibly human. Not so Mao.

Both Chiang Kai-shek and Joseph Stalin spread the notion that Mao was an ignorant country bumpkin. Nothing could have been farther from the truth. From his earliest years he had schemed and fought to rise above the brutal know-nothingness of the Chinese countryside. Throughout his life his restless mind explored every avenue of thought. He was a thinker and doer, *l'homme engagé* as the French put it. He loved knowledge so much he suffered taunts and humiliations to enter grammar school at an age when he should have been in college. For six months, he immersed himself in the library at his birthplace in Changsha, spending each day reading everything he could get his hands on. He knew more, in an unorganized way, then most university graduates by the time he enrolled in the teachers college there.

The question arises: How could such a highly intelligent, gifted man make the mistakes which marked his later career?

The answer is not an easy one. He was, it seemed to me, a complex, rebellious, driven individual. He had a peasant's shrewdness and cunning, the gentleness and compassion inherited from a loving mother, rebelliousness bred from resistance to a tyrannical father, a heart hardened against pain and suffering by years of battle. He could, by turns, be kind and cruel, passionate and cold, romantic and hardheaded, trusting and deeply suspicious, a realist believing strangely that his people could, simply by faith in his ideas, work miracles.

As he aged, the negative aspects of his persona became stronger while the positive ones withered. Pride, envy, and an insane jealousy took over. Flattered by those around him, he allowed himself to be raised to the status of a god. At first he believed everything his wife Jiang Qing told him. Later, even worse, he believed nothing. He might have found the truth somewhere in between. Worst of all, he lost touch with the aspirations and yearning for justice of the masses he prided himself on knowing so well. To divert them, he staged mass trials of those he and Jiang Qing regarded as enemies. He no longer was the confident, ebullient, rational human I had known in Yan'an or the man who, standing on the Gate of Heavenly Peace in 1949, proclaimed that the Chinese people had at last stood up.

As father of the People's Republic, he was idolized by millions sick at the injustices of the old regime and happy that China at last was free and independent, no longer preyed upon by the Western imperialists who had divided it up, for profit, among themselves. They would have followed him anywhere. He had only to say the word.

His first priority, it seemed to me, should have been healing the wounds of the civil war, bringing about a national reconciliation. Instead, he set one class against another, created chaos and fear when stability and general self-confidence were needed for the awesome challenge of reconstruction.

Jiang Qing, the woman who shared Mao's life in Yan'an, was his third wife. The first had been executed by the Kuomintang after being captured during the Long March, the second had become physically and mentally ill from the rigors of that epic retreat across China from 1934 to 1935. Both were dedicated Communists, highly regarded by the Red leadership.

It was not surprising, then, that the party elders opposed Mao's courtship of Jiang Qing. A Shanghai movie actress famous for her lurid love affairs, she was, they said, hardly the type to be the First Lady of Chinese communism. When Mao overcame their objections, they made her promise to be a simple housewife and not to meddle in politics.

When I met her, she was a demure model of housewifely reserve and propriety, a facade which concealed the agitated past neither she nor the Yan'an comrades wished to recall. It also hid an ardent nature which would be revealed in a startling way during a crisis in Mao's life and career, the Cultural Revolution.

Self-effacing, she smilingly consented to let me photograph her holding the hand of Li Na, her 6-year-old daughter by Mao. We met often, during the performances of the Peking opera, at the airport, during the dinners Mao occasionally hosted. Dressed in a beret, loose-fitting trousers and blouse, she was modest and pleasant, seemingly happy only to be at Mao's side. Nor was she inclined to play the grand dame of this primitive capital. She could have, if she wished, put on airs, be a touch arrogant as befitted her high place, but this definitely would not have gone down well with the other matrons of Yan'an, particularly Zhou's wife, Deng Yingchao, and other veterans of the Long March. Though married to Mao for seven years, her status beside him was a shaky one politically. She had not undergone the rigors of the Long March; those who did were members of an elitist club whose power and influence would last into the 1990s. She knew she could never be admitted to this inner circle and it made her both angry and careful.

He Zizhen, the wife she had ousted, had been active in party affairs and had the sympathy of the Long March veterans. Kang Sheng, the Red spy chief, whom I knew then, owed much of his later influence to the fact he approved of Jiang Qing's marriage to Mao. It was no coincidence that Liu, who opposed it, became one of her first victims during the Cultural Revolution. She had the crystal-clear memory of a woman much scorned.

During my months in Yan'an she and Mao behaved toward each other like affectionate, long-married spouses. There were no outward displays of love. In this period of calm between the scarlet life she had led in Shanghai and the stormy one she was to lead in Communist Beijing she seemed not to have a care in the world.

Whether she was merely acting or not no one, except perhaps Mao, could really say. During much of the time she was his personal secretary and must have known how he thought on many subjects, including political ones. Yet, for twenty-five years, she kept her word not to stick her nose into party politics. When she did millions regretted it.

But all this lay years ahead. Nether I nor anyone else in Yan'an could then have guessed what would happen.

When she flew off to Chongqing to be treated for dental problems, I could not resist writing an article contrasting her life-style to that of Madame Chiang Kai-shek, whom I met in Chongqing. The First Lady of China, she was one of its great beauties and was fully aware of it. She did everything any woman with money and taste would have done to enhance and show it off. She dressed in seductive silk skirts slit up the thighs, wore expensive furs and jewels, and knew the uses of lipstick, powder, rouge, paint, and mascara. I was in Washington during the war when she scandalized Americans by auctioning off her furs to raise money for the war effort. It did not somehow fit the American image of poor, suffering, starving China.

By contrast, Jiang Qing was the plainest of plain Janes. No one in Yan'an used makeup or dressed in rich clothes and neither did she. Her hair was, like theirs, cut in a revolutionary bob. Though she was an orchid among sturdy wild flowers, Mao would not have allowed her to do otherwise.

The story of her pre-Yan'an life contained enough material to fill several romantic novels or proletarian tracts on the virtues of poverty and the vices of excess.

She was born bone-poor in 1914 to an alcoholic carpenter and a woman already worn out by overwork. Apprenticed to a troupe of actors at an early age, she moved through bizarre stages to Shanghai where she became one of the most talked of and raciest of the racy inhabitants of this prewar coast city where sin, seduction, and glamour were no strangers. Yet despite several marriages and highly publicized love affairs, she drifted into leftist politics, saw herself as an emancipated woman, like Nora, the rebellious heroine of Ibsen's *A Doll's House.*

In 1937 she turned her back on Shanghai and, after a stop in Chongqing, went to Yan'an where she laid siege to Mao. Saddled with a wife half mad, and yearning for glamour after the arduous Long March, he fell for her like the merest love-sick schoolboy.

From 1938, when they were married, their stars were intertwined in one of the most extraordinary tales of love, ambition, cruelty, and death in Chinese history.

Mao and I met often during my two long stays in Yan'an. Sometimes we strolled the dusty streets together either alone, or with a single young bodyguard. It was interesting to reflect that Chiang Kai-shek had ten years earlier put a $250,000 price on his head, dead or alive, and that it had not yet been lifted. Mao invited me on several occasions to the Peking opera, an event of some moment in those rather austere days. Yan'an sat in the middle of a desert region which in the best of times had a lower living standard than other parts of China. The Kuomintang military blockade made an already bad situation worse. The people of Yan'an were so poor they could not afford rice. They ate millet instead, a coarse grain which those used to a daily diet of rice disliked intensely. Mao, as we have seen, and the other leaders, wore the same patched and worn suits year-round. They regarded themselves as no better than the rest of the population and shared their difficulties. They could hardly have commanded the loyalty of their followers and the Yan'an people if they had done otherwise.

For people leading such bleak lives, the Peking opera was a patch of bright color, a feast for the inner man, the part which did not live by rice alone. The opera was staged in a cavernous wooden building open to the icy blasts of winter and drew a full house. Mao and his wife, Jiang Qing, Zhu De, Liu Shaoqi, and other party leaders occupied the first row, stamping their feet and sipping cups of hot tea to keep warm. I sat in the row just behind them. The performers, dressed in a dazzling array of silks, their faces made up in red, blue, black, green, and white paint, singing in falsetto voices, against a background of vigorously banged drums and cymbals, swept Mao and his friends back to the Chinese past of emperors and empresses, generals, courtesans, heroes and heroines. It was make-believe at its most ironic when one recalled that the spectators had lived lives more romantic and adventurous than had the characters portrayed on the stage.

Love of the Peking opera, with its sumptuousness, its clashing cymbals and wailing string instruments, was one of the few things on which Mao and the Generalissimo could agree. I once sat through a performance in Nanjing attended by the Generalissimo which was so long it had to be staged on successive nights. Though the din and the caterwauling—or so it seemed to untutored Western ears—struck up reverberations in an ailing tooth which gave me a fierce toothache, I confess it held my attention. The Gimo and everyone else sat on the edges of their seats.

The Yan'an opera buffs took it seriously in contrast to those in the Nationalist areas where it was a noisy, high-spirited, festive affair, especially in the countryside. In Yan'an everyone sat quietly in his seat as the story unfolded, interrupting only for occasional applause.

The theaters in the Kuomintang areas were nearly as primitive as those in Yan'an but that was the only resemblance. There the audience was part of the show as hot towels flew through the air to mop eager but perspiring faces and dried water melon seeds opened up to expert cracking between tutored teeth. During the opening scenes the murmur of hundreds of gossiping voices drowned out the music. Once the heroine—usually a wispy-waisted young man—appeared on the stage and delivered his or her piercingly high falsetto aria, the tumult died down and the applause became thunderous. That done, the audience resumed its chatter. The applause and laughter erupted again as the acrobatic clowns somersaulted onto the stage.

Despite the absence of turmoil, or perhaps because of it, Mao quite obviously hugely enjoyed himself. The drama recalled the days of Old China which he had discovered in the *Romance of the Three Kingdoms* and other famous novels.

After one of these soirees I asked him whether, in accordance with his views on literature and art, the Peking opera as a whole might be revised to give a moral message to the peasants and workers. I hoped he would say no and he did. He made it clear that he was abundantly satisfied with the way things were in these ancient dramas.

"Maybe a small change somewhere to make them appeal more to the masses," he said.

Another, more restricted, social event was the Saturday night dance in the military compound. Held in a large hall from whose stage Mao presided over military and party meetings, it was attended only by high-ranking cadres and their families.

A small Chinese orchestra spiritedly attacked Western waltzes, foxtrots, and two-steps as the dancers, dressed in their padded cottons, moved around the floor.

A week after we arrived my three colleagues and I were invited to one of these affairs where most of the leaders and their wives, except Mao, were present. During the evening, several of them performed vocal or instrumental solos and we were asked to make a contribution to the fun. After hurried consultation, we did a ragged version of "Working on the Railroad." The unexpectedly vigorous applause owed less to our singing than to the fact the comrades, familiar with the number, regarded it as a worker's song.

I met Mao at one of these balls later on and complimented him on his dancing. In fact, his style was hesitant and awkward. In his padded cottons and clasping a girl in pigtails half his size in his arms he looked like an inflated doll. Zhu De, Zhou Enlai, and Ye Jianying were bolder and more skillful.

On the dance floor and in other social situations, the Yan'an leaders were at their best, light-hearted, quick to laugh, and relaxed. It was hard to believe these were the same "red bandits" accused by

Chiang of so many unspeakable crimes.

At one of the Saturday night dances, on January 25, 1946, a tall, handsome youth of 24, dressed in Russian cadet uniform and shining black boots, aroused intense interest. Mao introduced him to me as one of his sons, Mao Yongfu. He had arrived a week earlier from Moscow with two Soviet doctors assigned to the Yan'an hospital. The Generalissimo generously gave the Soviet plane and its human cargo clearance to enter Chinese air space but no one in Yan'an except Mao and a few others knew about it until this particular Saturday.

Others identified him as one of the three sons of Mao's first wife, Yang Kaihui, the woman it is said he loved most. The intelligent daughter of a professor at the Hunan Normal School which Mao attended, she was captured by the Nationalist general He Jian in 1930 and, after refusing to abandon Mao or communism, executed.

Years later, attempting to learn more about Yongfu, I came across one Western historian who described him as the son of Mao's second wife, the mentally unstable He Zizhen. This seems more likely. In any case, the story of Mao's children is a confused and confusing one with no two scholars agreeing about who was who.

When the sun set in the Gobi, Yan'an, already wrinkled with time, returned to the Middle Ages. The desert night, unrelieved by electric street lights, descended softly over the primitive buildings lining its modest main street. The flicker of flames from kerosene lamps and candles glowing through the paper windows and doors of thousands of caves turned the recognizable city of daylight into a suffused blur of light and shadow. A few paces into the desert plunged one into a pool of darkness where bright diamonds of light twinkling in the black velvet of the sky were reminders of the insignificance of man and his dreams.

If Mao and his friends ever paused for such philosophical reflections, they did not show it. For them the business of life was revolution and even in this remote cave city it kept them busy.

When they did relax it sometimes was in the Dixie Mission which alone luxuriated in electricity produced by noisy, evil-smelling gasoline-driven generators. The generators powered the missions's radio communications system which linked it to U.S. military headquarters recently established in Shanghai. Besides this it supplied light for the mission caves and its main recreation hall where vintage movies were shown. Mao, Zhu, and Zhou came over occasionally to see them. Mao's favorites were Charlie Chaplin and Laurel and Hardy.

The Dixie Mission caves were less caves than they were cave-like buildings whose far walls were the sides of the surrounding hills. In every other respect they resembled those the people of Yan'an occupied. Mine was 15 feet deep, 10 feet high, and about the same width.

Paper-covered windows let in a glimmer of light during the day. A naked light bulb of eye-strainingly low wattage hung from the curved ceiling. A small charcoal brazier set on the stone floor supplied an apology for heat. Casualties from the inefficiently burning charcoal were numerous; I once had to get oxygen to overcome a spell of dizziness it touched off in the close quarters of the cave.

Saw horses held up a spartan bed of wooden planks on which were placed a thin mattress, a heavy comforter and a pillow filled with sand. I have never slept so well as I did on this torture rack.

There was a wash basin and a pitcher of water but no inside bath or toilet. One trotted outside in the freezing cold for these conveniences. Water laboriously heated in an overhead drum can provided the weekly shower. A Rube Goldberg gadget of great ingenuity, it allowed water to pour out of punctured holes in the bottom.

Two straight-back wooden chairs and a severely functional table on which I installed my old portable typewriter turned my cave-dwelling into an office as well. My daily interviews, feature stories, and analyses were transmitted by the mission to the Shanghai Military Command where they were picked up by AP. Occasionally the Xinhua News Agency broadcast my copy to San Francisco where it was relayed to our bureau there.

Most of my meals were taken in the mission mess hall named after Capt. Henry C. Whittlesey, killed when he entered a village still occupied by Japanese stragglers. The Communists were reported to have sacrificed almost an entire battalion attempting unsuccessfully to get back the bodies of Whittlesey and the Communist Chinese photographer accompanying him.

The only other American in Yan'an besides those of the mission was George Hatem, better known as Dr. Ma Haide. Born in 1910 in Buffalo, N.Y., of Lebanese origin, he came to China when he was 23 and three years later accompanied Edgar Snow to Yan'an. He had attended medical school in the States but was not a qualified physician. Quiet and personable, he told me he was disgusted by the corruption of the Kuomintang and its reluctance to confront the Japanese. Finding on arrival how desperately the Yan'an survivors needed medical help, he stayed on, married Su Fei, a lovely Chinese girl, in 1940 and by then already had had one child.

Of medium height and swarthy complexion, he wore a black beret and the standard cotton clothing of the region. When he smiled, which was often, a light appeared in his dark, sunken eyes. He seldom talked politics and seemed content with his expatriate status.

In Yan'an, he concentrated on the public health aspects of medicine and helped run the Bethune Memorial Hospital, named after Norman Bethune, a brilliant but eccentric Canadian who died while working with the Red Army during World War II.

After 1949, Ma Haide finally gave up his American passport and became a Chinese citizen, the first foreigner to be naturalized by the People's Republic. Soon after, the Ministry of Public Health appointed him one of its advisers and he threw himself into the campaign to eradicate diseases of the skin such as cancer, syphilis, and schistosomiasis, the latter a parasitic disease of the liver common in China.

Ten years later, he turned to the fight against leprosy and this took up much of his life. In 1984 he attended an international leprosy conference in New Delhi as head of the Chinese delegation and was decorated by Lebanon for his contributions to medical and scientific research.

In 1984, when we dined together in Beijing, he suffered from a stomach problem and his hair had become gray but he had lost nothing of his quiet sense of humor. Few people have come to terms with their lives so successfully or adjusted to another society so well. Essentially modest and tolerant, he combined the best qualities of physician and humanitarian, virtues more powerful than any ideology.

The Bethune Memorial Hospital consisted of 110 caves dug into the loess hills and a new, brick building below used as an operating theater. Dr. Ma took me on a tour of this honeycomb of earth and stone where the sick, the dying, and the convalescent lay on beds of board tended by salaryless nurses and physicians. It had 150 beds and 300 staffers. Treatment in most cases was free.

It had become famous during the war for its improvisations. In the absence of city power, it used a gasoline-driven generator to power the X-ray machine. Lacking incubators, heated sandbags were packed around the bodies of abnormal newborn babies. A thin wire heated over the dull red glow of a charcoal fire substituted for an electric scalpel; it cauterized nearly as well as the real thing.

Short of antibiotics, pain killers, and a hundred other drugs, the staff researched the medical properties of Chinese herbs, discovering some unknown to the West. Acupuncture, the insertion of wispy needles of gold or silver at sensitive points in the body, performed astonishingly well as an anaesthetic. It also proved effective in suppressing the symptoms of malaria. I tried it, but having no ailments then needing attention, could not judge how good it was. Instead, I wrote a story about it which became widely circulated. The fascinating thing about acupuncture was that it was centuries-old but no one knew exactly how it worked. The needle insertion points were determined by ancient body charts which provided no explanations.

Dr. Ma introduced me to a dozen or so lepers then under treatment.

Pathetic creatures, their noses had been eaten away and some had stumps instead of arms. Considering their plight they were remarkably cheerful, probably because instead of being shunned as most were in those days they were being cared for and treated. Drugs for what has been renamed Hansen's Disease were appearing on the market. Some in small quantities were available. But to humans up to then under sentence of death, they represented something more powerful called hope.

Hope was what motivated Zhu De, commander-in-chief of the Red Army, master of guerrilla warfare and one of the most remarkable military men of this century. Hope that China could pull itself out of the mire of poverty and ignorance and become a modern nation. Dreams are not the sole province of the young and innocent. An early life of lechery, corruption, and opium addiction preceded Zhu De's. Like Mao, books changed his life. From them he learned that life need not be so poor or sordid or aimless. Later than most, he caught the Nationalist fever and from there, became a Communist. His was the fervor of the reformed drunkard, the unwavering faith of the born-again Christian.

During my first two months in Yan'an he stood in for the ailing Mao and we saw each other often. He was as friendly and comfortable as an old shoe, as loquacious as a proud grandfather speaking of his grandchildren.

Our many talks, interviews, and lunches were held in the Date Orchard Compound, a four-cave complex which served as bedroom, office, sitting room, and staff quarters. It got its name from the old date tree under which we sometimes sat.

He was nearly 60, one of the most raggedly dressed of a ragged band of revolutionaries. A fur-collared cape and winter army cap, whose earflaps were tied in a roguish bow under the chin, were a contrast to the standard blue cotton trousers and jacket but did nothing to improve his sartorial appearance. Even with them he managed to look like a rumpled bed. Though he was the equivalent of a five-star American general, he carried no marks of rank, only the white and blue badge of the Kuomintang on his cap, a reminder that in name at least he was a member of Chiang Kai-shek's staff.

When he smiled, which was often, his heavy black eyebrows tilted a bit higher, his wide, flat nostrils distended a little more and his lips parted to reveal a row of yellowed, uneven teeth. He had known everything a human could know, the pleasures, the pain, the struggle, and the disappointment, but instead of leaving him worldly wise and cynical it made him humble. I had never met a man of such stature endowed with such genuine humility. He lacked the dash and the charisma of some of his other comrades but it would have been a

mistake to dismiss him as nothing but a garrulous old man. Underneath the easy-going friendliness and the emotion—his eyes clouded
over when he spoke of his hopes and plans—one could detect an un-
shakable will. I had somehow expected him to be a modern military
figure, anchored to the present while thinking of the future. In Yan'an
the cult of equality ruled. Everyone talked and acted in a plain and
unvarnished way. The traditional ceremony and politeness which oiled
the business of living in the Nationalist areas were absent here, dismissed as vestiges of feudalism. But Zhu De's manners were
unabashedly old-world Chinese. He bowed, hands clasped together
in the old-fashioned way. When I offered him an American cigarette
he placed it between two fingers and inhaled the smoke through
cupped hands. I was impressed. The last time I had seen anything
like this was in an old movie called *The General Died at Dawn* whose
eponymous hero was Oriental, brave, and elaborately courteous.

In fact, Zhu De had not been so amiable during our first week in
Yan'an. Only a few days before Truman's announcement of the
Marshall mission he had called us together to denounce the United
States for siding with "China's enemies." He was specific, singling
out Chiang Kai-shek and his American friend, Henry Luce, the publisher of *Time, Life,* and *Fortune* magazines which had consistently
been hostile to Yan'an. China-born, like John Service and the other
political officers in the Chongqing embassy, Luce did not agree with
their assessment that communism was the wave of the Chinese future. He admired Chiang and Madame Chiang and refused to print
the critical dispatches his own correspondents wrote about the
Kuomintang.

One could almost measure the relaxation in Zhu De's manner after
the Truman announcement. He had attacked the United States more
in sorrow than in anger. That at least was the impression he left. Now
he was happy to praise rather than censure. Until then the Nationalist-Communist negotiations which had dragged on for months during
the closing phase of the war and into the first autumn of peace appeared doomed to failure. China's condition was terminal. Truman
revived it. Those who had gathered to mourn its demise now experienced a surge of hope. Zhu De was one of them.

He was up at 6 a.m. each day, ate a light breakfast then plunged
into a mound of dispatches from the Red armies. After a meager lunch,
he conferred with Mao in the military compound then set out on a
five-mile hike in the hills. Whatever free time he had was set aside
for reading books, newspapers, magazines and keeping up with national and international affairs through the radio and translated
articles in the few foreign newspapers which trickled into Yan'an. He
knew that this routine might be shattered at any moment with the '
outbreak of all-out civil war. As commander of the Red armies he

would have to fight yet another battle. The prospect of peace pleased him.

Zhu De loved children and several of them played around the Date Orchard Compound during our interviews. One of them was the bright-eyed, 11-year-old daughter of the New Fourth Army commander, Ye Ting. Crossing the Yangzi River in 1941, the army had been destroyed by the Generalissimo and Ye Ting imprisoned. This marked the final break in the 1936 United Front. His daughter was only 7 then but she shared his prison cell until the Kuomintang released her. In the more generous mood of 1945, Chiang had given Ye Ting his freedom. His little daughter, tense with anticipation, was at the airport with Zhu De, Mao, the rest of the leadership, and myself to meet him. The light faded from her eyes when word came that the American-piloted plane had blown up enroute. There were no survivors.

I had now met three famous survivors of the Shanghai Massacre and of the Long March—Mao Zedong, Zhou Enlai, and Zhu De—individuals of markedly different personality and background. The contrasts between Mao and Zhou could not have been greater. Mao was indifferent to the point of sloppiness in his personal appearance, he was a populist drawing his strength from his peasant origins, a dreamer with his feet in mid-air. He had never been abroad and got his knowledge of the world from books. Zhou dressed fastidiously, sometimes sporting a Western-styled fedora, was sophisticated, city-bred, pragmatic, an internationalist. Zhu De fitted into a special niche, an old warlord turned revolutionary, a shambling bear of a man, as likeable as a grandfather, as hard inside as nails. He had known every pleasure, every pain, and still burned with a passionate love for the common man. A dreamer, a pragmatist, a brilliant guerrilla fighter—these were the raw stuff of any revolutionary movement. Liu Shaoqi provided another essential ingredient: organization. Without it there would have been no recruits to swell the party's ranks.

Gaunt and of medium height with a face of almost sepulchral solemnity, he was 47 when I met him, one of the shadowy legends of Chinese communism, a mysterious figure of many aliases adopted and shucked off during dangerous years in the underground, organizing Communist unions under the noses of the Kuomintang and the warlords. His real name was Liu Zuohuang but he might reply at any given moment to Hu Fu, Zhong Hu, Xie Kang, Wen Cun, Shao Chi, Dao Shangxing, Chao Chi, Liu Shangbiao, Shang Dao, and just to add spice and an international touch, Mr. K. V.

We sat face to face for sixteen hours over a two-day period while he told me the story, until then unknown, of his life and gave me his views on the Communist party in which he ranked second, just after Mao.

Mao exuded confidence, Zhou geniality, Zhu amiability. Liu lacked their color, a fact which may have helped him survive in the desperate cat-and-mouse existence of his organizing years. Mouse-like would have been a good description of him. Dressed in standard Yan'an cottons and wearing a fur-collared overcoat against the cold, he never spoke above a whisper and his black cloth cap never left his head during our long hours of talk. I wondered idly whether he might be bald. Later I found he had a full head of graying hair combed straight back from the forehead. He spoke in a monotone, as though he had said what he had to say many times. But once in a while a spark would appear in his intense brown eyes and he would allow himself a shy, friendly smile. I understood then his reputation for inspiring loyalty, affection, even love in the simple, illiterate workers he proselytized.

Born in Hunan Province, not far from Mao's birthplace of Changsha, he came from a wealthy peasant family. His father, a school teacher, occupied a place of honor in the countryside.

An older brother who knew Sun Yat-sen and had been a company commander in the scattered military actions against the Manchus, kindled the nationalist spark in his young heart. Like many others later to become Communists, Liu first admired then followed the eccentric revolutionary.

"The stories my brother told and the hand-written tracts Dr. Sun had written which he possessed filled me with excitement," he said.

Like Mao, whom he had not yet met, Liu cut off his queue because it was the symbol of the hated Manchus. His friends and family, amused, called him "the young revolutionary." At Peking University, where he studied French, he joined the student marches against the World War I Versailles peace conferees who gave part of German-occupied Shandong Province to a new imperialist power, Japan.

The war brought about the collapse of Tsarist Russia and the emergence of the Soviet Union, inspired by the socialist theories of the German philosopher, Karl Marx. Its announced promise to destroy capitalism struck fear into the hearts of the Western industrial democracies.

But in China, it touched off a lively debate among the politically conscious young over the relative merits of Marxism and democracy. After months of argument with his Beijing student friends, Liu pooled his tuition money for the next semester with two of them and they set sail for Moscow to see for themselves.

It was 1919 and Russia was the other side of the moon, far away and mysterious. Liu spoke a smattering of Russian but the other two did not. (I met one, the gifted Ren Bishi, in Yan'an, then a member of the politburo. His sudden death in 1950 at the age of 46 ended a promising career. The other became a general in the Red Army.)

They spent seven miserable, seasick days on a small, dirty, and uncomfortable steamer from Shanghai to Vladivostok. Because they had no travel documents, they were suspected of being Nationalist spies and were thrown into jail. It was a period of flux when, attacked by the White armies of Japan and the United States, the fledgling Soviet Union feared it might be strangled in its cradle.

Faced with execution—justice was rough and swift in those days—the three students said they were members of the Chinese Communist party, which did not exist, and were released. Given a little money and train tickets, they rode the Trans-Siberian train, which paused occasionally to let the passengers gather firewood for its engine boilers, into Moscow.

All along the way they had witnessed scenes of poverty and desolation. But they were not prepared for what they found in the capital to which had flocked ragamuffin thousands hoping to taste the joys of the new order. They found misery and chaos instead. Food was scarce and expensive and no one seemed to be in command. "We were tired, excited but very happy," Liu told me. "But when we saw the beggars, thieves and numerous poor, filthy and in rags, our faith was shaken. We thought the revolution had been a failure."

Enrolled for a seven-month course in the new University of the Toilers of the East, they found their dormitory "cold and bare, the food heavy and indigestible." Smiling wanly, he said: "We were always hungry."

The university's furnishings were spartan. Since it had no chairs or desks, they sat on the floor. But meeting eager students from all over Asia, Europe, and the United States made them forget the discomfort. It was a breeding place for revolution.

"I studied Soviet economics and the international labor movement," Liu said. "We met Grigori Zinoviev, chairman of the executive committee of the Communist International, then known as the Comintern, at the first Far Eastern Labor Conference." (One of the earliest Bolshevik statesmen, he was liquidated by Stalin in 1936.)

Back in China in 1922, Liu joined the newly formed Chinese Communist Party.

"The disappointments and disillusion of Moscow did not shake my belief that Marxism could work in China," he said.

His labor studies in Moscow led him to labor unionism and Mao. After years of living and studying close to each other, they finally met in their native Hunan where Liu organized Red labor unions.

His work came to the attention of his hero, Sun Yat-sen, in Guangzhou where he arrived for a labor conference hoping to meet him at last. But Sun had died a few months earlier.

"It was one of the bitter disappointments of my life that I never personally knew this man whom I so much cherished," he said.

The Kuomintang in those days had a left wing, which cooperated with the Communists, and a right wing headed by Chiang Kai-shek. Sun's widow, Song Qingling, later to become a vice president of the People's Republic, was among the leftists.

"Because the left Kuomintang believed that strikes, which I had successfully organized, were powerful weapons against the Northern warlords, we became close," Liu said.

Fleeing for his life after labor unions were outlawed in Shanghai, he went to Hunan where he promptly was clapped into jail.

"My friends, including the left Kuomintang, protested and organized demonstrations," he said. "They wrote articles on democracy and the right to trial. I became nationally famous and the governor let me go, with an apology."

When Manchuria's "Young Marshall" seized the Soviet-run Manchurian Eastern Railway, Liu obeyed Soviet leader Joseph Stalin's order to fight back by organizing a strike in Mukden. Disguised as a worker, Liu was arrested and thrown into prison a second time.

"I was disguised as a worker and they didn't know who I was," he said. "Unable to get enough evidence to convict me, they let me go after two months of regular beatings."

Stalin rewarded him by giving him a top post in the Profintern, the international Communist labor organization.

For years afterward he lived in the twilight zone of the underground, a price on his head, moving constantly to avoid arrest, fearing that a careless look or word would cost him his life.

During the Long March he worked closely with Peng Dehuai as political commissar of his Third Army Corps. Unlike Mao they were pragmatists. It was not the Chairman's style.

"We ate grass for months," Liu said recalling the Long March. "Kuomintang planes strafed and harassed us all along the route. I could not begin to tell you of the agony and tragedy of this terrible journey."

In 1935, the year the marchers reached Shaanxi, he went into the underground again in Tianjin and Beiping to recruit new party members.

"I hid constantly," he said, "staying indoors during the day and traveling at night, always a step ahead of the Kuomintang's agents. I stirred things up by sending letters to newspapers under a false name and distributed inflammatory literature."

In 1936, he arranged Edgar Snow's entry into the Communist areas. "He never knew it and we never met," he said.

Liu's 1939 lectures to the Marx-Lenin Institute in Yan'an became popular under the title of "How to be a Good Communist." They revealed a mind less doctrinaire and more supple than Mao's, a realist instead of a dreamer. Yet, so secretive is the Communist system, their fundamental differences did not become public until the 1960s. The 1945 National Party Congress, held only a few months before I arrived in Yan'an, elected Mao party chairman and Liu the No. 2 man, a fact not publicly known until I reported it that year. Zhu De had until then been regarded as the party second in command.

Though Liu was almost tiresomely fulsome in his praise of Mao—he praised him repeatedly in his speech to the Congress—a more expert observer than I might have detected the issues over which they would later fall out. They were class struggle and the speed and route the party should travel toward the Communist utopia.

"If there is anyone who wishes to apply communism in the political and economic fields here, or even in the Kuomintang areas, our party would be the first to oppose it," Liu told me.

"Our present policy," he emphasized, "is political and economic democracy,"

"Policies which would abolish private property and private industry and create only one class in China are ones which we would oppose today," he said.

For Mao, class struggle was the cudgel with which he belabored his rivals. It led him inexorably to the bloody excesses of the Cultural Revolution.

In retrospect, Liu's public statement to me that he opposed class struggle, Mao's favorite weapon, seems bold to the point of recklessness. After all their years of intimacy, certainly he knew what Mao thought.

China in the future, he continued, would have the Western democracies as a role model, not the Soviet Union.

He said that Yan'an had had no contact with the Soviet Communist Party or with the Communist parties of any other nation since the dissolution in 1943 of the Comintern.

Saying the Chinese comrades would take steps independent of the Soviet Union, he added: "The policies of the Chinese Communist Party are not based to any extent on Soviet ideology. They rest solely on the Chinese economic and political situation. This is what dictates them."

He went a step further.

"At present we are learning more from the American revolution—Jefferson and Lincoln—and the French Revolution with their industrial, agrarian and cultural reforms than we do from the Soviet experience."

It is possible that he really believed this. Whether Mao did was another question. Later he would accuse Liu of being too enthusiastic both for a rapprochement with the Kuomintang and the United States. Looking back, I can see now that he indeed was Yan'an's chief advocate of the peace process and a gradual approach to the Communist ideal. He paid for this with his life.

One can see, in retrospect again, how Liu would have done it differently from Mao had he had the power. Not only did he countenance dissent, he favored an economic system in which private enterprises would have an equal role to play alongside cooperatives and state-owned industries.

This idea, as it turned out, was nowhere in Mao's vision of the future.

I wondered out loud how Yan'an, relying on primitive radio contacts, could control its hundred million people. Liu was an expert on party structure. He explained that the various areas were run by more than a hundred thousand cadres indoctrinated at the party school in Yan'an and especially trained for their assignments. They knew what they had to do, only occasionally consulted Yan'an on a particular problem.

During our spare time some of the soldiers of the Dixie Mission and I, joined by the crew of the monthly mission supply planes, hunted for pheasants. Yan'an was a happy hunting ground. It had been relatively quiet for a number of years with few shots fired in anger so the birds and other game lived in a fool's paradise, persuaded that man must be peace-loving. It was a mistake and they were soon disabused. They felt so secure that they refused to escape when anyone crept up on them. To save ammunition, the Red soldiers clubbed them to death. It was that easy. We did not, however, regard this as sporting. So we went after them with small-bore carbines at a distance of 200 feet. Normally, they would have had nothing to worry about from me. During my army days I had qualified as an expert rifleman—the highest achievement of marksmanship—but had difficulty hitting the side of a barn. (I had this exalted rating because I was the last man left to qualify, it was getting dark and the company would have had to march back in the heat of the next day if I failed to pass. So each time I fired, whether it was into the dirt or the air, it was registered as a bullseye. I may have had the highest score in the entire U.S. Army.) Had they behaved like normal, skittish pheasants and whirred into the air as they ought to have done at my first shot, a dozen of them would have survived. Instead, they looked around with a look of indignation and waited patiently for what might happen next. It was like hitting ducks in a shooting gallery. They were the best pheasants I have ever eaten, moist and tender.

Ye Jianying, the ruggedly handsome chief of staff of the Red Army and Yan'an's former liaison with the Kuomintang, tracked down bigger game. I came across him one day standing outside his cave home beside an enormous wolf, strung up by the nose, and photographed them both.

Durdin, Weller, Joelson, and I met him a few days before the news broke that Marshall would be coming to China as a mediator. It was none too soon. The military picture as he described it was critical. Civil war could not be avoided unless something was done.

"Civil war in China is not only a disaster for China but it threatens world peace," he said, pounding his fist on the table so hard the tea cups danced. "We do not want war, but we will defend ourselves. The Kuomintang said repeatedly it wants peace. We are working to see that it is realized. But time is running out and there must be a settlement before total war breaks out."

Ye had rare qualities for a military man. He was a brilliant strategist, respected and consulted by the Generalissimo during the honeymoon period of anti-Japanese collaboration, he was a patient negotiator and had a passion for the theater, shared by his wife Wei Gongzhi.

"Wolves," he said to me at the start of our interview, "are common in the Yan'an area. Once in a while we have to discourage them from coming too close." After seeing his huge and fierce-looking prey, I was grateful for the accuracy of his aim.

Sturdily built, dressed in well-pressed cotton clothes, his face had the weathered quality of someone used to long periods outdoors. When he smiled, which was often, the crow's-feet around his eyes crinkled in good humor. He was the kind of robust, self-confident man you would want in your lifeboat.

"He breathes vitality," I scribbled in my notebook.

The peace process, he said, would "depend on the help of foreign friends, especially America."

If it came to a showdown, he added, Yan'an could hold out at least for ten years.

He accused the Kuomintang of using the disarming of the Japanese as a pretext to penetrate the Communist regions and attack the Red Army. Not only that, he continued, they let the Japanese keep their weapons and ordered them to join in the anti-Communist campaign. By implication, he criticized Truman for airlifting Nationalist troops to the east coast and giving them a chance to resume the civil war. There was an edge to his voice when he talked of the Generalissimo. He gave us the impression that Yan'an would not wait much longer for him to begin negotiations in earnest.

He did not know it then, but within a month he would be in Beiping serving as Yan'an's representative at the Kuomintang-Communist-American executive headquarters set up by Marshall to monitor the cease-fire accord the American chief of staff so swiftly brought about.

When we arrived in Yan'an, Mao had only recently decorated him with a gold medal, first class, for his accomplishments during the war. One of these was a bloodless victory over the Generalissimo. While serving as Yan'an's liaison chief in Hankou, he managed to infiltrate Communists into the New Northwest Shanxi Army of Chiang's warlord ally, Yan Xishan, the Christian general famous for baptizing his troops en masse with a water hose. Marxism proved more powerful than Christianity this time and sixteen of Yan's regiments defected to the Communists.

Evans Carlson, the gung-ho commander of Carlson's Raiders which were active on the Burma front, met Ye in 1938 and described him as "a hearty, explosive individual, invariably good-natured." That description still fitted in 1945.

Ye was a Hakka tribesman from Guangdong Province, a minority famous for the broad-brimmed black hats it wore and its remarkable successes in the wider world. At the age of 17, he told me, he traveled to Singapore and Hanoi with his father, a well-to-do merchant, then entered the Yunnan Military Institute. Afterward, he went to Guangzhou, became a county magistrate, then met Sun Yat-sen who persuaded him, as he had so many others, to take the revolutionary road. He became an instructor at the Whampoa Military Academy where he was befriended by Zhou Enlai, escaped the 1927 Shanghai Massacre for the simple reason that he was not yet a Communist but made the leap later that year. He helped plan the uprising in Nanchang and when it failed fled to Hong Kong where he met Zhou again and helped nurse him through a serious illness. He failed a second time to stage an uprising, this time in Guangzhou, then recognized that if the Communists were to amount to anything they had to have an army of their own, not a hodgepodge force devoid of an ideological incentive. So he helped create the Red Army and set off, as his friends had done before him, for Moscow, Paris, and Berlin, in the pursuit of knowledge, both general and Marxist. He became a devotee of the stage and learned how to take unlikely material such as peasants and mold them into actors.

On his return to China this versatile military man became principal of the Red Army college in the east coast Jiangxi soviet and in his spare time organized a drama troupe. He was 33 when he became chief of staff of the Central Revolutionary Military Council, the highest military body in the soviets. He drew up the plan for the Long March retreat and when it got underway he continued to run the military college which became a regiment in the First Column, led by Zhu De. Now he found a valuable use for his young actors and actresses. Under his direction, they staged plays all along the gruelling retreat to rally the people of the areas they passed against the Japanese invader. The first of these plays appeared in 1934 and appears to confirm the Red claim that they were agitating for a united front two years before the Generalissimo agreed to it.

The Yan'an of 1945 to 1947 opened its arms to almost anyone with the proper credentials, foreign correspondents, scholars, writers, Catholic priests, even some lesser Nationalist officials. It preserved the myth of the United Front by allowing a Kuomintang liaison mission to set up office, a modest, much less publicized counterpart to Zhou Enlai's Eighth Route Army office in Chongqing.

Most of the visitors flew in for a few days then returned to Beiping or Nanjing or wherever they were based. Because I was more or less permanently installed there, my Dixie Mission cave—generously supplied with beer, cigars, chocolate bars, and other American necessities of life by the monthly U.S. military flights—became the unofficial hospitality center for foreign visitors.

Two women of formidable aspect, both writers, stayed longer, two weeks in each case. They were Freda Utley, a dedicated and self-proclaimed anti-Communist representing the *Reader's Digest,* and Anna Louise Strong, an equally devoted pro-Communist.

Freda Utley was not always so hostile. A school teacher, she married a Soviet engineer and sympathized with Moscow's aims. When her husband disappeared in the savage Stalinist purges of 1938, her attitude changed. Affection for communism turned to hatred and she wrote a number of books critical of Marxism. In Asia she became a supporter of Chiang Kai-shek and a critic of Yan'an. One might ask why, then, the Chinese Reds not only invited her to visit but rolled out the red carpet for her. The answer was that in those days Mao and his friends had chosen to seek a peaceful solution to the quarrel with the Kuomintang, welcomed the Truman initiative, and were eager to demonstrate to anyone willing to see that they were a disciplined, comparatively democratic, honest, and trustworthy political force capable of playing a major role in any postwar political settlement. Mrs. Utley had the advantage over other writers. Yan'an made determined efforts to influence its enemies; it took its supporters for granted, wasted no time on them. I fell somewhere between these two stools, neither friend nor enemy.

Mrs. Utley arrived on February 22, 1946, and bedded down in the Dixie Mission for the rest of her stay. Awaking from an afternoon nap, she came to my cave and, over Coca Cola and cookies, gave it as her considered opinion that Mao and his comrades were a good-for-nothing lot involved in a hopeless cause. She had been in Yan'an a total of four hours.

The following afternoon, after a brief tour of the city, she interviewed Yu Guangshen, then editor of the Xinhua News Agency, and did more talking than he did. She made two points in a somewhat pedantic manner, first that the Yan'an experience worked tolerably well in rural China but could not possibly be applied to the big cities, and second that Yan'an should condemn the Soviet Union for attempting to create a sphere of influence in Manchuria. This latter complaint seemed curious since it was not the Communists but Chiang Kai-shek himself who had agreed to this in a Sino-Soviet treaty concluded the previous August. It gave Moscow some of the privileges in Manchuria enjoyed by the tsars.

Yu replied that the Yan'an idea had been successfully applied to the city of Kalgan, population 150,000, in Jehol Province, and that he did not expect the Russians to ask for more concessions than those already granted by the Kuomintang. In this he was wrong: In 1949 they asked for and got more than they had from the Generalissimo, a fact which angered Mao.

After this discussion, Mrs. Utley announced that there was a direct Yan'an link to Moscow, the border region experience was too primitive to apply to all China, and that the Yan'an Reds were Communist first, nationalist second.

A somewhat stout, unsmiling woman of severe aspect, Mrs. Utley suffered from acute arthritis of one arm which forced her to carry it in a sling. Solicitous, the Communists assigned a nurse to her full time and expressed concern over her health and diet. Miffed by these attentions, she fixed her interpreter, the mild-mannered Ling Qing, with a piercing gaze and snapped: "See here young man, you know who I am, don't you? I'm against you people." Ling murmured that his superiors were well aware of her political beliefs but that as a guest in Yan'an they were eager to make her comfortable. She smiled a wintry smile and said nothing more.

Zhu De received her, in the closing days of her visit, in my presence. At the end of the long talk she said, "Well, General Zhu, I want to say that so far I have seen nothing to seriously criticize. You seem to be doing things right. But I'm afraid it won't last. It's only temporary, like the Soviet New Economic Policy."

This referred to the introduction by Lenin in the 1920s of capital incentives. Regarded as a deviation from Marxism, it helped revive the flagging economy then, under criticism, was abandoned.

The old marshal paused to consider this judgment, put his arm around Mrs. Utley's shoulder and said, "Don't worry, Mrs. Utley, everything's going to be alright."

Miss Strong was as jolly as Mrs. Utley was severe. A brilliant graduate of one of the leading American colleges for women, she dedicated herself to revolutionary causes early in life. Disillusioned with Stalin, she spent most of her adult life among the Chinese. She died in Beijing, much honored and praised by the Chinese, at an advanced age.

She came to see me in Shanghai's Broadway Mansions, where I was staying following my first Yan'an assignment, and peppered me with questions about life there. When she got to Yan'an Mao used her, in an interview, to propagate his pet theory that men not weapons won wars. The atom bomb, he said, was a paper tiger and not to be feared. To anyone able to see what one, small atomic bomb had done to the city of Hiroshima, this was palpable nonsense. But then, Mao had expressed the equally nonsensical opinion that the Soviet entry into the war and not the American atomic weapons had forced Japan to surrender.

Not all Chinese saw it Mao's way. They thought modern weapons indispensable to the Chinese Communist army. The germs of a bitter quarrel over this issue existed in the Yan'an of 1946 waiting to explode.

I had returned to Yan'an when Miss Strong made her second visit. Like Mrs. Utley she had few doubts about communism. After a drink in my cave she announced that nothing could be more beautiful or perfect or delightful than Yan'an. A large woman with legs swollen by phlebitis, she burbled. In the next few days she went about town on a guided tour of the prison, the hospital, the university, the party school, the kindergarten, and the news agency. Everything was splendid. She said it with a girlish smile and great conviction. Her good humor was contagious. You wanted to share her enthusiasm and I felt churlish for harboring unspoken reservations.

Hers was a mood of calm optimism. Like Voltaire's Dr. Pangloss, she thought all was for the best in the best of all possible worlds. She meant, of course, the Marxist world not the capitalist one she had abandoned.

The Communists were not quite sure how to deal with so large and ebullient a woman but they did everything they could to make her welcome and comfortable.

The Reds attracted foreign women writers. One of them was Edgar Snow's first wife, writing under the pseudonym Nym Wales. She wrote movingly of the suffering of women and children in the old Chinese society. Another was Agnes Smedley, an American, who portrayed the plight of the poor and the struggle for women's rights. I did not meet either of these two women in Yan'an. But in 1949, during home leave in New York City, I went to an off-Broadway play and put my name down on a waiting list for a ticket. Miss Smedley was there and did the same, noticed my name and introduced herself. She was writing a book on Zhu De and asked me to tell what I knew of him. After the play, we talked into the early hours in a Greenwich Village coffee shop. An intelligent, sensible woman, I was saddened to read of her death a few years later.

Correspondents came and went, most of them staying overnight. In the first few months they asked for an interview with Mao but, because of his illness, got Zhu De instead. Robert "Pepper" Martin of the *New York Post* and Henry Lieberman of the *New York Times* were among the visitors. Pepper was a seasoned, highly respected reporter who knew a great deal about China. He had a wry sense of humor. Lieberman, though a comparative newcomer, had a reputation for toughness. He asked sharp questions in news conferences, liked to talk out of the side of his mouth, and delighted in unusual headgear. He smoked cigarettes through a long, Roosevelt-style holder.

The three of us spent several hours with Zhu De and afterwards I knocked my story out on my cave typewriter. They stopped me before I could send it to Shanghai via the mission radio. They explained they were too tired to write theirs.

"Give us your story," Hank said, "and we'll send it for you when we get to Beiping. That way, no one will have an advantage over the other."

I hesitated. They were old China Hands compared to me. Could I trust them to keep their word? I hardly knew them and it seemed risky to do so. I had been a foreign correspondent little more than a month.

"Okay," I said, stifling my doubts. "But be sure to send it out as soon as you can."

Hank smiled and said, "We'll draw lots to see which will go first."

As insurance, I secretly gave a carbon copy of my story to their pilot, whom I knew, and asked him to deliver it to the AP bureau chief in Beiping. Unaware of this arrangement, our intrepid correspondents arrived in Beiping, decided again that they were not up to writing the story and put it off till the next day. That night they were awakened by telegrams from their editors:

RODERICK SAYS YOU PRESENT AT CHU TEH INTERVIEW. WHERE OURS PLEASE.

The AP Beiping chief had dutifully sent my carbon copy on to New York where it appeared in both their papers. They were furious with me but I thought of myself as the injured party. After all, they had not kept their side of the bargain. They did not speak to me again for six months. With the benefit of four decades of foreign correspondence I can say confidently that I would do it again.

Mao's paranoid fear and suspicion of political rivals included the homely, outspoken deputy commander of the Red Army, Peng Dehuai. He had a mind of his own and that did not go down well with Mao, who preferred to be surrounded by yes-men. Peng annoyed Mao back in 1927 by creating his own Red Army, aroused more unfounded suspicion when one of his military units rebelled against Mao, then became a national hero in 1940 with a massive assault on the Japanese.

Regarded as one of the most brilliant of many brilliant Yan'an military commanders, his life had been one of danger, turmoil and tragedy. He told me he was 50 but he looked and acted like a much younger man. We talked from early morning to late evening in front of his cave which, unlike the others, was bright with flowers growing in a window box.

A shaved head, heavy features, and a jutting lower lip gave him a bulldog look. When he talked, he gestured expansively and parted his wide, laughing mouth in an impish grin. His hands, thin and expressive, were those of an artist rather than a military man. Dressed in a faded cotton tunic, black sneakers, blue cotton trousers and a black cap, he paused occasionally in the strong winter sunlight to wipe away the sweat glistening on his face.

He did not share the general euphoria following Truman's decision to send Marshall to China. And he was not so optimistic about the U.S. role.

Washington, he said, could hardly claim to be neutral when it had helped the Kuomintang move twelve armies, six of them American-trained, into areas where they were bound to clash with Communist forces.

Nor did he believe that Chiang Kai-shek had changed his spots overnight. Peng accused him of planning a full-scale attack by March 1946, aimed at dislodging the Reds from the city of Kalgan. In fact, when this did happen months later the civil war began in grim earnest.

Everything, he said, without much enthusiasm, depended on Marshall. He clearly doubted that he would succeed in ending the fighting. The Communists were willing, he said, but Chiang was not. Yan'an had intended to slash its army by a million men when the war ended, he continued, but Chiang's repeated attacks had made this impossible.

"We could take Beiping without much trouble, but we won't do so because it would reduce General Marshall's chances for successful negotiations," he said.

There was much talk during the war that the Generalissimo had pulled his punches in fighting the Japanese to save himself for the anti-Communist campaign. I asked Peng for his evaluation.

"From 1936 to 1938, the Kuomintang did do some fighting," he said. "But after Hankow [Hankou] fell on October 25, 1938, it stopped. From that time onward, it followed a policy of fighting us and resisting the Japanese about equally. Today, it is entirely anti-Communist."

Born in 1895, in Mao's Hunan Province, Peng lost his mother at the age of six, received periodic beatings from his teacher, responded by hurling a stool at this worthy's head. At the age of 9, his grandmother, furious because he had kicked her container of opium from the stove where it was warming, had the family condemn him to death.

Rescued by a kindly uncle, he successively became a coal miner, cow-
herd, sodium miner, and dike builder, then fell in love with his uncle's
daughter. Leading a famine-stricken rabble, he attacked a rich farmer
who refused to sell his rice, tossed a bomb at the cruel governor of
Hunan, joined the Kuomintang Army, became a spy, was tortured,
and went to prison. Getting out, he hoped to marry his cousin but
found she had died.

His independence, unwillingness to accept Mao's infallibility, and
stubborn insistence, years later, that the great man had made serious
mistakes, set him apart from the rest of his fellow Communists. These
were sins which Mao never forgave or forgot.

Returning to Yan'an in 1981 I found that the primitive cave capital
which I knew 36 years before had faded into history, replaced by a
noisy, nondescript city. The old airfield had been enlarged and there
were several new buildings. The Tang pagoda stood on its loess hill
as it always had except that now it was surrounded by a beautifully
manicured park bulging with flowers. Macadam had replaced the
old dirt road and there were three bridges across the Yen where there
had been none. There were guest houses for visitors who did not come,
factories, a university, two movie theaters and far too many jeeps
and trucks. The made a din never heard in the old days.

My young guide knew about my past residence and treated me, to
my surprise, almost arrogantly. He was of the new, Deng generation
and possibly resented anyone faintly connected with Mao. He was
aware that I was on a nostalgia trip and obviously had no time for
such rubbish. All business, he whipped me around the city with hardly
a pause. Fortunately, he was replaced the next day with someone less
brusque and unfeeling.

My home for those few days was in a new guest house which had
the spartan cleanliness and simplicity of the one I stayed in centuries, it seemed, ago. My bedroom was cold but I warmed it with my
memories.

I was seated alone for dinner in a large, empty room. My guide and
the hotel staff sat at the next table. They only reluctantly, at my insistence, joined me. The same procedure was repeated at each meal until
I gave up and dined by myself in solitary grandeur.

The tiny old main street and its modest shops, even the two-story
bank, had survived, maintained like a museum for the historically
curious. Strolling down its modest width, I returned in my mind's
eye to the past. Sure enough, almost as though it had been staged, an
82-year-old graybeard with little, twinkling eyes, stopped to talk. He
said his name was Feng Yuxing and that he had met me in the 1940s.
Looking like a sage, he gratified me by making a sagacious observa-

tion: "Heaven and sky rotate. Heaven is different." Translated, this meant that a lot had happened since we last met.

A primary school occupied the site of the old Dixie Mission. Everything had gone except one or two caves marked for destruction. I posed in front of one of them for a photograph not entirely sure it was the one I had once inhabited. No one in the neighborhood remembered the Americans. I began to think we were an eminently forgettable race. But the mood was one of cordiality with the exception of my first guide.

Visits to the caves once lived in by Mao Zedong, Zhu De, Liu Shaoqi, Peng Dehuai, the confident flag bearers of a fatally flawed revolution, brought me back to the 1945–47 period. All, including the auditorium where we had had our Saturday night dances, were preserved as relics of the Yan'an period. The old date trees in the Date Orchard, gnarled but still healthy, reminded me of the hours spent talking, eating, puffing endless cigarettes, and drinking hot tea with men and women now dead.

During my tour, I had a strange feeling that something was missing. Then it came to me. I was alone. There were no crowds of tourists, no merely curious people milling around what should have been a popular shrine celebrating communism's finest days. The feeling of isolation deepened as I strolled through the caves and stared at desks no longer used, chairs gathering dust, beds no longer slept in. Neatly lettered signs said Mao wrote his works here, that Zhu planned his campaigns from this room, but even though I had known them it was hard to resurrect them. I asked myself: Is this what it is all about? Do the pain, the struggle, and the overflowing passion end up at last in dusty rooms and lifeless interiors, seldom visited?

It was as though Mao and his comrades never existed. Once it had been a mecca for the faithful, a symbol of the revolution and the early days of thrift, frugality, and high ideals. Mao himself praised the Yan'an Spirit which, to him, meant self-reliance. In 1981 it was an unfashionable slogan. Deng Xiaoping wooed the world, invited foreign countries to contribute to Chinese modernization. Unlike Mao, he believed in the open door.

During the 1966–76 Cultural Revolution, launched by Mao to purge the party of pragmatists such as Liu and Deng, the inhabitants of Yan'an behaved tawdrily. The fanatic young Red Guards touched off an orgy of Maoist terror in the big cities which reached out even here, the symbol of a once-united party, to find victims. The story, given to me over beer in the guest house by a succession of old men, told how, driven by fear, friend turned against friend, colleague against colleague. There were endless struggle sessions, beatings, torture, humiliations.

"It was a time of shame," said one grizzled veteran of the civil war.

After it had ended, most of the bullies returned to their old jobs, unpunished.

"It is hard to meet them every day as though nothing had happened," said one victim. "But what can one do? Life goes on."

A morning visit to the university, on the banks of the Yen, produced the kind of surprises one associated with the greater freedom of the Deng era. The students brought me to their classrooms and, in high spirits, thirty or forty of them peppered me with questions about the United States and the workings of democracy. Back in the 1940s party students also spoke of democracy but only to demonstrate they knew about it and American history. They had no desire to replace socialism/communism with American-style democracy. It was different with the 1981 students. They genuinely wanted to know about the democratic process and thought it probably applicable to China. In the post-Mao period, many vaguely regarded democracy as an alternate system, just as their fathers and grandfathers were attracted to Marxism. The seeds of the Tiananmen pro-democracy movement had been planted, but few people knew how it functioned.

In Mao's old capital, young and old in 1981 dared criticize him for allowing the excesses of the Cultural Revolution. The people of Yan'an in the 1940s would neither have dared nor have wished to question the Chairman's credentials. It would have been blasphemy. Mao then had had faults but his virtues far outweighed them. He had led his small band out of the wilderness and was the only real hope of an embattled minority. Without him there would have been no People's Republic.

I remember thinking in 1981 that Deng had made progress in trying to make socialism work but that the odds were heavily against him.

My last stop was a building with a long name: Museum on Chairman Mao's Direction of the Chinese Revolution in Yan'an. I was met by the curator with warmth and toured the seven rooms of documents, photographs, paintings, and relics from Yan'an's thirteen years as the Communist capital. Most startling was Mao's white horse, stuffed, which in life he had ridden on the Long March. A photograph showed him astride it. There also were heroic-sized paintings showing the arrival of the first troops after the great retreat as well as papers and photographs about the United Front with the Kuomintang, the army's self-reliance, Mao's first purge, called the Rectification Movement, and finally victory over the Nationalists.

A one-story building, with wings sprouting from a large central hall, it originally had the more modest name of Yan'an Revolutionary Museum when it was built in 1950 and stood inside the city. In 1973, at the height of Mao's deification, it was moved to the more prestigious Military Compound area. Resolutely up to date, it had an oral history room and the curator, pleased at catching yet another prize, sat me down and we talked in English for more than an hour dredging up my memories of Yan'an's halcyon age.

After this dip into the past, I returned to the airfield and in an hour was back in Beijing. Because it was part alive and part dead, Yan'an in retrospect seemed to me not quite real. I would not want to live there, though my personal and professional memories of it are warm.

3

War, Johnny, and Sin

Gen. George Catlett Marshall, the man military experts credit with having done most to defeat Adolf Hitler's armies, arrived in Shanghai on December 20, 1945, one of those shiveringly cold, bleak days which make winters in that great port city so miserable. He was met by Gen. Albert Wedemeyer, Stilwell's replacement, a friend of many years' standing.

According to one biographer, the general had barely taken off his overcoat when Wedemeyer told him bluntly he had been given an impossible mission. Neither side, he said, was willing to give up power.

Marshall, 65, exhausted from the long flight, reddened then, in a hoarse voice, replied equally bluntly that he would succeed and Wedemeyer was going to help him do so.

It was an extraordinary assignment, something that had never happened before, an American effort to persuade the lion to lie down with the lamb, though which was the lion, which the lamb was not quite clear.

Working in his quiet methodical way, listening to everyone but refusing to show his own hand, he brought about a cease-fire in remarkably short time and got both sides to agree to a multiparty conference to work out the political problems of a coalition government.

Even Wedemeyer, abandoning his original pessimism, conceded that the old man had done the impossible. Truman ordered Marshall home for consultations on what to do next. Before leaving, he stopped off overnight in Yan'an to meet Mao.

The date was March 4, 1946, a clear, dry day with the air as heady as wine. From the crowd I caught my first glimpse of Marshall as he descended the steps, an erect military figure in full uniform exuding confidence. With him were Zhou Enlai and Zhang Zhizhong, the government's representative in the negotiations.

All of Yan'an turned out for the arrival carrying banners welcoming the three in Chinese and English.

The way Mao Zedong, Liu Shaoqi, and Zhu De were togged out underscored the importance they attached to the visit. Instead of the usual baggy, patched cottons they wore tailored woolen jackets and well-pressed trousers. Mao even wore shoes.

After Mao and Marshall reviewed a military honor guard, the two clambered into the back of a Dixie Mission three-quarter-ton truck, supplied by Yeaton, and moved in stately fashion to the Wangjiaping military headquarters where the first formal talks took place.

At a banquet that night in the unheated military building, the Americans and Chinese dined sumptuously by candle light—there was no electricity—and drank toasts in baigar from white porcelain tea cups. A chorus sang the "Yellow River" cantata, and the event was preserved for posterity on flimsy brown paper programs topped by crossed American and Kuomintang flags—the United Front fiction was being maintained. Everyone except Marshall, who was bareheaded, remained buttoned up against the freezing cold. Mao prudently kept his new cap on his head throughout. Figuring that Mao was setting the social tone, I did the same.

Mao, in a brief speech of welcome, thanked Truman and Marshall for restoring peace and seeking to realize Chinese political unity.

Replying, Marshall told the dinner guests in his direct, honest way that the time for fighting was over and China must now channel its differences through the soon-to-be-realized free press and elected legislatures.

"I am impatient of failure and don't believe in playing favorites," he added.

If China wished to take its place among the great powers, he said, it had to achieve some kind of unification. The American public, he explained, would not approve continued economic assistance to a house divided.

The record of their private talks, released by the State Department in 1972, on the eve of Richard Nixon's historic visit to Beijing, reported Marshall told Mao he was gratified by Yan'an's attitude and particularly appreciative of Zhou's "fine show of cooperation, straightforwardness and friendliness."

As the man in the middle, Marshall ruefully observed to Mao that he had run into "considerable reluctance and mistrust" from both sides.

He then spoke of the extreme right-wingers in the Kuomintang, whom he called "irreconcilable elements," trying for selfish reasons to block unification. This referred to the "CC Clique," the wealthy and powerful brothers Chen Lifu and Chen Guofu, who believed that in a military showdown the Kuomintang would win. Because of this, they saw no reason to make concessions to the Communists. These elements, Marshall told Mao, could not be tolerated.

The two discussed the question of Manchuria where the Kuomintang and the Communists were locked in a race to gain control of key areas. The Nationalists held Mukden and Changchun, while Lin Biao and his forces were in Harbin and much of the countryside.

Marshall called the situation there "a potato almost too hot to handle." Both sides backed and filled over whether the newly created truce teams, based in Beiping, should monitor the peace in this vast area, next to Russia.

Mao initially had said the truce teams should keep out. But in his meeting with Marshall he reversed himself, saying he hoped the teams—Kuomintang, Communist, and American—would go there and enforce the peace. This caught Marshall off-balance. Annoyed, he asked Mao rather sharply what was behind this about-face. Was it a political maneuver? He said if it was he did not want to get involved. He apparently feared the Kuomintang would believe the decision had resulted from the Yan'an talks. Marshall had scrupulously avoided taking sides in the negotiations. The last thing he wanted to do was give advice to either of the antagonists.

Realizing the delicacy of the question, Marshall added that Mao did not have to answer it. The Chairman chose not to.

In the event, the Generalissimo decided that Manchuria should be left out of the cease-fire agreement. Marshall told Mao Chiang feared the presence of the Americans on the truce teams "might give the Russians excuses and precipitate international complications." The truth appeared to be that the Gimo believed he could defeat the Communists in Manchuria and did not want the teams to hamper the movements of his forces.

On his way back to Nanjing, Marshall stopped off at several other cities. As human as anyone else, he could not resist messaging Truman he had become a peace hero. "My reception everywhere was enthusiastic," he said, "and in the cities, tumultuous." The Chinese, weary of war, saw him as their savior.

The prospects for permanent peace seemed so good that the Kuomintang reporters accompanying Marshall asked Mao to pose with them in a group picture. Years later, after Mao had won, they would pull it out from some secret space in their desk and show it to prove that they had been in at the creation.

I spent a few more weeks in Yan'an then decided to see for myself what was happening in Manchuria. Marshall's departure for Washington gave me the chance I wanted to do so.

Manchuria held the key to peace or civil war in the China of 1946. The withdrawing Russian armies left in their wake a vacuum which the Nationalist and Communist forces rushed to fill. The Nationalists, headquartered in Mukden, ordered the Communist commander,

Lin Biao, to hand over the portion he held, a suggestion he ignored. Another American correspondent and I hitched a plane to Harbin, Lin Biao's capital, for a first-hand look. Lin put us up in his official residence, a massive, four-story Russian mansion with high ceilings, panelled walls, and an imposing central staircase. It was our home for two weeks.

The meals were gargantuan, on a Russian scale, stewed meat and potatoes, borscht, black bread, and cakes, all washed down by red and white wines, vodka, beer, soft drinks, and mineral water. Caviar was an occasional delicacy.

A town of 40,000 in 1897, Harbin mushroomed in population after it became the transportation center of northern Manchuria. Five railways met there linking it with Russia, Korea, and China. Steamships and smaller boats plied between it and other big cities along the broad Sungari River. In 1946, it had a population of nearly a million.

Under the tsars it had had a glittering history. A luxurious train connected it to Moscow and on to Paris. It was a center of European culture with ballet, opera, and the symphony.

At night, however, none of its past grandeur came through. Coal to power the city electric system and gasoline for buses and automobiles were in short supply. Dimmed street lights turned it into a city of shadows one strolled through with a certain trepidation. We drove around town in a big, black charcoal-burning sedan through a depressing and desolate cityscape.

Though they had developed its resources, there was little evidence of the more recent Japanese presence except the shells of factories looted of their machinery by the departing Russian army.

Lin Biao gave us a long interview soon after we arrived. Dressed in a baggy uniform, he did not look what he was, an authentic military genius, one of the great commanders of Communist China. Nor could one read in his mousy appearance any clue to the dramatic future he saw for himself. Short, slender, and shy, he rarely smiled, but when he did, managed to look almost boyishly young. At 39, you could hardly call him old compared to his Yan'an comrades, most of them in their fifties.

Born in a village not far from Wuhan, he got involved while still young in the radical life of the big Hubei Province city. By the age of 18 he was a member of the Kuomintang and enrolled in the new revolutionary Whampoa Military Academy. There he studied under the Generalissimo, its commandant. In 1925, ordered to choose, he abandoned the Kuomintang and became a Communist.

After the Shanghai Massacre, he escaped to the Jiangxi-Guangdong-Hunan border region along with Zhu De and Chen Yi where they joined Mao and Zhou. He was 20. The following year he commanded a Red regiment and at 23 headed an army.

On the Long March he led the First Army Corps to capture Zunyi in Guizhou Province where, during a celebrated conference there, he backed Mao's bid to become party chairman.

He became internationally known after winning a rare victory over the Japanese in Shanxi Province.

Frail and sickly, he was sent to Moscow to be hospitalized, took part in the defense of Leningrad and received a handsome revolver from Stalin. He also acquired marked Soviet sympathies. That was a formula for trouble. It was an enthusiasm Mao did not share.

At the Seventh National Communist Party conference in Yan'an in April 1945 he delivered a speech and became a member of the Central Committee. He was on the way up. Soon after the Japanese surrender, he set out for Manchuria with 30,000 men. On the way he picked up thousands more. These, added to the guerrilla forces already in place, gave him an army of 300,000. He told me he was ready to incorporate them into a new Kuomintang-Communist national army if a coalition government could be hammered together.

Though he was the commander-in-chief, he took orders from three high-ranking Communists. One of them, Gao Gang, either committed suicide or was murdered ten years later after being accused of trying to set up his own, Soviet-dominated empire in Manchuria. Despite the surface indications, the Communist Party, even then, was not united.

Lin said he had held an election in Harbin soon after taking it over. It named trade and industrial leaders, poor peasants, and ordinary citizens to the city council. There were even Kuomintang members, he said, without explaining where they came from.

It was not, he said, democracy in the American manner, but it did give the people of Harbin a greater voice in their affairs than they had had before.

Lin said that despite all the fighting and misunderstanding, Yan'an was willing to work with the Kuomintang and share political power in the local governments the Reds had set up. He complained that Chiang had snubbed this offer and abolished local governments in the areas he had occupied.

"It is still possible," he said, "to reach a political rather than a military settlement."

After our talk, I wrote that the Communists were in Manchuria to stay and that nothing short of armed force would root them out.

I talked to one of the few Russians who had chosen to remain behind rather than accompany the Soviet troops to Moscow. An employee of the old British-American Tobacco Company, he had relatives in

America and recalled Harbin's salad days when it was a center for tsarist refugees. Ex-archdukes and other noblemen, he said, lived handsomely there rather than driving taxicabs in Paris.

In 1946, the Russian influence, despite the presence of the Chinese comrades, began to dwindle, like a collapsing hot air balloon. Those electing to remain preferred to take a chance with the Chinese rather than risk an uncertain future in the Soviet Union. They were called, contemptuously, radishes, red on the outside but still white on the inside. They stubbornly refused to alter their life-style which was much higher than that of the more numerous Chinese.

One of the things to which they clung was the Russian Yacht Club on the wide Sungari River. It had been the brilliant center of White Russian social life for decades. Now it was an oasis in a drab desert. Blue and white with spacious verandas and immaculate public rooms, it looked like a miniature fairy-tale castle, startlingly out of place in this sordid-looking city. We were taken there for a splendid Russian supper and a lively cabaret performance by Russian girls in bright new costumes. Our escorts plied us with vodka, matching us in toast after toast without so much as blinking. This aroused my suspicion. Most Chinese become fiery red after drinking alcohol and otherwise show its effect. These did not. When they went to the toilet, I sampled the bottle they had been using. Ours was genuine vodka, theirs ice water.

The audience was entirely Russian, obviously members of the club and very much at home in this atmosphere. Throughout the evening they stared at our small party which included the American colonel of the truce team in uniform. I feared they might become hostile. Little by little as the general level of vodka consumption rose they inched closer and closer. I went out to the toilet and met one of the Russians who stammered, "Excuse me" and thrust a piece of paper into my hand. I opened it and saw it was a note addressed to an uncle in Connecticut.

Returning to the table, I found that one of the Russians, bolder than the rest, had introduced himself. That broke the ice. A score of others speaking hesitant English surrounded us and began talking all at once. They too had messages for American relatives. The mood became extravagantly friendly as the Russians clambered onto our tables and did Cossack dances. The vodka and the bonhomie overflowed. Our Chinese hosts, forced to drink the real stuff, mellowed and embraced the Russians they had only a little earlier kept at arm's length. On the way home, much besotted, I passed out in the charcoal-burning limousine.

The letters we mailed for the White Russians reestablished contacts broken for many years. Because of them, many in the yacht club that night eventually found their way to new homes in the United States.

My Harbin visit and several other trips to Mukden, Changchun, and Szepingkai, persuaded me that the Nationalists could hold on to Manchuria only if they allowed free elections. This they did not appear prepared to do.

In December 1946, I returned to Yan'an for my second long stay and encountered a mood of pessimism bordering on despair. The smouldering sparks of war in Manchuria had burst into flame and the Communists blamed the United States as well as Chiang Kai-shek. Mao was furious after the Americans and Nationalists concluded a commercial treaty, leaving Yan'an out. He gave me a statement which called it "China's new National Humiliation Day."

On this second long visit to Yan'an I stayed from December to March, just before it fell. The momentous events of the first made my three months there pass with the speed of light. The Marshall mission had been hailed as a messenger of peace and life had taken on a rosy glow. It seemed wonderful just to be alive and a witness to what promised to be a critical watershed in modern Chinese history. To be American was to be immensely popular in Yan'an then. We would never be so well regarded by the Communists again.

By contrast, my second sojourn among the Red cave-dwellers, which lasted nearly four months, went slowly, on leaden feet. Because the coalition talks had broken down, there was a sense of impending doom. The black clouds of failure had shut out the sunshine of the previous year.

Christmas 1946 in the Dixie Mission was a half-hearted affair which none of the Communist leaders attended. The year before, Mao and Zhu De had appeared in a festive mood drinking toasts and accepting small presents. Because it was a Chinese custom, I sent Mao a modest gift at New Year. It was returned with a politely cold note that Communists did not follow the old ways.

I spent much of my time, as before, in interviews, the longest with Xu Deli, Mao's snaggle-toothed old former teacher. Many of the others had left, among them He Long, the famous "red bandit," to take up positions for the impending civil strife which now seemed inevitable. A sense of purpose and determination penetrated the Yan'an gloom. It now was engaged in a familiar exercise: preparing for battle.

Even Zhou Enlai, always so cordial, greeted me with an air of gravity. He was particularly angry over a military loan granted Chiang Kai-shek by the Truman administration. He argued that Marshall had originally intended this money to be used to create the new Kuomintang-Communist coalition army. Now, with the negotiations on the rocks, it was clear the funds would go solely to the Kuomintang. Though the loan agreement stipulated it not be used for civil war, in effect it represented American aid to the Nationalist army, he said. He saw it as encouragement for the Generalissimo to go on the offensive.

"The United States," Zhou said to me in an emotional voice, "should recall its own struggle for freedom and independence with shame if it fails China at this critical moment."

Yan'an, he went on, clung to one slender hope, that Chiang would reconsider his refusal to accept the two conditions Yan'an regarded as vital to the continuation of the talks. The first was that the Nationalist forces give up the gains they had made and return to the January 13, 1946 lines which had been agreed to after Marshall brought about a cease-fire. Dissolution of the rump National Assembly—it included no Communists, only the Kuomintang and some minor parties—was the other. If Chiang bowed to these demands, the negotiations could be resumed in earnest, he said. To demonstrate its good faith, Yan'an would order its army withdrawn from Harbin, its Manchurian headquarters, and other key points in the Northeast provinces.

Chiang had a clear option: war or peace. He refused to reply and the dogs of war, held at bay for so many months by Marshall's patience and dogged determination, slipped their chains. Three more years of hardship and bloodshed for the long-suffering Chinese people lay ahead.

The amiable Zhu De walked around with a long face, unhappy over this fatal turn of events. Though he blamed the Kuomintang for the impasse, he said Washington should share the guilt.

Referring to the American military loan to the Nationalists, he asked, bitterly: "How can you negotiate between two antagonists while giving a helping hand to only one of them?"

To make matters worse, three Kuomintang armies converged on Yan'an itself. The Communists began packing for their second Long March. I asked my New York office for permission to accompany them on this new adventure. Never very imaginative, the big brass there decided that if I did so I might be out of touch for months. (Ling Qing told me in 1980 that the Communists had never lost contact with the outside during the two-year trek.)

Like me, Anna Louise Strong wished to go into the underground with Mao. She recognized, as I did, that it was a great story. And she did not have any bosses to tell her not to. But, as it turned out, the Communists were embarrassed at her request. They asked me to intercede.

"Please try to persuade her not to come with us," they said. "She is a wonderful woman and we love her. But she would not be able to cope. We will have to strip down to bare essentials. Food will be scarce and there will be fighting. We will have to walk a good deal and climb mountains. She is a heavy woman and her legs would not hold up. We cannot spare any horses and we could not carry her."

She saw the logic of this argument and left Yan'an with regrets.

I packed my own bags, said my farewells and was driven to the airfield for the flight to Beijing. Mao was there to meet someone on the incoming flight. I approached him and after some small talk observed that with Yan'an falling and a new retreat beginning the situation for the Chinese Communist Party looked bleak.

"Luo-de-li," he said, using my Chinese name, "I invite you to visit me in Beijing two years from now."

When I expressed surprise at this evidence of optimism, he went on to say that the Communists would win but that once they got to Beijing they would face new and greater problems than those they had dealt with in Yan'an because of the temptations and corruption of the big cities.

These two statements were evidence not only of Mao's unruffled calm in the face of crisis but of his prescience. He was in Beiping (which he renamed Beijing) within two years.

A month after our talk, the Communists evacuated Yan'an and plunged once more into the wilderness.

The collapse of the negotiations all but doomed the Marshall mission. The Generalissimo drove the last nail in the coffin by capturing the Communist-held city of Kalgan in Jehol Province. Yan'an had warned this would be the last straw.

With the Manchurian situation rapidly deteriorating into full-scale war, the situation looked irretrievable. Despite all his efforts, Marshall had failed. In January 1947 he officially announced, in a plague-on-both-your-houses statement, that he was going home. I wrote then that the hatred and suspicion were too deep for the antagonists, even with Marshall's patient help, to overcome.

I covered the first six months of the Marshall negotiations in Nanjing and Shanghai and went with him on his visits to the Generalissimo in his mountain retreat, where they discussed some of the major problems which had arisen.

But it was not until the secret record was released in 1972 (*Paper Relating to the Foreign Relations of the United States, 1946*) that I realized how patient, and persevering, Marshall had been. It disclosed his determination to explore every avenue that might lead to peace, no matter how round-about, even though he was aware that both sides were trying to use him to their advantage.

The papers contained some astonishing information we had not known in 1946. One was that the bulk of the negotiations took place between Marshall and Zhou. The Generalissimo, or his representatives, saw the American envoy infrequently and when they did threw roadblocks, or diversions, in the way of agreement, the papers said.

Chiang stubbornly and unrealistically insisted that Lin Biao surrender his armies in Manchuria before any political settlement had been reached. Not surprisingly Yan'an refused and said they would turn them over only to a coalition government of all China.

Though Marshall tried to disabuse him of the idea, the Generalissimo apparently believed the United States would back him in any prolonged civil war. As it turned out Chiang was right. The Communists were embittered by the significant material, technological, and advisory aid Washington gave him. Rightly or wrongly, they blamed Marshall.

The 1972 papers contained something of a bombshell, a fact kept secret until then. They reported that Joseph Stalin had invited the Generalissimo to Moscow to discuss ways of averting war in Manchuria. Without consulting Marshall, the Gimo declined.

With the infallible benefit of hindsight, it seems a pity that he had not made the trip. We know now that Stalin had nothing but contempt for the Yan'an "land reformers" and regarded them as potential trouble-makers. He had concluded a treaty with Chiang which gave him important rights in Manchuria and may have felt, as it later turned out, that a victorious Mao would rescind them. Having the Yan'an Communists on his long border was not a prospect which enthralled him. He foresaw the trouble that would result.

In the long run, he probably believed, the Nationalists would be less bothersome.

The Cold War had not yet begun and Marshall, unhappy over the way things were going in Manchuria, told Chiang he would have welcomed the Moscow visit, especially if Stalin could persuade Yan'an and Lin Biao to reach a reasonable agreement with the Nationalists.

"We were working for peace, not special privileges," Marshall messaged Truman, "and I, for one, would welcome a helpful intercession by the Soviets to compose the Manchurian crisis."

In the event, we may never know what the wily Stalin had up his sleeve. Whatever it was, it could not have been worse than what happened. When Manchuria fell to Lin Biao, the war was all but over.

Before Marshall left China he ordered the U.S. Marines, based in North China, to return home.

Theirs had been a tough and controversial job. Many Americans thought the Marines should not have been sent to China in the first place. By their very presence the United States had unquestionably taken sides in the civil war. That they were ordered to help one side and not the other made things worse. They were not numerous enough to make a difference in who won but there were enough of them to be an irritant to the Communists. They had been put in an untenable situation. They only way to extricate them was to send them home.

"I'd like to kill all those yellow bastards," said one Marine to me. It was the frustrated reaction of American military men to Asia and the Asians due to be repeated some years later during the Vietnam War. To the Marines, the Chinese were inscrutable, something out of the American comic strip, "Terry and the Pirates." They were prepared to like them, but when they found the "chinks" ambushing and killing them they responded in an understandable way. They did not see much difference between Communists and the Nationalists. They were all "gooks."

Maj. Gen. Samuel Howard had no comment when I approached him for his reaction to the withdrawal order, but the Marines themselves were less reticent. They received the news with mixed but strong, emotions. They were a special breed of Americans based in China to take orders, not question them. That did not mean they did not have some very strong opinions of their own on this strange and distant land.

"My idea of China is—it stinks!" said a private from Syracuse, N.Y. "I am very glad to be leaving here. I have been thinking of the day when I would leave, even if for another base in the Pacific. Anyone interested in duty in China just doesn't have any sense. I don't like it and many of my buddies feel the same way. I always imagined it to be a clean, quiet, civilized place. I now know it is a lot different."

A sergeant major from Harrisburg, Penn., thought it was an interesting experience, "neither good nor bad," while a corporal called it "good duty" and found the Chinese generally "okay" for coolies and ricksha pullers, a class the Marines encountered most often.

One private who did not want to be named said, "I guess the Communists were right when they said we were interfering in the internal conditions here. We don't do nothing but sit around and pull a little guard duty once in a while. We certainly prevented them from attacking Tianjin or Beiping just by being there."

A Raleigh, N.C., pfc. was glad to leave. "I just don't seem to mix with these chinks," he said.

The prospect of going to a place "where the streets and people are clean and where, when you buy a girl a drink you don't have to pay the house rent," enthralled a Marine from Oakland, Calif. "I'll leave China to the missionaries," he grinned. "They got more guts than I have."

The news saddened the White Russian girls who made a profitable living selling their charms to the Marines. "We are going to be lonesome without them," said one startlingly blonde blonde. "Of course we had boy friends before and we will again. But they'll have to be civilians now."

"Les Girls" were something of a triumph and a defeat for the Marine command. Alarmed at the high rate of venereal disease among the men after contacts with unsupervised Chinese prostitutes, it created "approved" houses where Navy medics regularly inspected the ladies of the evening. A Marine officer told me, with a touch of pride in his voice, that thanks to this the venereal disease rate of the First Division had plummeted and was the lowest in the entire U.S. armed forces.

It was too good to last. A young Marine came down with gonorrhea from a "free lance" Chinese girl. He told his parents he got it in the approved Marine house. Mom wrote her congressman and the house was abolished. The VD rate, not astonishingly, climbed back to its old heights, among the highest in the service.

During most of 1947 I covered North China and Manchuria from Beiping. The civil war raged with no holds barred and foreign correspondents covered it the best way they could. Barred by the government from going to the fronts—and there were many—they had to rely on official briefings and communiqués, educated guesses from American officials and the Chinese press, which regarded its role as one of entertainment rather than the supply of hard news. The Xinhua News Agency, still broadcasting from the underground after the fall of Yan'an, supplied bits and pieces of information which could neither be denied nor confirmed.

The pivotal battle of the Manchurian campaign was that of Szepingkai, an important rail and industrial center. The Nationalists pushed Lin Biao's forces out after a devastating battle which lasted a month. I got there the day after his retreat, the first foreign reporter on the scene, and was told by the Nationalist commander that he could not afford another such victory. It had cost him 25,000 casualties and he had had to fight the Reds block by block. The city looked as though an earthquake had hit it. The charred timbers of destroyed houses and factories stuck up like burnt fingers on a dead hand. The rest was desolation.

The thing that doomed the Kuomintang in Manchuria was the fact that the attackers withdrew laden, like a file of ants, with all Szepingkai's grain stores. The Kuomintang had planned to survive for three months on these reserves. When they disappeared, resistance began to crumple. A few months later, Lin Biao returned to the city and found it like a tree hollowed out by termites. It took little more than a push to topple it. Changchun and Mukden followed.

Reporting on these developments from Beiping, with an occasional trip to Manchuria, represented the very height of genteel war reporting—no slogging in the mud, dodging bullets and mortars on frozen battlefields, sleeping in drafty tents or surviving on military rations. In fact, though it was only a few hundred miles away, the war seemed distant and unreal as one sat around the swimming pool of the Peking Club and ate fresh strawberries. It was hard to believe that countless thousands of soldiers and civilians were dying each day. The citizens of Beiping, long used to war and commotion, went their unhurried rounds seemingly oblivious to the momentous events unfolding outside their walls.

The city which now is the capital of the People's Republic has had a bewildering variety of names. Two thousand years ago it was a tiny garrison town called Qi, soon wiped out by the first emperor, Qin Shi Huangdi. It was Yanjing under the Han Dynasty which succeeded Qin, then a tribal center called Yuzhou several hundred years later. It once was called Nanjing and then Chong-tu. When the great Mongol emperor, Kublai Khan, made it his capital in 1276 the world came to know it, thanks to Marco Polo, as Khanbaliq. In 1644, the Manchu took it over and called it Beijing, which means Northern Capital. When they fell, the raffish northern warlords whom Chiang Kai-shek and the Communists had fought, claimed it as their own.

Unhappy with these past foreign and freebooter associations the Generalissimo made Nanjing his capital. It means Southern Capital. Since there obviously could not be a southern and northern capital, Chiang changed the name of Beijing to Beiping (Northern Peace).

Mao had no such scruples. Or perhaps he, in turn, did not want to be associated with Nanjing and Chiang. So he set up shop in Beijing.

I have known both cities in my day. During Chiang's rule, it was Beiping, a dusty city of quiet enchantment. It has become more grandiose, noisier and less attractive today than before.

Coming from wartime Kunming, the grubby wartime capital of Chongqing, and primitive Yan'an, I was not prepared for the mixture of grandeur and simplicity which was the Beiping of that time.

The old walls still stood and I entered it through one of its massive gates to find myself in a city of walls, those of the Forbidden City, and thousands of smaller walls surrounding the homes of its inhabitants. One knocked at one of their bright red gates and walked into a secluded world, tree-shaded courtyards separated by walls pierced with moongates into which none of the city's noises penetrated. Looked at from above, the city reminded one of that charmingly puzzling Chinese creation, nests of boxes within boxes impossible to open.

The rhythm of Beiping in the 1940s was slow, almost languid. There were few automobiles, a handful of jeeps, buses which never seemed to appear, some bicycles pedalled by students and professors, and thousands of rickshas. The city throbbed slowly to the muffled sound of the straw-sandaled feet of ricksha coolies. These were the main form of locomotion, serving restaurants, hotels, municipal offices, and homes. It was not unusual to see them piled high with the detritus of living—trunks, mattresses, boxes, and lamps. I once saw one moving a piano. A line of rickshas waited in front of the Grand Hotel des Wagons Lits where I stayed on my first visit. Like London taxi drivers, the coolies knew every corner of the city and were said to have prodigious memories for past clients.

During my year's residence, I maintained a ricksha puller, as did everyone else. Spindly legged, his skin as brown as old parchment, he wore a constant smile and not much else. He took me to my appointments, delivered my stories to the telegraph office, and otherwise dozed in his ricksha outside my home. He could have been 30 or 50. It was hard to tell. Dressed in the flimsiest clothing in summer or winter, he seemed unaffected by the heat or cold. After one got over the initial discomfiture of being pulled around town by a fellow human, the sensation of moving in almost total silence through the streets became a pleasurable one. It had all the joys of sailing a yacht rather than a noisy motorboat.

Despite their spare physique, the pullers had remarkable stamina. They trotted around town all day without signs of fatigue. A diet of raw garlic was said to be the secret. Sensitive passengers held handkerchiefs to their nose as they were wafted through the streets.

That year in Beiping was an experience so satisfying that I wanted it to last forever. Its slow, thoughtful pace, its intelligent Chinese and expatriate residents, its walls shutting out the distractions of everyday life, and its history all appealed to me. I could see myself whiling away the rest of my days there, sampling its varied cuisine, picnicking in the Western hills, sauntering bemused through the courtyards of the Forbidden City, drinking in the sights and sounds, engaging in witty conversation with friends, and reading.

How could one not be enchanted by a city whose narrow hutungs (lanes) echoed with the cries of the noodle vendor, the scissor sharpener, and the peddler of caged crickets? Where could one still indulge the hobby of incense sniffing and of training pigeons to wheel in the sky, with flutes attached to their legs, so that sunset became not only a visual but a musical revelation? In a frenetic world, we all have our Beipings, places of refuge and concealment, of escape from the things and the people we want to forget, communities where we can live controlled, graceful, unhurried lives, and be taken, tolerantly, at our own estimated value. I glimpsed all these possibilities during my first short stay. A year of residence reinforced these impressions.

I took over from Tom Masterson, the resident AP man who had been reassigned to Singapore but was reluctant to leave. In fact, he did almost everything he could to get the transfer canceled. I did not have any sympathy for him then but I do now. He maneuvered and stalled for a month while I waited, impatiently, with nothing to do but eat, drink, and sightsee. Comfortably installed at the Wagons Lits, time dragged its feet. I felt loaded down with chains. My first fifteen months as a foreign correspondent had sped past like a hundred-yard dash. Between my Yan'an assignments I had worked in Shanghai, hiked off to the borders of Tibet in pursuit of the savage Lolo, journeyed to Manchuria to meet Lin Biao, put in six months in Nanjing covering the Kuomintang side of the Marshall negotiations. Suddenly, all this feverish activity came to a grinding halt.

It was early spring and the weather was cold and dry, full of electric sparks and high tension. American style, the hotel was overheated. To pass the time, I entertained Chinese friends, mostly Nationalist air force pilots I had known in Kunming. We dined richly and drank deeply. I walked around with the frustrated, pentup energy ticking inside me of a small atom bomb which refused to explode. Eating, for the Chinese, is an adventure. They enliven it with games, toasts, and laughter. Zhou Enlai loved to play a game in which the players shouted their guesses of the total number of fingers flashed simultaneously. Another one was scissors, stone, paper. The loser's penalty was to *ganbei,* to down his drink in one gulp. My friends paid me the compliment, reserved only for friends, of trying to get me drunk. When the games became too slow, they fell back on simple toasts in *shaoxing.* It was so pleasant to the taste and so seemingly innocuous that one did not notice how deadly it could become. We began by drinking from small wine cups about the size of an egg cup, then graduated to teacups, and finally to rice bowls. This strenuous exercise night after night unravelled my nerves. I could not sleep. Awakening in the middle of the night to go to the toilet, I became dizzy, turned ashen white, and had to stagger back to my bed. I had nightmares, dreams of frustration so severe they jolted me out of my sleep. I do not know how long I could have kept up this life of pleasantly suicidal dissipation but deliverance came one day when Masterson, defeated, packed his bags and left. I moved from the hotel to his house and began writing. Recovery after that was rapid. I am convinced that work, within reasonable limits, is therapy.

My house was in one corner of a walled compound at 16A Datianshuijing off what used to be Morrison Street and now is the busy shopping center of Wangfujing. My landlord was Dr. Jean Bussiere, head of the French hospital. The lane's name meant "Great Sweet Water Well." Muddy and narrow, it was superior to the nearby lane of the "Small Sweet Water Well." During periods of drought the wells had saved many lives.

My new "house" was, more accurately, an apartment perched on the second floor of a building whose basement was used chiefly for storage. It consisted of a bedroom, a living room, bath, and small kitchen. The decor was blue—blue curtains, deep blue carpeting, blue bed covers. It was altogether as snug as a bug in a rug and much more luxurious than anything I had yet experienced in China.

I had my meals with Dr. Bussiere and shared his six servants. For this I paid the equivalent of $35 a month. AP bore the extra expense of the ricksha.

A stretch of pavement and an oak tree separated my house from Dr. Bussiere's large one. It had a big living room, several bedrooms, a kitchen, and servants' quarters. An additional room served as office and consulting room. Both buildings were roofed in tile.

The good doctor was 75 when I knew him, ruddy-cheeked, bushy-browed, eyes sparkling with good humor. He had the face of a well-fed French provincial, one who had lived well, seen much suffering but continued to regard life through twinkling blue eyes with good humor and compassion. There was something of the Mr. Pickwick in him. His generous white mustache gave him the look of Esky, mascot of the American magazine *Esquire* in the thirties. He spoke Chinese and had a knowledge of the people based on intimate observation over a period of thirty-five years. As healthy as a horse, he worked every morning at the hospital and spent part of the afternoons cycling the rounds of his patients in Beiping and the outskirts. He donated both his time and medicine to the poor, among whom were a number of Communists. He was hardly one himself. That might have entailed giving up a gourmet style of life. Besides, he came from the haute bourgeoisie. A sister in Paris was a countess.

"I never ask my patients about their politics," he said. "To me they are only one thing. They are sick. I do my best to cure them. What else should I do?"

A widower, his most devoted companion was Johnny, a Scots terrier. He went wherever the doctor went. They were a pair. Old and wise-looking, Johnny was extraordinarily intelligent. He lived in his own world but humored his human hosts. One of his tricks was to stand on his hind legs with a piece of bread balanced on his nose, patiently waiting for the doctor to clap his hands. When he did, he tossed the bread into the air and caught it in his mouth. It was a star performance.

The doctor returned one day from his afternoon rounds looking tired and defeated.

"It's Johnny," he said, "he's disappeared. I was afraid it would happen. He was round and plump. The temptation was too much for those poor people. I'm sure they have eaten him."

Anyone else might have cried or cursed or damned the Chinese race. The doctor did none of these things. Johnny's fate pained him deeply but the only sign of it was a Gallic shrug of his shoulders and a deepening line in his face.

Dr. Bussiere's closest human friend was a French sinologue named M. Bertrand. Dressed in formal black jacket and wearing a tie around his stiff collar, M. Bertrand spent his days with his nose buried in obscure Chinese tomes. He was a scholarly expert on China. Every Wednesday he came by the doctor's house for lunch, a ritual which they had observed religiously for three decades. I had the pleasure of being included in these weekly visits during which I learned a good deal of arcane things about Beiping. The conversation was lively, the food excellent but the wines less than distinguished. This astonished me since, on other occasions, when we dined alone, the doctor brought out some of his most treasured wines, sunshine in cobwebby bottles. I asked him why M. Bertrand only got *vin ordinaire.*

"Well, Jean," he said, "you must remember that he is an old, old friend. An old shoe, you might say. No need to do anything out of the ordinary. He wouldn't expect it. But you are a guest in my house. You are an adventure. It pleases me to see how you react to these old bottles. I like to try them out on you."

I came home one day in June to find the doctor in the courtyard standing in front of a pile of wood which he soon set alight.

"Come," he said. "We must leap over the fire, it is St. John's Day."

It was the first time I had heard of this peculiarly European custom, of St. John's fire. After jumping over the flames a few times we celebrated with still another bottle from the doctor's well-stocked cellar.

Long residence, a jovial manner, and good works made Dr. Bussiere widely known in Beiping. He treated many of the Chinese leaders, including the various warlords who came and went over the years. His most interesting patient, he told me, was a living god, the Panchen Lama of Tibet. During a state visit to Beiping his holiness contracted a toothache and Dr. Bussiere was hastily summoned to do the necessary. Though no dentist, he skillfully extracted the offending molar, an impacted wisdom tooth. Asked to present his bill, the doctor smiled and said, "If you wouldn't mind, I should like to keep the tooth. There is no charge otherwise."

When I knew him, the tooth rested in solitary splendor in a glass cabinet which contained the doctor's collection of Chinese antiquities. He delighted in showing it to visitors.

"How many people can say they possess the wisdom tooth of a living god?" he would ask with a glint in his eye.

The Panchen Lama never got back to Tibet. Caught up in a dispute with the Dalai Lama, he died on the border in 1937, aged 54, minus his wisdom tooth. In 1948, I met his 12-year-old successor in the Lamasery of Kumbum in Qinghai Province. He had all his teeth.

Beiping was not all Shangri-la. It had its ugly side. One of them was the deadly rivalry between Nationalist and Communist, or leftist, students. I went out one day to investigate a killing on one of the smaller campuses. Nationalist students in the pay of the government had gunned down another student suspected of Communist sympathies. I made the hour-long trip in one of the new tricycle pedicabs which were beginning to replace rickshas. With me, in another one, was Chris Rand, then with the *New York Herald Tribune,* later a *New Yorker* magazine writer.

Having picked up whatever information we could, we were being pedalled back to the city center when two grim-faced youths emerged from a ditch and pointed ugly-looking Mauser pistols at us. Our pedicab driver understandably came to a sudden stop. We sat there for an uncomfortable five minutes trying to look unconcerned.

"Roderick," shouted Chris, "do you have a camera with you?"

"Yes," I replied.

"Then take a picture of these two thugs," he said.

"I tell you what," I said, "I'll throw the camera to you and you take the picture."

He declined.

The youthful gunmen sputtered a language neither of us could understand. I finally ended the impasse by producing my card and handing it to them.

"Oh, oh," one of them cried in broken English. "Americans. *Meiguoren.* You can leave. We apologize. We thought you were Russians."

The language they had been attempting to speak was Russian. They were Nationalist agents.

Chris Rand was one of the reasons I found Beiping so endearing. A New Englander, graduate of Harvard, he wore a blond mustache and seemed determined to live down his white Anglo Saxon, Protestant heritage. I thought him the very image of a carefree bachelor only to find that he had a wife back in Boston and five children. Dining out with him was a thrilling experience; he was an expert in Chinese cuisine. He also was a brilliant raconteur and a formidable drinker. There is a saying that God protects fools, drunkards, and children. I thought of that when he returned, with a pal, one night to his compound in an advanced state of inebriation. Almost dead drunk to put it plainly. The door was locked and he had misplaced the key.

"Not to worry," he said. "Just climb over the wall." Which they did. The next day I inspected the wall in question. Like all Beiping walls it was covered in broken glass to deter burglars. They were not even scratched.

Chris went through phases. In one of these, he became devoutly Buddhist. He refused to eat meat or fish, made sure he stepped on no

insects or other living things and avoided the use of leather. Most
Buddhists are not so strict. But Chris always did things totally, never
by halves. The leather bit proved inconvenient. It meant he had to
replace his leather belts with rope tied around his middle. Since rope
did not hold as well as it might, we often were fascinated during a
cocktail party or other standup encounter when his trousers slowly
began to descend. Before they reached his ankles he pulled them up
and tied the knot a bit tighter as though nothing worth noting had
happened.

Everyone I knew admired Chris and was proud to be regarded as a
friend. He was, as Dr. Bussiere put it, an old shoe, comfortable to be
with, always stimulating. He did not seem to have a problem in the
world. The shock was great when, sometime in the mid-1950s, I picked
up a paper and read that he had killed himself.

One of the more flamboyant of Beiping's residents was my chief
competitor, the United Press chief, Reynolds Packard, better known
as Pack. A large, bulldog-shaped man, he had been bureau chief in
Paris and Moscow, had covered the Abyssinian war and was the author of a much-quoted book on news agencies called *The Kansas City
Milkman*.

On news stories, he went to great lengths to make sure he got an
"exclusive angle," one AP did not have. When two planes were assigned to carry the press corps anywhere, he always insisted that we
travel in separate ones. During these trips he thoughtfully sipped gin
from a flask concealed under his trenchcoat.

A prodigious drinker, he became philosophical as the evening wore
on.

"What is truth?" he would exclaim. "You people at AP claim to be
writing the truth because you are objective. But isn't objectivity just
as much an exaggeration as a bit of subjectivity. Who is the custo-
dian of truth?"

He was impressed by the Chinese press, which regarded news as a
form of entertainment, something to be invented for the amusement
of its readers. It may have been only a bit ahead of its time. Knowing
this propensity, most of the Beiping correspondents treated stories
in the Chinese papers with caution. Not so Pack. He enthusiastically
picked up reports of human-headed spiders and atomic explosions on
Lake Baikal and relayed them to his New York office.

Pack enjoyed life to the full. In the absence of his wife, he picked
up a jolly, peasant girl from Manchuria to keep him warm nights. I
met her in the Wagons Lits on the shoulders of a visiting AP executive. She had an engaging habit of stripping naked and admiring
herself in the mirror.

When Pack's wife, Pee Bee, arrived the three set up housekeeping together. We never learned what happened, but on one occasion Pee Bee came down to breakfast with razor marks on her wrist.

One of the Americans in Beiping was a former missionary from my state of Maine. Of a practical turn of mind, he abandoned the gospel for a more rewarding career buying and selling Tianjin carpets. With the considerable fortune thus collected, he built the ideal residence for foreigners, ferro-concrete affairs in Chinese style, complete with moongates, which had the added advantage of central heating. Pack and Pee Bee moved into one of these luxury homes and seemed quite content. There was one drawback, however. The missionary's wife ached to know what was going on in her houses. She would burst into them without advance notice to see whether the furniture had been disturbed or anything else was out of order. This, obviously, was a source of some annoyance to the Packards. They decided to do something about it.

One night, when the landlady strode into the room in the usual way, she was shocked to see Pack and Pee Bee standing in front of the fireplace sipping dry martinis. They were as naked as jaybirds. The effect was heightened by the fact that Pee Bee was as tall and rangy as Pack was large and square.

The landlady screamed.

"What is the meaning of this?" she shouted, trembling.

"Well," said Pack, lowering his glass but making no attempt to otherwise conceal himself, "we regard our home as our castle. We like to relax without any clothes on. If you insist on breaking in without warning, I'm afraid you'll have to put up with it."

She stomped out in fury but never bothered them again.

When, one day, United Press messaged Pack that he was fired, there was general gloom in Beiping. He was, despite his occasional eccentricities, a first-class newsman. In the expatriate society of Beiping, he was liked for his good humor and his imagination. Life was never boring while he was around. A few days before he left, the foreign press corps gave him a farewell party at the home of *Time* correspondent Jim Burke. At its height, Pack picked up the engraved pint-sized silver flask we had presented him, put it to his lips, and drained its contents of gin without pausing for breath.

Leaving China, he and Pee Bee spent the rest of their lives in Italy as correspondents for a New York newspaper.

Besides Rand and the Packards, the Foreign Correspondents Club of Beiping included some more than ordinary journalists. One of them was Walter Bosshardt, correspondent of the *Neue Zuricher Zeitung*. He lived in a splendid Chinese-style house whose living room of painted beams contained a fitted, circular Mongolian carpet of great size. White-haired, jowly and distinguished looking, he acted more like a captain of industry than the brilliant reporter he was. In a long lifetime, he had hiked into Tibet and written books about it, had reported on China both before and during the war. He had a habit of clearing his throat before speaking which gave what he said an extra touch of gravity. His cuisine was superb and invitations to dinner sought after. When he retired it was to a chalet in the mountains of his native Switzerland. Few people had witnessed so much of China's modern history.

Seymour "Cy" Topping, later to become managing editor of the *New York Times,* was there stringing for the International News Service (INS). A story for INS had to be urgent to be telegraphed. Most of his articles, analyses, and features went by airmail.

He lived in a large compound with several other young Americans studying Chinese on the GI Bill of Rights, legislation which provided free education to veterans of World War II. By pooling their modest resources they were able to hire a rotund cook of formidable ability and to entertain on a scale equal to Bosshardt. It was at their compound, under the trees, that I first met the famous scholar-historian Hu Shi.

One of the GI Bill students sharing the compound was Robert "Bob" Burton, Pack's successor, on a part-time basis, as correspondent for United Press. Bob was still in his twenties, blond, outgoing, and highly intelligent. He was one of the best-informed reporters in Beiping.

He suffered acutely from asthma which attacked him at unpredictable moments leaving him gasping and out of breath. I became adept at jabbing him in the leg with a medication which gave him almost immediate relief. We became close friends not only in Beiping but in Shanghai and years later in Hong Kong. After I left Beiping in 1948, I received a letter from him which described one of the traumatic events of his life. He was on the scene, covering a demonstration against the Nationalist government in Beiping when soldiers opened fire on the withdrawing students. One of the bullets hit one of the students, a close friend, in the back, killing him instantly. A few days later, in despair, Bob took an overdose of sleeping pills.

He was unconscious and had reckoned, as he said, without the U.S. Marines. They sent a plane to Qingdao and brought back antibiotics which restored him to life, an event he had not foreseen. Could I loan him $800 for the trip home via the Middle East? I was in Transjordan then and wired the money, which he later repaid, at once.

Bob went to Hong Kong for the Voice of America broadcast people and there became a friend of Zhang Guotao, the aging former chairman of the Chinese Communist Party, one of the first victims, in 1938, of Mao's paranoiac fear of potential successors. Sensing that the moment was right, Bob undertook to write Zhang's biography. He had dozens of interviews with him and set about preparing the manuscript. Everything pointed to the success of his project. But there was a problem. In Hong Kong he had met a Chinese gentleman of the old school, wispy-bearded and dreamy. The dreams were induced by opium which, while providing escape, had made him cadaverously thin. Always prone to experiment—most correspondents including myself had at one time or another tried smoking opium—Bob joined the old man in his dreams. He found that it not only alleviated the asthma but gave him a serenity that, despite his outward affability, he did not in ordinary life have. It did not take long for him to become an addict and later, as he told me, to move up to something far more deadly, heroin. Enroute to taking an America-bound plane with the manuscript, he lost much of it. Breaking the drug habit, he said, was one of the most painful experiences of his life. But he did.

After Hong Kong, he became head of the Chinese department of the University of Kansas which published the Zhang book in two volumes under the title, *The Rise of the Chinese Communist Party*. He put in months filling in the missing pages. The result was a valuable contribution to the history of the Communist party and Zhang Guotao's not inconsiderable part in it.

Bob became a leading member of a scholarly committee promoting closer ties with the mainland in 1979 then returned to Hong Kong to become director of the international division of the highly successful Chinese motion picture company which introduced Kung Fu and Bruce Lee to the world. Its president, Raymond Chao, was Bob's friend from his Shanghai days. During this period he lived in unaccustomed opulence. The salary was dazzling and the perks impressive. Raymond offered him a Rolls Royce so he could move about Hong Kong in style. Bob modestly refused. He settled for a Bentley.

After several years of this, he returned to Kansas, where he had two adopted sons and their families, and went into business. He died in 1987 at the age of 65. His love affair with life and tolerant amusement at its absurdities never waned.

Among my Chinese friends perhaps the most amusing was a Beiping student at the Catholic Fujen University named Liang Tsaiwen. Fascinated by the great Venetian traveler, he had taken the English name Marco Liang. A younger brother became Polo Liang. They were the children of a prosperous banker and his tiny, old-fashioned wife who lived in a hundred- room compound in one of the best parts of the city. It had once been a prince's residence and when they left, after the Communists took over, it became a hospital. There were gardens and lily ponds but not all the rooms were occupied. Some held the compound's stockpile of coal.

The Liangs adopted me and brought me into their home. Through them I learned much more about Beiping than I might otherwise have done. We went on picnics in the Western Hills, climbed Coal Hill, rummaged through antique shops, visited their friends, went boating on Bei Hai, the Winter Palace Lake, and explored old temples in the countryside. At New Year's we watched the devils in their ferocious masks being driven out of the Tibetan Lama Temple. They introduced me to a Mongolian barbecue restaurant down winding alleys where the rotund owner, naked to the waist, greeted us on arrival and bawled out for all to hear how much we had spent when we left.

What happened to the Liangs after the Communists came illustrates, in a small way, the resilience of the Chinese in the face of adversity. The eldest son already was installed in New York as representative of a Nationalist trading company. Polo joined him there and enrolled in a New York university. Despite the language handicap—he spoke good but not fluent English—he earned a doctorate in chemistry. Since there were still problems about his permanent visa, he decided to continue his studies and took a doctorate in a totally different subject. Today he is a university professor.

Their sister went to Taiwan where she married a man who became Nationalist ambassador to the Vatican.

Marco's career had its ups and downs. He also initially went to Taiwan. Having majored in chemistry he undertook to manufacture soap. After several years of this, he went to Denver, Colorado, where he opened a shop dealing in Chinese antiques. Then he hit on the idea of introducing pedicabs to Denver. He contacted me in Hong Kong to acquire the gaudiest looking pedicabs I could find and engaged Denver college students to peddle them. They were an instant success, so much so that the taxicab association launched a formal protest. There was too much competition. In the land of capitalism, where imagination and enterprise are said to reap rich rewards, he was defeated. The business collapsed. He went back to Taiwan and opened an English language school which became locally famous.

I took another of my Chinese friends, a venerable 80-year old scholar of the Mandarin class, to the Peking Club. The war had interrupted its activities but this equally venerable British establishment had regained its stride. It was an oasis for the foreign community, its library stocked with new books and recent periodicals, its swimming pool surrounded by chairs and tables where the members—few of them Chinese—sipped lemonade or ate strawberries and ice cream. I took my old friend to the tennis courts. It was his first glimpse of the game. We watched a couple of the large and sweating members chase after the ball for a while then I asked him what he thought of it.

"Well," he said with a small smile, "We have coolies who do that sort of work."

The Peking Club stuck to its colors, which were true blue, even when the Chinese Red armies closed in on the city. Lin Biao's forces were almost literally knocking at the gates but the news which made headlines in the *Peking Chronicle,* published by Tom Masterson's British wife, had nothing to do with this jarring event. Foreign attention was focused on a much more alarming development, the great debate over the status of women in the club. Since its inception they had been tolerated, but only just. They could visit but they must use the back door.

The headline of the *Chronicle* summed up the new order: Peking Club Votes to Admit Women by the Front Door.

It was a belated blow struck for women's rights. The members need not have bothered. Once the Communists took over they turned it into an international club and anyone, including women, could come in the front door.

In the closing months of my stay I came down with a mysterious illness which began with a chill, developed into a fever, and graduated into splitting headaches, aches in all my bones, and a pain in the back. I coughed up blood and lost twenty-five pounds in a month. Dr. Bussiere took an X-ray and a Chinese specialist said I was suffering, at the age of 33, from hardening of the arteries. Some hardening! They are still functioning forty-five years later. An American Navy doctor examined me and said it was a bad cold. It left me as suddenly as it had arrived.

A message arrived from Fred Hampson, my boss in Shanghai, at this stage. It asked me to return to Shanghai and be replaced by Moosa. I resisted, sent him Dr. Bussiere's diagnosis of my condition and a suggestion that the dry cold air of Beijing was more salubrious than the heat and humidity of Shanghai. He insisted, hinted there were pressing professional reasons he needed me there. I later discovered the truth. His wife, Margaret, could not get along with Spencer's wife, Nina. Fred solved the domestic dilemma by shipping the Moosas to Beijing. History is made by trivia like this.

Dr. Bussiere regretted my departure and opened one of his finest vintages to send me off. His own personal situation had improved. The 18-year-old Chinese girl of good family he had hired as secretary and housekeeper became his wife. Before I left she presented him with a boy. The Communists had short memories or lacked gratitude, an essential of life. When the three left for Paris they refused to let him take his Chinese antiquities with him.

The Correspondents Club gave me a farewell dinner and presented me with a print of a Chinese kitchen god and his seventeen attendants. They appended their signatures to it and typed in an inscription which said:

> The Foreign Correspondents Club of Peiping
> Presents to its Frail Brother
> JOHN RODERICK
> With concern for his Heart and Weight this
> KITCHEN GOD
> Which We Expect Will Enable Him to Defeat
> Disease, the Evil Spirits of Land, Sea and Air and
> U.P.

The kitchen god is on a wall in my Kamakura farmhouse not far from my only other valuable souvenir of Beiping, a Tang dynasty three-color glaze official, bought from Plaut, the noted collector across the lane, for $250. Together they remind me of an existence once cherished but now gone forever.

I spent six months in Nanjing, reporting on the slow, joyless dance of negotiations which continued after the failure of the Marshall mission, and another year in Shanghai, which like Beiping, became a base from which to travel to other parts of the country. I returned to Chongqing, tracked the savage Lolos of Sikang, met a Moslem warlord, and interviewed the Panchen Lama in Qinghai Province.

After each trip I returned to Shanghai still yearning for the dusty charms of Beiping. Instead of living in a walled compound, shut off from the noises of the street, I occupied a fourteenth-floor apartment in the Broadway Mansions which looked down on the Bund, an uneven row of Victorian-style buildings and trading offices lining the teeming waterfront. Devoted to the unabashed accumulation of money, Shanghai was brash, supremely confident, in a hurry. It was a foreign enclave at once admired and hated by most Chinese for the Western progress it represented and the arrogance with which it flaunted it. Shanghai was New York or London of the thirties devoid of the culture of those cities. Beiping was Chinese in ways the Shanghailanders could never understand, quiet, withdrawn, unostentatious, and scholarly.

The French, the British, and the Japanese had dominated the prewar life of Shanghai. Now it was the American turn. The Navy took over the Glen Line Building on the Bund and American sailors and soldiers were bedded down in the Cathay and Park Hotels, their interiors pure art deco reminiscent of John Held, Jr. and the age of the flappers, Tiffany lamps and Tiffany windows. The departing Japanese had ripped out the plumbing and some of the fixtures but they were soon replaced. Worse had been expected.

Wherever the Americans went they were met with smiles and applause. Victory after so long a deprivation was sweet. Even the children

got into the act, tagging after the servicemen, grimy hands outstretched, shouting: "*Tinghao, tinghao,* you good, Joe. You got chewing
gum, please? You want pretty girl, cheap? How about my sister?"

The Yanks were loved not only for themselves but for the scarce
goods they brought with them, penicillin and Lucky Strike cigarettes
and cling peaches in the can. These soon became units of exchange,
hoarded against the rising inflation.

The relics of Shanghai's glamorous past still existed—the French
Club with its heated swimming pool, dance floor on springs and string
quartets, the Race Track taken over by the Armed Forces Radio people
which my Mormon reporter friend, Jack Anderson, had joined, and a
huge, gangster-run entertainment complex called the Great World.
All these gave postwar Shanghai a certain liveliness but its vices
were workaday gray rather than purple. The old French city and the
International Settlement, run by the British and Americans, had been
abolished and the new openness discouraged hit-and-run crime. The
Chinese pickpockets and slit purses, small-time thieves and drug
dealers had once found asylum in these international enclaves. Now
they had nowhere to run to. It discouraged business.

A new enemy, inflation, stalked the city's markets, department
stores, and restaurants. Prices changed hourly as the situation wors-
ened. Within months it took several hundred million Chinese dollars
to buy an American dollar. Chiang sent his son, Chiang Ching-kuo—
later to be president of the exiled Republic on Taiwan—to see what he
could do. He lined up speculators and had them shot, then introduced
a gold certificate pegged at a thousand to one. It did not work. The
price of a bottle of aspirin or atabrine used to control the symptoms
of malaria rose to astronomical heights. Public confidence in the government swiftly eroded. There were comparisons to the inflation which
destroyed the German Weimar Republic after World War I.

The Broadway Mansions which the correspondents shared with
the U.S. Army was an island of stability in this furious sea of inflation. An eighteen-story, brown brick apartment hotel built by the
Japanese, it looked down on the British consulate, the Whampoa River,
Soochow Creek, and the Bund. Hampson, and his wife Margaret, had
a spacious apartment on the seventeenth floor with a splendid view.
From it in 1949 she was able to give a running account to AP of the
entry into Shanghai, after a brief battle, of the ever-victorious Communist army.

After the Chongqing press hostel and the caves of Yan'an, my small
apartment was luxury incarnate. All it lacked was Shanghai Lil.

I hired a 70-year-old Chinese cook of almost cadaverous thinness
and worried that he might not appreciate the joys of good food. When
I ordered lobster for my first dinner, he reeled off a dozen different

ways to prepare it. He was a genius with a wok and made invitations to my modest table much cherished. The other correspondents worked their cooks harder and paid them between $25 to $30 a month, a princely recompense in those inflated days. My happiness was so great that I paid my saturnine cook $40. My colleagues and their wives greeted this show of munificence with indignation. They told me heatedly that I was betraying my class, pricing the help out of the market.

Before the war, Shanghai had justly enjoyed the reputation of being a city of sinister excitement, sin, and depravity. A delicious shudder coursed down the spines of Americans as they came ashore from the warships of the Seventh Fleet, or arrived from West China by plane, to get their first glimpse of the city.

The reality proved less titillating. The International Settlement and the French Quarter, where much of the fun had taken place, now were submerged in the new Chinese city administration. There were bars and dance halls with White Russian hostesses, but somehow the war had taken the zip out of sin. In the scramble to survive in the postwar period, few people had the time or the money to spend on high life.

There were, however, some human relics of those bawdy, careless old days. One of them was Du Yuesheng, tsar of the prostitution, protection, and opium rackets. He had done his old friend and fellow gang member, the Generalissimo, an unusual service in the 1927 break between the Kuomintang and Communist parties, ordering his thugs into action when the Gimo's troops proved unable to reach the fleeing Reds. It was they who carried out the massacre. The thugs were members of Du's Green Gang, an old and infamous secret society which ran Shanghai. Because it had patriotic pretensions it was glad to help Chiang, a member, in what it considered a good cause.

Self-exiled during the war to Hong Kong where he continued to direct the Green Gang's activities, Du hoped to return in triumph to Shanghai, his city, the one he ran practically single-handedly with gun and knife, through bribery and blackmail but with a Robin Hood–like streak of generosity. Instead, demonstrators bearing placards crying "Down with Du Yuesheng" waited at North Station to greet him. Chagrined and disillusioned—he could not recognize that Shanghai, along with the rest of the world, had changed—he got off the train before it reached the terminal and went home.

When I arrived he was the talk of the town and the subject of many news articles. He was vintage Shanghai, the opium king paradoxically chairman of the Opium Suppression League, a government post. The Americans cultivated him because he was staunchly anti-Communist and a friend of the Generalissimo. He kept a low profile even though he was on the board of directors of at least fifty companies, including the leading newspaper. But he wanted the speakership of the city council which he regarded as his own creature. In the voting, forty ballots were unmarked, more signs of protest. It had never happened before. Ashen-faced, he withdrew, pleading ill health. The worst blow fell in 1947 when he learned that a trusted lieutenant, an officer of the Hong Kong labor association, had turned Communist and was babbling of human rights, free trade unions, and communism. He celebrated his sixtieth birthday with a party at the Lido Ballroom attended by more than five thousand guests but the music was drowned in his own mind by the drums of the advancing armies of Mao Zedong.

When the Communists moved in they let it be known, indirectly, that he would be more than welcome to remain behind and, like others who had defected from the Kuomintang, could expect a responsible post in the new order of things. But he had had too many pleasures, too many complaisant young opera singers, too much good food, and too much power to give all this up for the gray austerity of communism. In May 1949 he sailed for Hong Kong where he died in 1951. He was buried in Taipei.

Another unseen, but deeply felt, presence in postwar Shanghai was Wang Qingwei, once leader of the Kuomintang, Sun Yat-sen's heir-apparent, and more notoriously, puppet president of Japanese-occupied China. Handsome, intellectually brilliant but fatally indecisive, he waffled and wavered after Sun's death and thus allowed the Gimo to seize leadership of the Kuomintang. Sprayed while premier with bullets from a gun ingeniously hidden in a press camera, he survived. Ironically, the assassination attempt was mounted by an anti-Chiang faction in the Kuomintang which mistook Wang for the Generalissimo. This revelation—for years anti-Japanese patriots and Chiang himself were suspect—appears in *Old Shanghai* by Pan Ling.

On his death the emperor of Japan sent a wreath and the body was flown to Nanjing where amid such ceremony it was buried at the foot of Purple Mountain. Two years later, at Chiang's order, the tomb was blown open and the body burned.

Madame Wang Jingwei survived, a dumpy little woman of imperious mien who paid her husband the supreme compliment of believing unwaveringly in his cause. On April 16, 1946, her trial for treason began in Suzhou, the city of canals a few hours by train from Shanghai. I covered it.

Daughter of a rich family from Penang, she met Wang during one of Sun Yat-sen's fund-raising trips to Malaya. Defying her father, she went with him to Beijing where, after an aborted attempt on the life of the Prince Regent, he ended in prison. She was his accomplice. They were married when the Manchus fell in 1911. After her husband's death she became a power in Guangzhou and was tricked into surrendering by a false report that she would be received by the Generalissimo in Chongqing. Instead she was smuggled at midnight to Suzhou to face her accusers.

The crowds were dense inside and outside the magistrate's yamen, or court. Pushed and shoved from the rear, I stood throughout the proceedings while taking notes. Wearing sunglasses, her hair cut short in the kind of bob affected by the revolutionary women I had met in Yan'an, she stared straight ahead, defiant to the point of arrogance. Charged with espionage, serving the Japanese in Guangzhou, and the murder of resistance fighters, she acted as though the judges and not she were on trial.

She portrayed herself as more heroine than traitor, selflessly and patriotically dedicated to saving lives by dealing skillfully with the enemy. These were her husband's arguments which she had totally adopted. She hinted darkly that there might be others as guilty as she who should be in the defendant's box. The audience understood her to mean Chiang Kai-shek himself and to refer to his own extensive and suspect contacts with the Japanese during the war.

There were murmurs of guarded approval when she spoke, often angrily and using expletives, of her own integrity and total devotion to her husband. She had loved Wang as no other woman had—despite his good looks and intelligence, he never took a mistress—and in the dock she defended him as much as herself. I would be reminded of her thirty-four years later when Mao's widow, Jiang Qing, defiantly refused to admit her guilt and gave her tormentors more then she got.

Sentenced to life imprisonment, she refused to appeal. Like Jiang Qing later, she would not repent and berated her jailers for daring to use the familiar form of her name instead of Madame Wang. In 1949, when the Communists took Shanghai, Mao sent her a message offering to free her in return for a signed confession. She replied haughtily that her husband's cooperation with the Japanese had been no worse than Mao's friendship with the Russians. She would stay, she said, where she was. She died thirteen years later in June 1959, about the time Mao himself was being put on the shelf. Her children scattered her ashes over the sea.

I remained in Suzhou to visit American friends and attend an execution the day following the trial. It was a sample of what might have happened if Madame Wang had been sentenced to death. The hapless criminal, condemned for theft and murder, was paraded through the city his arms tied behind his back. His crimes were listed on a flat piece of wood thrust between the knotted ropes. The immense crowd—larger than that which had attended the Wang trial—was in festive mood. They might have been at a carnival as they strolled about, sipping their jasmine tea and chatting with their friends. Taken out of the truck, the condemned man, a youth in his late twenties, was roughly shoved onto a large field and forced to kneel tied to a post about six feet high. The executioner came up behind him, passed a rope around his neck and twisting a stick, as one would a tourniquet, garroted him. A policeman gave him the coup de grace, a bullet in the head. At the sound, the vast crowd burst into polite applause then returned to its tea and gossip.

The gulf between rich and poor in Shanghai was depressingly great. The cooks, drivers, and maid-amahs in the Broadway Mansions were the lucky ones. Their salaries were protected against inflation. And they could obtain scarce things like soap through generous employers. But the situation was desperate in the rest of the population. Most lived at the edge of starvation or died of diseases induced by malnutrition. Trucks went around every morning to pick up the corpses of the night before. Today Shanghai's waterfront is a pleasant, antiseptic, tree-planted promenade devoid of commercial activity. The unloading of ships has been transferred upriver. But in 1946, freighters discharged their cargoes in the middle of the city, on the Bund. The waterfront pulsated with activity as thousands of Chinese stevedores staggered under heavy loads from ship to shore over temporary wooden bridges. They got a pittance for their hard work and often were cursed or beaten for not moving faster. The Bund was like a bee hive, swarming with industrious people. The stevedores, thin and frail rather than big and brawny as they are in Western countries, were bundles of rags. They often slept in the open, near the big ships, ready for the next day's labor. The ricksha boys were hardly better off. Like the stevedores they were victims of the insane inflation, but at least they had somewhere to sleep. At night one saw them, wrapped in a thin cloth, curled up in their rickshas. These were the tip of the poverty iceberg. The big textile factories employed thousands of workers. One boasted of 80,000. They spent their days, and often nights, amid the thunderous din of the looms, exposed to industrial accidents and pollution. Like the stevedores and coolies, they earned barely enough to keep a spark of life alive in their emaciated bodies. For them, life was brutish and short.

If we correspondents lived well and cheaply, the military did even better. One night I attended a buffet dinner given for a departing American colonel. It was warm but a cool breeze wafted over the lucky guests. The buffet was one of Lucullan splendor. It included lobsters, crab, fish, chicken, pork, beef, game, ham in aspic, an assortment of salads, soups, and desserts. Tiny electric lights glowed from the antenna of the lobsters, a sight I had never seen before. I counted the dishes. There were fifty-seven. The next day I wrote a story about it, noting that it took place directly above a kind of sampan city in the creek below where poverty-stricken boat people lived on scraps, drank the muddy water, and washed and defecated into it. It was lucky none of my military friends read it. They would have accused me of being a Communist.

But you did not have to be a Communist to sympathize with the plight of the all-too-prevalent poor. Many Americans tried to do something to help but it was a problem for governments not individuals. Nanjing did not seem able to cope with it.

The Communists, forty-five years later, fenced off part of a now-scrubbed, sanitary, and prospering Shanghai as a reminder of the sordid past. This is what I wrote about it:

> Pumpkin Lane is a wound in Shanghai's side, carefully kept open as a reminder of the bad old days—a museum of unhappiness. A 79-year-old former ricksha puller and a street cleaner's 65-year-old widow are, in a sense, the custodians of that museum.
>
> He is Wang Fu-hsing and she is Wang Lan-hua. Their family names are the same but their only relationship is the shared misery of life in the 1920s and 1930s in Pumpkin Lane, a super-slum.
>
> Today, it is an uninhabited relic hidden behind high walls, a sample of the many mud and wattle huts and matsheds—lean-tos of straw which kept out neither rain nor cold—which housed 15,000 of the poorest people in China.
>
> It looks today like an archeological discovery, a primitive village illustrating the spartan way humans lived 20,000 years ago. The communists maintain it to show foreigners ignorant of Shanghai's seamy past and Chinese who may have forgotten or never known how bad things were even in comparison to their present spartan life styles.
>
> Wang Fu-hsing and Wang Lan-hua live in comparative splendor next door in small apartments built as part of a large development in the early 1960s. But when visitors like myself arrive, they swing open the heavy gates to Pumpkin Lane and relive their miserable past.
>
> Ricksha-pullers, street cleaners, dock workers, cripples and beggars along with their swarming families inhabited it then. Dressed in rags, they suffered through the bone-chilling cold of Shanghai winters and the miasmic heat of summer. With nothing to drink but ditch water it was little wonder few survived into old age.
>
> In spite of the poverty and the suffering there was time for poetry. Mrs. Wang recalled one:
>
>> We took the sky as our blanket
>> The ground as our bed
>> The winds to sweep the earth
>> And the moon as our lamp

Japanese bombers in the early days of World War II added to the hazards of life as they laid their deadly eggs in the Chapei district in which Pumpkin Lane is located. It was during one of these air raids that Mrs. Wang gave birth to her first child in a matshed, practically in the open air.

"It was 1937. The bombers had come, destroying houses everywhere. I was 21, alone and afraid," she recalled. "My mother couldn't be with me; she was begging in the streets. On the day the labor pains began I was scavenging for food on Peking Road, in the British Concession. My husband was cleaning streets. The pains lasted all day, Dec. 25. A neighbor lady helped with the delivery. But when the baby came, it soon turned blue from the cold. I had to hold it against my bare breast for 24 hours, otherwise it would not have survived."

The money her husband earned was not enough to keep her and the children who followed, so Mrs. Wang became a beggar.

"I managed to pick up some discarded vegetables once in a while. But more than once we had to eat leaves from trees," she said.

Old Mr. Wang, a spare bird-like man with skin stretched taut like parchment across his face, spent 60 years of his life in the Pumpkin Lane area.

"I was 18 when I became a ricksha man in 1921," he said. "I was poor, didn't have any education and so couldn't do anything else. I ran 50 kilometers (31 miles) a day, mostly in the British and French Concessions, working from 1 a.m. to 1 p.m. The rented ricksha cost me one silver dollar a day (50 cents U.S.). On good days I earned 60 or 70 cents, not enough to afford luxuries like rice. Usually I ate corn flour and dried sweet potato. Meat once a month, maybe longer."

In 1949 the communist city government organized ricksha pullers into a union and he learned that for 27 years he had been engaged in a degrading and inhuman occupation; it had never occurred to him before. Like many others, he switched over to pedalling three-wheeled pedicabs. These too were phased out of existence in 1966—thanks to the Red Guards—but by that time he had retired.

The municipal government replaced the matsheds in 1963 with 35 five-story apartment buildings housing 7,600 people, among them 600 survivors of Pumpkin Lane. Workers, doctors, teachers, and government functionaries occupy the others. They pay an average of $2 a month rent for a single room, toilet and shared kitchen. The complex includes a nursery, bookstore, bank, barber shop, clinic, primary school, grocery and bath house.

The retired ricksha puller and the former beggar dote on their children and grandchildren. All read and write, have graduated at least from middle school and have reasonably good jobs. One, I am told proudly, speaks fluent English.

Mrs. Wang served for years on neighborhood and district committees, the lowest common denominator of urban life. Mrs. Wang lavishes his time and affection on a pair of caged canaries.

4

Lolos, Macbeth, and
a Living God

A story so strange it sounded almost like fiction sent me back to West China. It was common knowledge that many American military transport planes had crashed in the Himalayas during the war. I was made acutely aware of this when I flew from Assam to Kunming. Now a rumor flew around Shanghai that five downed American pilots had been sighted in a remote area of West China, turned into slaves by savage Lolo tribesmen. The report sent a shiver through America very much like the emotions aroused decades later when American soldiers missing in action were said to have been seen in the hands of the Vietnamese Communists.

An American graves registration team got orders from the Pentagon to check out the report. I set out to join them in Chengdu.

Nearly half the land space of China, the vast unexplored hinterlands and seldom seen mountain fastness, is inhabited by tribal minorities, nations within a nation, living their own lives independently of the Han majority. In 1946 they numbered about 40 million of the nation's 450 million people. Some of their tribes are mentioned in Chinese history as far back as 1,000 B.C. Far from being uncivilized, some showed skill and organization in fighting the Chinese. The Liao, the Mongolians, and the Manchus are prominent examples.

Others like the Lolos, however, were unassimilated. Their lives resembled that of prehistoric man. Superstitious, quick to frighten and to anger, they were deeply suspicious of the Han. Concentrated in the Sikang area, the Lolos were said to have been there for two thousand years. Nomadic, they lived chiefly by hunting, wore flat, black turbans, and dressed in loose-fitting black clothing. They were in almost constant warfare with the steadily encroaching Han Chinese. It was these primitive people who, rumor had it, had enslaved white men from the most advanced civilization on earth. The story fascinated readers all over America.

My first stop, with AP photographer Julian Wilson, enroute to Sikang was Chongqing where I spent a few days exploring the war-time capital. It had only been abandoned a few months before for Nanjing but, except for the almost total absence of foreigners, its streets were crowded with surging humanity. I found the restaurants filled and dance halls packed. Prices had stabilized and the cost of consumer goods was half that of Nanjing and Shanghai. Why this extraordinary prosperity? The answer was a bumper rice crop in Sichuan Province, where Chongqing is located, and famine elsewhere. Now that it was no longer a profitable market for American goods, the black market had all but disappeared. That helped curb inflation.

There was little evidence of the war that had so recently ended. A few old snapshots of American soldiers hanging in photo shops, the abandoned caves where the population used to shelter during air raids, the occasional Chinese dressed in an old U.S. Army shirt. That was all.

The American Army compound, Wedemeyer's headquarters, had been returned to its original owners, the Chiu Ching Middle School.

The Press Hostel was almost unrecognizable in its run-down, ne-glected condition. The banana trees were rank and tall, choking the inner courtyard like a jungle growth. Converted into a dormitory for middle school teachers, it was an eyesore, the floors dirty and partly torn up, the walls soiled, windows broken. In what had been the liv-ing room the pencilled autographs of the great and near-great survived. "Jinx Falkenburg, Oct. 31, 1944," one proclaimed. "Paulette Goddard, March 1, 1944," said another. They were film stars of a vanished era.

The China-American Graves Registration Team No. 5 was in Chongqing preparing to check out the Lolo reports. They were the right choice. Young and personable, the four Americans had combed the often-trackless mountains of West China for the bodies of airmen killed flying "the Hump." This was the first time they had been asked to look for possible survivors and, like us, they were excited by the hope of finding them alive.

Capt. William Uphouse of Port Angeles, Wash., headed the team which included Sgt. Ralph Chan of San Francisco, Cpl. Edward L. Koziel of New Salem, Penn., and Cpl. Toby McMunn of Harrisburg, Kansas.

The facts in their possession were skimpy but they seemed to tally. A Chinese herbalist and a French Catholic priest had heard in differ-ent places at about the same time that two B-29s had crashed in the mountains near Yuexi, in Sikang, west of the southward hook of the Yangzi River, in the latter half of 1944. The Lolos, their informants said, captured them and moved westward. There were no eyewitnesses.

In Chengdu, the capital of Sichuan, I met Dr. Davis C. Graham, an American missionary who had spent thirty-five years in China and

knew the Lolos well. He said they numbered around 500,000 and occupied an area of 9,000 to 10,000 square miles.

There were two kinds of Lolos, he said, the black and the white.
The black Lolos were the masters and the white their slaves, prisoners taken during the tribal wars which sputtered and crackled in the
mountains over the centuries.

They slept on the dirt floor of their houses and ate around a central
fireplace. One room was reserved for animals and slaves. Always ready
for battle, they wore shields of untanned leather ornamented with
designs in black and yellow. The Lolos had never risen higher than
the clan system and this accounted for their backwardness.

An article by two Chinese scientists in the scholarly journal which
Dr. Graham edited gave further details. They spent eighty-eight days
among the Lolos in 1943, and found them warlike and hostile. They
ate field rats and malaria was endemic. After a good deal of research,
they speculated that they had descended from the fifth-century tribe
named the Tsouan whose chief was a whore named Lulu.

Wilson and I flew to Sikang from Chengdu aboard a Chinese air
force plane over seemingly endless miles of dense forest and towering mountains, a sight so compelling I wrote that it "stirs in the
observer something of a feeling of fear for the mysterious unknown
mingled with awe at the magnificence and power of nature."

Taking off, the earth below looked idyllically beautiful, the sun's
rays glinting off rice paddies as though reflected by a million diminu-
tive mirrors. An hour out, we suddenly hit the mountain belt and the
earth took on a life of its own as countless, jagged mountain peaks
burst from the tortured land. We skirted past Da Liang Shan, one of
the most rugged mountains in the Tibetan foothills. Mountains rang-
ing from 15,000 to 20,000 feet loomed in the near distance. The muddy
Yangzi below looked like a slender ribbon. Clouds opening and closing like a fluffy curtain revealed thousands of acres of closely packed
forests, devoid of roads, trails, or apparent human habitation. I shuddered whenever the plane did as it strained to gain altitude. We had
no oxygen and as we climbed I became feverish and light-headed.
Chinese airforce planes were notoriously badly maintained. It did not
help to reflect that even a successful crash landing in the dense forests would leave us miles from nowhere among less than friendly wild
animals.

"Look, the Rock of Gibraltar!" exclaimed one of the crew. Sure
enough, dead ahead rose an immense, knife-edge mass of stone 14,500
feet high which could have come out of an advertisement by the Pru-
dential Life Insurance Company. As our plane flew close to it, I felt
the terrible insignificance and loneliness of man in the presence of a
cruel and uncaring nature.

From a hidden shelf, a high waterfall tumbled into the forest below, a silver thread which looked hundreds of feet high. Then, a few miles further, the first human dwellings appeared, Lolo villages of from ten to forty families, perched near the mountain peaks. Seen at closer range, they reminded one of giant anthills. Block houses, like those built by frontier Americans, protected some of the villages. Getting too close was not healthy. A few days earlier the Lolos had peppered another Chinese plane with gunshot as it flew over. I saw the holes and met the shaken pilot in Chengdu. But there was no outward sign of life as we roared over.

Suddenly, a great metallic lake appeared in the west, another eerie spectacle in an empire of silence. Flat and gray, it seemed like a lake on an uninhabited planet waiting to be discovered and explored. It lay at the bottom of a huge bowl hollowed out by some giant hand. Next to it was the city of Sichang.

On landing, we saw that the forests halted abruptly within a half mile of their bases. The woods had been burned away over the years to allow a free field of fire against the rampaging Lolos.

From the airfield we could see Mt. Lo Chi where, two weeks earlier, a Chinese passenger plane crashed killing all thirty-two aboard, including its American pilot. This was the land of rumors. First reports, solemnly avowed, said all survived and were being sheltered by friendly Lolos. The truth was that all died instantly and the Lolos had stripped the plane of its valuables.

Mt. Lo Chi was being fought over by a Nationalist regiment and hostile Lolos when the plane crashed. No one could get to the crash scene while the fighting continued. The fourth son of the mayor of Chongqing, a bridegroom of only three weeks, was one of the crash victims. He carried with him his wife's dowry, $3,000 in silver money.

Not all the Lolos were savage. A group of tame ones had been talked out of their belligerence and persuaded to accept Chinese life. They were at the airfield when we landed. They fitted the descriptions I had heard in Chengdu. Their black leather shields, flat, black turbans, prominent beaked noses, and leathery faces stood out against the fair-skinned, small featured Chinese. They had never seen an airplane at close range and it clearly impressed them. They measured this strange, metallic bird with outstretched arms then posed, agreeably enough, for photographs. Through an interpreter, they conceded that they neither washed nor bathed and that they had the utmost contempt for the ways of civilization.

A city of 20,000, Sichang looked like a village set down in the Bavarian mountains. Its wooden bungalows were gracefully constructed and, like those of the German Alps, artfully decorated. The occupants of these fairy-tale houses, however, were grotesque. Huge goiters protruded from their necks. They were victims of a diet lacking in iodine, which comes from salt. Sichang was far from the sea and other sources of salt.

During our two-week stay we lived in the French Catholic mission in clean rooms of spartan simplicity. The fathers produced an admirable red wine in this remote corner of China, one which went superbly with the French country cuisine.

The Nationalist commander, Gen. He Guoguang took a keen interest in the search for the American "slaves," but was openly skeptical about the story. He dispatched a runner to a distant Lolo village to investigate but learned nothing.

"I'm ninety percent sure," he said, "that no unaccounted for American plane crashed in this area during the war. Chinese villagers rescued twenty-three of twenty-four B-29 survivors in another area, but not this one."

The general, a genial type, yearned for company. We were his guests at sumptuous Chinese banquets on several occasions. But he had a weakness which marred the pleasure of his company. That weakness was the mission's red wine. Instead of toasting in thimblefuls of smoky Chinese wine he insisted on glasses of the mission red. "*Ganbei!* Down the hatch!" he would cry and drain the full glass in one gulp. It pained me to mistreat so good a wine in this way. After a dozen or so *ganbei's* the pain turned into a migraine headache.

Chinese generals never want to sound alarmist. Ho assured us, despite the evidence of the fighting which delayed discovery of the Chinese passenger plane, that all was peaceful as far as the Lolos were concerned. But only a few days earlier, the heads of a half dozen captured Lolos lolled in the dust of the city square, a cautionary exhibition halted just before our arrival.

The most indefatigable Lolo fighter was Col. Luo Dayin, a Nationalist officer who himself was a Lolo. It was he whose campaign in the mountains made it impossible to reach the crashed plane. He commanded a regiment.

But Colonel Lo was not the regimental boss. That role was played by a little, old Chinese *grand-dame*, the widow of Lolo general Dun Xiuting who during his lifetime struck terror into the hearts of the savage Lolos whom he helped subdue.

I met Madame Tun at General Ho's. Surrounded by fierce-looking Lolo guards, she was dressed in a square velvet cap, serene and magnificently poised in her great old age. She carried herself like a queen but in the Chinese manner, aware of her power yet courteously deferential to strangers.

The son of the mayor of Chongqing who had died in the plane crash was her son-in-law. It was her regiment, under the persistent Colonel Lo, which had been busy killing Lolos while he died. Her daughter was not aboard.

During our conversation she, too, doubted that any Americans had survived to serve as slaves to the Lolos. Her influence over the tame Lolos was great. And through them she got a good deal of information, none of it suggesting that the savage Lolos held any foreigners.

The American graves registration team, now headed by Col. Herbert Wurtzler, ran down a dozen different leads without success, interrogated French missionaries and Lolos in nearby villages. Now it set out on October 8 on a week-long trek to gather more information, particularly in the vicinity of the two B-29s reported to have crashed in late 1944. Wilson, lugging his heavy cameras, went with them.

They made an arduous ascent of the 14,500-foot Mt. Wu Tai in the Liang Bao Shan range where it was believed one of the planes had crashed. Starting off with fifty friendly Lolo bearers, they were reduced to six as the terrain took its toll near the top. Bursting into the open, they came upon a strange sight, the four engines of a B-29 imbedded in the hard rock of the summit. The rest of the wreckage was strewn over a ten-square-mile area around it.

Neither there nor in talks with Lolo chieftains in the villages enroute to the summit had they found anything to confirm the story of the enslaved Americans.

The team remained in Sichang for another few weeks but every clue it tracked down proved false. Finally, they called off the search, reasonably sure that no American slaves were in Lolo captivity. But the story died hard. The rumors persisted. It was a mystery never likely to be unravelled. If there indeed were slaves, they must long ago have perished from the hard labor and the primitive conditions of their lives.

It had been a futile search, but it was one which had to be made, one which the Chinese themselves never totally understood. Their history was replete with instances of thousands wiped out or lost without a trace. Why bother to look for them? The individual counted less than the mass.

Failure was perhaps not the word for it. No missing Americans were found, but the exhaustive hunt had indicated almost conclusively that there were no survivors. That was an accomplishment of sorts, not the happy one everyone prayed for, but at least it injected a note of certainty into what had been little more than rumor and speculation.

The graves team, in the course of its search, uncovered some additional details on the lives of the Lolos, a small contribution to human knowledge which might, who knows, prove useful in saving lives in some future time.

The Lolos counted their wealth in rifles, no matter how old or ineffective. Chief Meh Lo-yu in the village of Lanchang, 10,000 feet up the mountain, controlled 800 families and 1,000 rifles. He owned 40 rifles himself, which included German, Czech, Belgian, and Chinese makes. There were some American carbines. Where they got the bullets to fit these varied weapons was not made clear.

The chief's house was forty feet long, twenty feet wide, and made of stamped mud. There were no windows. Since the doors were three and a half feet high, one had to crawl into the house. A vent in the roof allowed smoke to escape from the central fireplace below. The fire and the stones surrounding it were regarded as sacred. A graves team member tossed a match in and it was fished out with tongs after he had been roundly cursed. Aside from the light it gave, the room was pitch black. The Lolos never cooked their main dish until after dark, and if there was game, it was killed just before eating. The team was offered a rooster which was promptly killed in the middle of the floor, followed by a goat whose throat was cut with crude knives, like meat cleavers. It was butchered on a mat and the blood caught in a bucket. The Lolos like their meat almost rare and their vegetables half burned.

The chief lived in a loft with his wife and family at one end of the house and the hogs, horses, chickens, cats, and dogs occupied a room at the other. Fleas were abundant.

The neighboring Chinese village of Lo Yao lived in terror of the Lolos. Sentries kept watch all night above it. It had been raided three times the previous twelve months.

The Lolo men on the mountain wore trousers, a shirt, a tobacco pouch on their belt, and a black cape. Ammunition belts and rifles were regular wear. Their ear lobes were punctured and colored wooden cylinders inserted in them.

The women wore skirts of a gypsy-like gaiety with silver bands on their wrists, silver ornaments on their blouses, and silver necklaces about their necks.

Most of the Lolos lived in houses perched on the edges of small cliffs.

The men were the hunters and providers of food. Women were their servants. All were illiterate and depended on the tribal priest for simple reading and writing.

Death was an almost impersonal thing. The body was turned over to the priest and he disposed of it. The survivors never knew where or when it had been buried.

Both men and women smoked long-stemmed pipes whose bowls were larger than the tiny Chinese ones.

Finally, there was a certain amount of quality. The only distinction between slaves and masters was that only the masters wore the black turban. The slaves got the same amount of food as their betters and, being a hereditary class, got the easier work, such as cooking and housework. Women, less fortunate, did the heavier work of fetching water or fuel and carrying the tribe's possessions when it moved. In special cases, the chief called on the slaves to fight as well as work.

Our final few days in Sichang were enlivened by a night at the theater, a performance specially arranged for us. Staged in a good-sized hall filled to capacity, the first half of the program was one of music and Western classical ballet, surprisingly well danced.

The second half featured tribal songs and dances by a band of youthful Lolos. The evening reached an unexpected climax with an animated performance of the "black bottom" and the "Charleston," hip-shaking, knee-bending American dances of the 1930s. After we recovered from our astonishment, I asked our guide how such esoteric dances had reached so remote a corner of the earth. We got the answer from a slight little man in steel-rimmed glasses beaming proudly over his charges. He was a Chinese professor who had won loving cups in "black bottom" and "Charleston" competitions while at the University of Chicago and thought it only fitting to introduce them to the Lolos. We may have been the first Americans to reach Sichang in years, but American civilization had preceded us.

The urge of an American ballpoint pen manufacturer to gain publicity for his product brought me to Lanzhou, the capital of Gansu Province in West China. The manufacturer learned that some mountaineers, climbing in the Himalayas, had taken photographs of K3, one of the peaks in that majestic range, which suggested it might be higher than the 29,028 feet which made Mt. Everest the highest in the world. Because of light refraction and various other factors, including snowfall, accurate measurement of all the Himalayan peaks was not then possible. He got the idea of measuring K3's height from an airplane. With much fanfare and newspaper publicity, he bought an old U.S. Army bomber and hired a professional pilot to fly it. The plane was to go to Lanzhou ready—after the press showed up—for the adventure which would, it was hoped, rewrite geography and, incidentally, sell more ballpoint pens, a new product at that time.

I reached Lanzhou, a primitive city of 400,000 at an altitude of more than 5,000 feet, in March ahead of pen pusher and pilot. It seemed the old flying crate was having mechanical problems. Various modification had been made to allow it to fly higher than 30,000 feet, a height achieved with difficulty in those days.

There seemed to be more camels than people in Lanzhou, which lay astride the land route from Europe to China. We stayed in an old Chinese inn where camels filled the courtyard. The atmosphere was very much like Yan'an, the air full of desert dust and the atmosphere exhilarating. While waiting for the K3 people, I wandered in the outskirts and, in a small open air restaurant, had the best noodles I have ever eaten. Beaten, pounded, stretched, and pummelled by a bare-chested cook of generous proportions, it was flavored with a mountain herb which gave it an incomparable taste. I have searched Asia in vain for anything so delicious.

At another time I spent two days in a leper colony run by two elderly and beatific Philadelphia missionary ladies. They made scrumptious toll-house cookies and brownies. The lepers, despite their deformities—noses eaten away, stumps of hands or arms—were remarkably cheerful, inheriting, I suppose, the good humor of these truly saintly women. Highly civilized, full of the zest of life, they found happiness in caring for the most despised and feared of God's creatures. I admired them deeply. They told me the story of how new drugs had made cures possible and how, whenever a cure took place, there was a special "graduation" ceremony. But not everyone was so humanitarian when it came to caring for lepers. Gansu was governed then by Ma Hongkuei, a Moslem of ferocious habits. I later learned the horrifying story of how he had, some years previously, dealt with the leper problem. Told by Madame Chiang Kai-shek to do something about it, he corralled the 600 or so lepers then in the province, had them dig a large ditch, and shot them. This was not what the Madame had in mind and she gave him a scathing piece of her mind when she found out about it. But leprosy was endemic, and soon there was another batch for the good Philadelphia ladies to look after.

It was full to capacity with forty-five lepers when I visited it. Another thirty-five had to be turned away. Tibetans and Chinese were the principal patients.

The women were divided from the men. One end of the Great Wall of China poked its nose into the women's section, a 2,000-year-old visitor from the past. The Chinese in 1948 had thrown up a "great wall" against their lepers, treating them as outcasts. The stories one heard were pathetic. Mothers turned their children out into the street when they got the dread disease. Wandering in rags from place to place, they were everywhere shunned by other humans who set the dogs on them.

I met a 19-year-old Mohammedan girl, her face swollen red and purple. She had no feeling in her hands and feet. A burning coal placed on them created no sensation. A sweet-tempered child, she had the shyness and embarrassment of the sick who feel that somehow they are to blame for their affliction. The "Hiroshima Maidens," young survivors of the first atom bomb to be used against humans, were similarly shy and embarrassed when I met them years later.

Then there was Tsaru, a 13-year-old Tibetan boy. He had been turning a prayer wheel ten days the other side of Lhasa, in Tibet, hoping for divine intercession to cure him. His mother decided that medicine was more effective than prayer and set out on the terrible journey over the mountains to Lanzhou and the missionary colony. She, Tsaru, and another son wearily plodded the mountain roads and trails for six months before they reached their destination. When she got there it was discovered that all three were leprous. Yet they did not despair.

In the small chapel where one of the ladies, a Miss Lester, taught scripture, we talked about the lepers and Christianity, an alien faith to most of them.

"No, we do not coerce them into becoming Christian," she said. "But once one becomes Christian, he has hope for the future. The leper hates the world and the world hates him. His mother has turned him out. He is a beggar before he comes to us. He often fails to respond for months. We just let him sit out in the sun. When we come up to him, he puts up his arms. He is afraid of dogs. The Chinese put dogs on them. So we just let them sit and soak up the atmosphere. When they regain their confidence, we stretch out our hands to them."

Giving them something to do proved an effective therapy. All were illiterate when they came to the leprosarium, now all could read.

"Great sorrow can bring on leprosy," said Miss Lester. "Emotional strain and a poor diet also contribute. It is not inherited. They say that it breeds in moist, dirty tropical climates. But how can you explain why it is endemic in this dry, desert and mountain region?"

I thought of Yan'an and the work being done there by the Communists to combat the same disease. Here was an example of people believing in diametrically opposite ideologies working for the same humanitarian end. Was it not possible for men and women everywhere to do the same?

The story of the Lanzhou leprosarium was not all bleak. Miss Lester told me about the arrival one day of a mother and her 11-year-old daughter. Both were infected. The gatekeeper kept their presence secret, knowing that the leprosarium was overcrowded. He shut the gates in their faces. For two weeks they moaned and wept. The lepers inside threw them pieces of bread to keep alive. Finally the ladies learned of it and brought a doctor. He found the mother dying but the girl, who looked five or six, was less seriously affected. In four years she was cured and was taken into the home of the Philadelphia ladies. They lavished love and tenderness on her. One day a medical assistant in the hospital asked to marry her even though she had pock marks on her face.

"You don't want to marry me," she said. "I'm ugly."

"I don't care," the suitor replied. And they were married and were living happily when I met them.

The ballpoint pen manufacturer and his plane finally arrived and I took a couple of flights with them over the Himalayas, still a breathtaking sight. But though we flew close to it, we made no attempt to

measure K3. That was to be for another day. In fact, mechanical difficulties and a growing conviction that K3 after all was not that high,
doomed the undertaking to failure. After a week of flying around the
area, the pilot found he could not make the desired altitude and the
expedition was called off. When last heard from, the manufacturer,
dunned for airport fees, flew out of Beiping scattering ballpoint pens
on the tarmac to throw pursuers off the scent.

Relieved of my story, I decided to try another one. The governor of
neighboring Qinghai Province was Ma Bufang, cousin of the cruel
governor of Gansu. He was benign by comparison and something of
a socialist. The Panchen Lama, god-king of Tibet, also lived in Qinghai
and I hoped to meet him.

I had to get permission for the land trip to Qinghai from the Northwest Kuomintang chief, Gen. Zhang Zhizhong. A flush-faced, erect
soldier of considerable warmth, he invited me to a banquet during
which he revealed that he loved Western classical music. He had a
few old 78 rpm records which he played. After the dinner, he put a
jeep and driver at my disposal. He was the same General Zhang who
had represented the government in the Marshall negotiations. In 1949,
he chose to remain in China rather than flee to Taiwan and spent the
rest of his life honored by the Communists. (After I returned to Shanghai I sent him some Mozart recordings. He kept them for twenty years,
until the tone-deaf Red Guards confiscated them as "rotten bourgeois
music" in the Cultural Revolution.)

I set out next day with a Chinese reporter for Xining, capital of
Qinghai. The soldier assigned to drive the jeep in the twenty-four-
hour trip over the mountains had the instincts of a racing driver. On
the long descents he threw the engine into neutral and coasted at
about 60 miles an hour making our hair stand on end as we skittered
close to the edge of precipitous gorges with inches to spare. During
the moments free from terror, we saw some spectacular mountain scen-
ery broken dramatically by great wooden water wheels on the banks
of the Yellow River.

Qinghai is in the lowlands of Tibet. Sparsely populated, its nearly
300,000 square miles of area contained only a million people in 1948
when I visited it. About 90 percent of the area is made up of mountains and plateaus. Tibetans, Mongols, and Kazakhs raised yaks and
sheep for their hides and wool. Yaks also provided milk and butter.
Xining, the provincial capital, had about 50,000 people, many of them
Tibetans.

Ma Bufang, already warned of our arrival, received us in handsome style. He put us up in a guest house which, he said, had been
built only a few weeks before. It was entirely of wood, unheated and
smelled strongly of mutton, the favorite dish of this Moslem area. He

plied us with banquets whose centerpiece invariably was mutton.

A square-shouldered man of imposing height, he dressed in black woolens, very similar to those worn by Mao in Yan'an. His head was close-shaven and a wispy beard fringed his face. His nose was large, his eyes small and squinty, but he smiled often. A few days after our arrival, he drove us in an American Buick of ancient vintage to the base of a hill just outside the city. Like the rest of Xining it was innocent of trees, shrubs, or grass, a somewhat forbidding mound of dusty rubble. As we stood expectantly at the foot of the hill, Ma produced a whistle and gave it several sharp blasts. Suddenly, over the brow of the hill appeared an army of men carrying saplings. There must have been thousands of them. They raced down the hill like the soldiers in Macbeth carrying Birnam wood to Dunsinane, then came to a halt, laughing and panting, in front of us. The governor greeted the leaders with a bear hug and blew another whistle. At that signal, they set to work planting the saplings. More far-sighted than his cousin, Ma recognized that something had to be done to reafforest the depleted land. But like his cousin, he favored decisive measures to meet a problem. His was to order the entire adult population to stop everything it was doing and take two weeks off to plant the new, young trees. By the time I arrived, he had planted a million, he said, and the program had only just begun.

Ma made available to us his private bathhouse, a welcome gesture since our inn contained no baths. The building was an elaborately carved wooden structure reserved, it was said, only for the male officials of the government. During a relaxing massage after the hot bath we were served tea in elaborate cups; mine, hastily washed, betrayed the presence at some recent time, of a woman. It was smudged with lipstick.

As in Sikang, I was one of the first Americans to reach Qinghai after the war and, though I insisted that I was a mere journalist, the governor privately believed that I represented, in some way, the United States government. He was eager to obtain modern arms from Washington and told me so. I said I would include this in one of my articles.

A few days later he asked me to have an early breakfast and accompany him to the military parade ground. When we reached it, I was astonished to find three thousand soldiers lined up awaiting our arrival. They came briskly to attention and I then undertook an inspection of what seemed like the entire Qinghai army. Only three years before, I had been a rather unorganized, somewhat dishevelled sergeant in the OSS, the least military of people. Now I found myself walking beside a full colonel in the provincial army, stopping with an approving look to examine a soldier, clucking when it seemed right, as I had observed other, higher-ranking mortals do. There was a shortage of machine-guns and those Ma possessed were vintage affairs. I noted that there was a dozen soldiers in each machine-gun rank, a bit more than usually called for. Those in the rear had a special function, however. As I walked past they uttered staccato noises like machine-guns firing. "Rat-a-tat-tat," they cried. I nodded sagely and walked on.

The most impressive of the military men were the 400 young and handsome members of Ma's personal guard. They were dressed in smart uniforms and well educated by the standards of the day, having graduated from middle school. They normally served until they reached the age of 40.

After the inspection, there was an impressive march past. No visiting president or prime minister has ever been treated so handsomely. I now know how it feels to review an honor guard at the airport, a privilege reserved to few of us. As I had long suspected, the ritual made one feel slightly silly and a little bit pompous, something admirably suited to polish the ego of visiting premiers, heads of state, and other ham actors.

Horses were the great assets of Qinghai and the troops I reviewed were Ma's dismounted cavalry. Sitting in his carpeted and richly panelled headquarters afterwards, he told me he had supplied the Gimo with 50,000 horses during the anti-Japanese war. He was constantly buying the sturdy horses of the province and when they were not being used he set them free to graze in the foothills of the mountains. The soldiers used wooden saddles. He said they were better than leather, and cheaper.

Ma's name meant "Horse of Fragrant Steppes," and he had the toughness of men born to the saddle. Politically, he was hardly a socialist. But he had some ideas which were intended to raise the low standards of living of his people. He was, in short, a somewhat enlightened warlord, better than his ferocious cousin. He did not smoke or drink and disliked those who did. His passions were riding, hunting deer, blue sheep, bear, and rabbits, and composing Chinese music. He was up at 5 a.m. each day, breakfasted at eight on mutton and noodles, then carried out a full day of inspection of projects he had started. There were no conferences in his scheme of things. He gave orders and they were obeyed. An aide told me that he talked very little, never asked for opinions and had his own ideas about everything. He avoided social activities and had little time for friends.

He spent a good deal of time talking to city elders and *xian*, or county, magistrates, the people who carried out his law. He shared his meals with his close subordinates and was in bed by eight or nine o'clock at night.

He was not popular, an aide, somewhat daring, confided because he worked hard and made others do so.

He had the advantage of family; his father was the governor of Qinghai, then called Ninghai, before him. Graduating from the military academy, he rose swiftly to the rank of general. He commanded a Nationalist army group when I met him, but the Generalissimo was chary about distributing modern weapons to his warlord followers. His alliances with them were uneasy. They were opportunists and so, in a way, was he. They paid allegiance to him because he had American money and backing, and more soldiers under arms. In his dealings with the warlords, Chiang rode the tiger's back; if he fell off, he risked losing his head.

It was too late, in any case, to beef up the military strength of Ma Bufang, or any of the other warlords. The Communists were rolling to an inevitable victory and these old crooks knew it. Some escaped to the United States. Others flocked to Mao's banners; opportunism never has been a nasty word in China. Mao knew how to treat them. He heaped them with empty titles and honors and emasculated them militarily. In a way, he was something of an old warlord himself.

The Panchen Lama, political and spiritual leader of 9 million Tibetans, was regarded by the faithful as a living god. At the age of 12, he was the fifteenth incarnation, having been chosen three years after the death of his middle-aged predecessor, the saintly man with a toothache who donated his molar to Dr. Bussiere in Beiping so many years before. Pro-Chinese, the old Panchen had been driven out of his capital of Shigatse in Tibet by the then Dalai Lama, a tool of the British in the civil war these shrewd imperialists stirred up at the top of the world. He fled to Qinghai, later became the guest of the Nationalist government which sponsored his Beiping trip. Thanks to the British, the Dalai Lama became the better known of the two god-kings, but in fact in the good old days they were more or less equal in Tibet.

Astrologers chose the new Panchen, the only son of a Tibetan farmer living in Qinghai, on his second birthday. He showed an absorbed interest in the old Panchen's spectacles.

A Living Buddha of Limitless Light, the holiest of the holy, he was an Asiatic pope without his flock. Installed in the centuries-old Kumbum Lamasery in the towering mountains near the great salt lake of Kokonor, he was a protegé of Chiang Kai-shek, a pawn in the game of empire still being played by the Chinese and British in the 1940s. Unable to return, except on London's terms, he was being kept in reserve by the Nationalists for the future. Ironically, it was the Chinese Communists who finally restored him and the Dalai Lama to their thrones in the land of the Lost Horizon. But the Reds were inept as rulers of a proud and sensitive people steeped in religion. The Dalai rebelled against them in 1959 and fled to India where he still lives while the Panchen was publicly honored and used by Beijing until his death in 1987.

Over teacups and dried persimmons served by a slovenly soldier in sloppy uniform, I interviewed the boy-saint in the lavishly decorated throne room of his red-walled palace. On its walls hung dozens of Buddhist scrolls. Through the open window the sunlight fell in symmetrical patches on the richly carpeted floor. There were low thrones in the room, one for the absent Dalai. Throughout our audience young monks in obvious need of a bath poked their head in to see the red-nosed foreigner. The Panchen's three black poodles wrestled and barked incessantly.

Flanked by two aged advisers, the Panchen Lama walked briskly into the room and stood under the green, scarlet, and gold canopy of one of the thrones. Bowing, I presented him with a blue silk ceremonial scarf, the Tibetan calling card. He smiled slightly, returned the bow and gave me a scarf in return. When he sat down his gold and green slippered feet barely touched the floor. A handsome, intelligent-looking boy with deep black eyes, he was dressed in flowing scarlet robes of rough wool; under them was a gold-embroidered jacket, its edges dark with the stains of yak butter which Tibetans use for washing. He was bareheaded, sat straight-backed and dignified throughout the talk. There was a sadness in his eyes which haunted me. But, once in a while they lit up with a mischievous glint. There were dimples when he smiled. He had the subdued air of a well-mannered child. His voice was husky and hurried and he leaned forward when he spoke.

Was the Panchen interested in other countries, I asked. Did he wish to visit America?

"Yes," he replied gravely, through two interpreters, one Chinese, one Tibetan, "all these things are attractive. Some day I should like to visit Shanghai, Nanjing, and the United States."

He added: "But now I must devote my time to study in order to become a religious leader. I have little time for anything else."

Each day of his disciplined life began at 4 a.m. and ended at 9 p.m. largely spent poring over the 108 volumes of *Kangyur*, the Buddhist litany. For recreation, he played table tennis or strolled with his three Tibetan poodles.

Among the pictures in his home were some English country prints, gifts ironically from the British throne.

In those days, he and his advisers faced a dilemma. The victorious old Dalai Lama invited him to return to Shigatse. If he had done so Tibet would again have been united—under the British, of course. The Gimo had not taken the bait.

Replying to my question he said, "I will return if and when China asks me."

But it was a different China which finally invited him back. And when he did return he took, for a while, the same rebellious path as the Dalai Lama. Placed under house arrest, his fortunes looked up with the post-Mao rise of Deng Xiaoping in Beijing. He became a member of the body which brings religious and national minorities together there, no longer treated as a living god by his Chinese masters but still regarded with awe and respect in his native Tibet.

"*O mani padme hum, O mani padme hum*—Oh the Jewel in the Lotus, Oh the Jewel in the Lotus!" The words were the same and the ritual unbroken since the days of Tsong Kaba, the great reformer of Buddhism who established the Kumbum lamasery in the fifteenth century. The faithful murmured their prayers as they turned prayer wheels or flung themselves on the pavement in front of the main temple, a pavement worn smooth by countless thousands of such prostrations over the centuries.

Kumbum is a dazzling collection of temples, the main one roofed in gold and its pillars wrapped in yellow, red, and blue carpets. It sits on a hillside above the Chinese village of Lusa within sight of the snow-capped Amne Machin mountain range. From the foot of the hill on which it is perched, seen through a screen of trees, Kumbum's low white buildings look like a giant wedding cake. At its entrance a row of dagobas, bottled-shaped bits of architecture, stands like sentinels beckoning to the traveler and the pilgrim. Tibetans in conical hats and long robes ornamented with silver and brass moved among the Chinese and the Mongolians. Some wore monstrous long earrings of metal punched through the lobes of the ear. Lamas sat pensively outside the temple gates mumbling their incessant incantations. Close-shaven, some gray-haired, they wore a rough scarlet robe tied across the shoulder like a toga. On their feet were leather boots or sandals. Their faces were bronzed from the sun and smeared with successive washings of rancid yak butter. They greeted the stranger with a low bow and continued their prayers.

There was an eerie quiet to Kumbum. Amid splashes of man-made color and under the cathedral-like canopies of tall trees the faithful went about their devotions in near silence. Outside the gates the world hurried unthinkingly on its way.

The central structure, because of lavish use of gold in its architecture, was called the Temple of the Great Gold Roof. Burned in 1913, it was restored to its ancient grandeur. Man-sized gold figures and engraved pillars sat like sentinels on the golden roof. Underneath it, the golden Buddha to which the faithful paid homage was dressed in the hair and clothes of Tsong Kaba himself. Votive flames flickered from a single wick set in huge brass urns filled with yak butter. Clouds of incense rose through the yellow cloth folds of the great statue to its apex thirty feet above the floor.

The throne of the Panchen Lama was set in another great hall where the monks worshipped. Long, richly woven prayer rugs, raised from the floor, formed a series of twenty parallel lines from front to rear of the room. Scores of great pillars covered with ornate dragon-inscribed rugs gave this low, dimly lit chamber the atmosphere of a Druidic forest. Long cloth canopies of many colors hanging from the ceiling added to the splendor and richness of the scene. Along the walls thousands of small Buddha images peered out inquisitively from individual cupboards.

In the adjacent Temple of the Little Golden Roof all the barbarities and strangeness of Lamaism were exhibited. There were stuffed animals owned by the predecessor of the then abbot, A Gya Hutukutu. I was startled to look up at the courtyard balconies and see long-dead cows and oxen gazing down at me through unseeing eyes. On a heroic-sized painting, death's heads sucked out the souls of women from their bodies while mad beasts swallowed naked men alive. Nothing here was natural. The flowers were elaborate creations in colored yak butter, minor masterpieces made for the New Year festival. Admired for a day by throngs of the faithful, they were thrown to the live cattle to eat.

The wild magnificence of Kumbum is a monument to the greatness of Tsong Kaba, an Asiatic saint.

The story of his life is half fact, half fanciful legend. The legend is that he was born near Kumbum, the son of a shepherd and that at birth he had a white beard and spoke with the profundity of a grown man. At the age of three he gave up the world and turned to religious life, shaving his hair which he threw to the ground outside his tent. Legend continues that a tree miraculously grew from this hair and its leaves and bark bore the characters of the Tibetan language. In one of the temples I saw a small grove of trees which supposedly were the sacred ones. On the bark were numerous Tibetan markings.

Tsong Kaba was adopted during his wanderings by a western lama, who might have been a Catholic priest. From his teachings, I was told, he grew up to see the error of the old Buddhist ritual. The old religion was called the Red sect because of the red robes which were worn. He introduced the Yellow sect which stood for increased sacrifice, celibacy among the monks, and abstention from smoking or drinking.

When he died in 1478 he left behind two disciples, the Panchen Lama and the Dalai Lama, with orders that they be reborn from generation to generation to carry on his gospel.

Because they were chosen as children they had to have regents. This made their lives precarious. Many never survived to rule. Poison in the soup guaranteed the continued tenure of the regent. Like the later Empress Dowager in Beijing who assassinated her rivals, they were unable to resist the attraction of power.

In this century, the Dalai and Panchen Lamas survived their regent ironically because of foreign interference. Britain and China had vested interests in them and the regents dared not tamper with the soup.

The regent in 1948 was Lo San Chien Zen, an old man with a long white beard, dirty black fingernails, and small blue veins outlined against a slender neck. He wore a resplendent gold jacket and a long, wide skirt. He guided the Panchen skillfully through our interview, emphasizing that he could not reply to political matters, dodging the political potholes and spitting noisily on the floor.

Kumbum means "ten thousand images," and refers to the tree which sprang from Tsonbg Kaba's hair with its numerous written characters.

Any Tibetan family in Qinghai at the time which had two sons had to enrol one as a lama. If there were three, two had to go. In 1948, there were six thousand at Kumbum.

In 1984, on a visit to Beijing, I was pleased and surprised to see a television documentary in color of the Kumbum Lamasery, as it is today. The Communists not only had preserved it, they also had added to its splendor. In its present state it remains a Holy See fit for a god-king.

During my stay I sampled one of the staples of the Tibetan diet, a concoction called *tsamba*. I went to the trouble of getting the recipe but must confess that I have never used it: "Pour hot tea into a bowl and add a large lump of yak butter. Let it dissolve. Add a large spoonful of yak cheese. Let it dissolve. Add a heaping teaspoon of whole wheat flour. Drink off most of the tea, leaving the flour residue. Add three or four more spoonfuls of flour and using the fingers, massage the paste counter-clockwise into a putty-like substance. Revolving the bowl, use the hands to create a cup-like indentation. Into this pour a hot sauce and eat like bread." A generation more interested in health food and exotic cuisine may be interested. After all, it keeps Tibetans alive under the most trying geographical conditions anywhere. The Tibetans much admire this delicacy, though I could not discover why. It tasted flat and uninteresting to me. It is essential, to get the authentic taste, to do like the Tibetans and not wash one's hands before creating this dish. They have been known to smear it on their face. On long journeys through the Himalayas, they put it under the horse's saddle. This gives it a fragrance much prized but which it was not my good fortune to taste.

I left Yan'an a couple of weeks before Mao gave up the cave city which had become the symbol of Chinese Communist survival. The evacuation began March 18, 1947, in an orderly fashion after

Kuomintang bombers returned to their bases following a devastating attack on the city and the airfield. The survivors of the epic Long March who had straggled into Shaanxi twelve years earlier left their footprints on the twelve inches of snow which had fallen the night before, a transient record of the end of an era.

Back in Beiping, the reports I received on this new Long March were scanty. Only years later did some of the details leak out. What we did know, through Xinhua newscasts monitored in Tokyo and elsewhere, was that the leadership was intact and the civil war, far from ending, continued unabated.

Reporting on their struggle in such indirect ways, I often wondered what had been the thoughts of these few men and women who had turned revolutionary in their youth, endured a thousand battles, and now in their middle years were once more thrust into the wilderness. They were young, almost in their prime, when they undertook their first long flight from the east coast. The resiliency of youth and faith in their cause had helped them to survive. But now they were in their fifties, accustomed to a safer and better life, some like Mao, running to fat. What were their chances now?

For two years the evacuees, men, women, and children, dodged the three Kuomintang armies sent to exterminate them. Scattered accounts published much later gave some inkling of what they had gone through. One, surprisingly, was a television documentary, which I saw, done by two British Communist nurses who accompanied them on part of the retreat.

The reports indicated that these two years were not as terrible as the single year of the original Long March. For one thing, they had ample supplies laid in during months of preparation. Another was that they were protected by crack regiments of a now-large and well-disciplined army. It was not so much a Long March as a game of hide and seek.

One column of 20,000 remained in the Shaanxi area, which they knew so well, finding shelter with sympathetic peasants and villagers. Mao Zedong, Jiang Qing, and Zhou Enlai were in this column. Another, led by Liu Shaoqi and Zhu De, moved to the Beiping-Tianjin area to join Red units there.

They traveled by night and slept during the day. Ultimately food became scarce and medicine in short supply. They had not banked on so long a hegira. Mao, weakened by hunger, fell ill and had to stop walking, which he preferred, and go on horseback. While they circled around, giving the Kuomintang the slip, they managed to inflict some casualties on their pursuers.

One source said it was a happy time for Mao, back in his peasant element and freed from the exhausting process of negotiation. He used his time to write more papers on military strategy, land reform, economic policy, and democracy, Chinese Communist style.

In one essay, he advocated killing landlords guilty of serious crimes but noted that since there were 36 million of them in a population of 425 million, it might be better to remold and save them. The task, he said, was to abolish the feudal system, to wipe out the landlords as a class, not as individuals. What caused him to change his mind we may never know. Had he stuck to these ideas, I reflected, millions of innocent Chinese might have escaped a cruel death.

In Manchuria, the Generalissimo had gambled and lost. Ignoring both his Chinese and American advisers, he attempted the military conquest of all Manchuria, a vast and inhospitable area. His lines were overextended. Lin Biao captured Szepingkai, the devastated city I had visited earlier, and seized the Nationalist grain stores there and in Changchun and Mukden which soon fell. It was all over but the shouting. No army had ever survived on an empty stomach. Chiang's was no exception.

After Manchuria, the next pivotal battle took place at Xuzhou in Jiangsu Province, the dividing line between north and south. A million men on each side fought for months. Though the Gimo had American-made warplanes and other sophisticated weapons, he was outmaneuvered and lost half a million men. The Communists had neither an airforce nor a navy.

After that the Kuomintang position in North China became untenable. Gen. Fu Zuoyi surrendered Beiping and Tianjin without a fight and, joining the winners reaped his reward, the ministry of Water Conservancy in the new government.

In April 1949, a million Communists crossed the Yangzi River in one of the greatest battles of Chinese history. They captured Nanjing then swept on to Shanghai where the defenses consisted of a 25-mile long wooden fence erected around the perimeter. By then, I was in Amman, Transjordan, reporting on the Arab-Israeli quarrel.

Bands parading down the Bund gave rise to rumors the Kuomintang forces had defeated the approaching Reds. Flags flying, the Kuomintang musicians headed for the docks where they sailed off to exile in Formosa, now Taiwan, instead.

The debate over who lost China raged throughout most of the 1950s in the United States led by the China Lobby, Nationalist sympathizers, and the notorious Senator Joseph McCarthy. They blamed Truman and the Democrats.

Actually, the Generalissimo bore much of the blame. Blinded by hatred of his old foes, he refused to join them in a coalition which could have guaranteed China years of peace. Another was that he refused in military matters to listen to anyone outside the clique he had taught at Whampoa Military Academy. One of those ignored was Gen. Du Youming, his Manchurian commander. When I met him in

Szepingkai, after he had repelled the Red attack, he said he had asked Chiang to give him the word and he would take Harbin, Lin Biao's headquarters. The word never came, he said.

China's last Confucian, the Gimo had few contacts with the common people or intellectuals who, like Mao, he despised. He lacked the broad view and his old revolutionary instincts had atrophied. By demanding personal loyalty, he turned his subordinates into yes-men. Finally, he failed to give enough attention to the country's economic difficulties.

Another problem was corruption in the armed forces. Unscrupulous generals collected money from the central government for ten battalions when they had only five. They pocketed the difference. This worked profitably for the generals but not so well when their nonexistent battalions were ordered into the field.

Underfed, underpaid, and generally scorned, the rank-and-file of the army suffered from low morale. When the Communists tempted them to surrender by letting them go home with a little cash in their pockets, they jumped at it. Many joined the Red Army.

How much had the Russians contributed to the victory of their Chinese comrades? All told, it seemed, very little. Stalin, somewhat obtuse behind his genial, mustachioed exterior, trusted the Kuomintang more than he did Mao. He advised Mao not to try to take over the whole country but be content with half, leaving the other half to Chiang. He did not, to say the least, believe Yan'an's prospects were bright. The Soviet Red Army did time its withdrawals from Manchuria to give Lin Biao's troops a chance to move in after it. And it left behind heaps of Japanese arms and ammunition which proved useful only for a while. Zhou Enlai wrote caustically in his memoirs, which appeared in 1982, that the most rewarding source of Red arms were the American ones left behind by fleeing Nationalists. Challenging the Americans to come to the support of the Generalissimo, he wrote that they would not last long once they ran out of Coca Cola, chewing gum, and toilet paper.

Truman, far from losing China, did all he could to save it by pushing for a peaceful settlement which would have avoided the civil war. His China advisers, later pilloried by McCarthy, told him the Communists would win. They turned out to be right.

Once the Marshall mission failed, Truman did what the China Lobby should have applauded. He supplied large amounts of economic and military aid to the Generalissimo. He wanted the Kuomintang to win because he wished to establish military bases in China to deter Stalin's Asian ambitions. Truman and Marshall were as anti-Communist as their hysterical critics, but they were reasonable men and did not consider the prospect of restoring peace in China a crime.

Considering the millions of lives involved, it was a gamble worth taking.

Finally, and most significantly, the Communists won because they were better trained, better disciplined, better prepared, and more motivated than their enemies.

It was a formula for success.

Having assessed the probable reasons for the Communist victory, the question arises: How clearly and how perceptively did the American press corps report the events which led up to it?

This is a hard question for me to answer mainly because I saw very few of the published stories of other correspondents. What I do know is that, like me they often worked around the clock to get the story and cable it to the United States. I have never labored so hard, before or since, in the journalistic vineyards.

5

China Watched

From 1945 to 1949 reporting in the Nationalist areas proved frustrating but not entirely unproductive. Neither the Nationalists nor the Communists were wholly open in their dealings with us but there were other sources, among them the biggest minority party, the Democratic League.

Its ranks included liberal politicians, professors, writers, and journalists. Harried, persecuted, and sometimes hunted down by the secret police, it relied on us to get its message across. There were some in China, and in the United States, among them General Marshall, who thought they might rule China better than the Nationalists or the Communists. The question was academic; they had no army, the others did.

Caught in the middle, eager to enlist the support of the United States, they readily told us what they knew.

We got our news from many other sources, among them diplomats who, like ourselves, were trained observers of the political scene. Some correspondents maintained a close, personal relationship with officers of the U.S. embassy with whom they sometimes exchanged information. I never enjoyed the confidences they said resulted from these ties. But when I came to a city for the first time, I did not hesitate to ask for a briefing from the American consul or vice consul. Since they knew a great deal about the local situation, it saved time to talk to them before undertaking research on one's own.

There were no bans on travel and, as these pages indicate, I did a good deal of it. Since I was young and did not have a family to worry about, my chief, Fred Hampson, kept me on the move. This suited me down to the ground.

The Kuomintang had its own newspapers and wire service, the Central News Service. But both in Chongqing and Nanjing, it allowed independent newspapers to publish.

The most influential of these was the liberal *Dagong bao*. Even though their sympathies were somewhat left of center, they understood and sympathized with American ideals of objective reporting. They came closer to telling the truth than any of the other major papers.

Until 1949, Shanghai was the foreign news center. Correspondents had apartments in the top four floors of the Broadway Mansions and those with staff of four or five, like AP, occupied offices downtown. At one time or another, I worked out of Shanghai, Nanjing, and Beiping. My travels, which were frequent, did not go unnoticed. My old buddies in the OSS approached me with an offer hard to resist.

"We have noticed that you travel to interesting and unusual places," they said. "Our proposal is simple. Let us have a copy of the stories you write and we will match your AP salary."

It was the second time OSS had tried to co-opt me. I had refused to work full-time for them at war's end behind the cover of a correspondent. I was a reporter *pur sang*, not an intelligence agent. I refused. This time, they were offering me a chance to serve both God and Mammon. AP was not notorious for its financial generosity. I was tempted. But again I said no. My life had been straightforward enough until then; I did not want to turn it into a lie.

That there were American correspondents working for OSS and the later Central Intelligence Agency was indisputable. They tended to be those taking the same out-of-the-way trips I did but whose stories seldom appeared. Fred Hampson thought he knew the identity of at least one of them and said so publicly. It was a mistake. Threatened with prosecution for libel, he fell silent.

In Europe and the Middle East, I knew a number of British and French reporters who played the dual role of correspondent and spy. They regarded it as a patriotic and glamorous game. But it came as a shock years later to learn that there were more then a few Americans in the same boat. We were aghast when their names were published. It seemed to us that they had tarnished the integrity of our trade. We did not deny that there was a need, especially in wartime, for gathering intelligence. But we believed then, as I still do, that the reading public would lose confidence in the press in general and in individual correspondents if it suspected they were part of the intelligence establishment.

During my seven months in Yan'an, only one of my dispatches was censored. It was about a continuing battle. But that did not mean that I operated as freely as I did in the Nationalist areas. There were no independent newspapers in the third of China the Communists controlled. I learned a lot, in dozens of sometimes interminable interviews, about the past lives and experiences of Yan'an's leaders. But they were mum when I asked them about day-to-day events. They played their cards as close to their chests as did the Nationalists. There were no non-Communist journalists with whom I could speak. The men and women in the countryside talked willingly enough but they steered away from politics; they trusted no one with their thoughts.

Xinhua News Agency and the *Jiefang ribao* (Liberation daily) parroted the party line. That line had been reached in lively and sometimes heated debates within the Central Committee. But once adopted, criticizing it was forbidden. It was what the party called democratic centralism. This lack of public dissent made Yan'an a dull place for a daily reporter. It did not matter to me. The big story, I thought, was that of this hardy, tough-minded little band of revolutionaries, grown old and middle-aged since the 1927 Shanghai Massacre, poised to share power with the hated enemy. Time was my enemy as I worked feverishly to piece the story together.

History has always fascinated me. It thrilled me to realize that I was, in this primitive cave city, a witness to history in the making. It compensated for the frustrations of daily reporting.

Lack of communications hampered all of us in our coverage of postwar China. Telephones were almost nonexistent and the telegraph unreliable and slow in the rural areas. The press corps hunkered down in Shanghai because it was the terminus of the Pacific cable. Since it cost as much as 50 cents a word to transmit, I wrote my stories in "cablese," eliminating the prepositions and running two words together when possible. The foreign desk in New York put the missing words back in but sometimes was baffled by too much terseness. "How please?" it would message, asking for clarification. Cablese also meant that the New York editors supplied historical or geographical background from their files.

As a news agency, AP not only supplied stories for its member papers and radio-television clients in the United States but distributed its news all over the world. After a while, it acquired a block of communication time which it could use not only to send the AP file to Shanghai but to receive dispatches from us. On that happy day, to our relief and that of the New York editors, we abandoned cablese and began sending stories in full. It also meant that we could no longer rely on New York to supply the background. We did it ourselves.

After China fell to the Communists in 1949, the Nationalist China Lobby in the United States convinced Senator Joseph McCarthy that the State Department, its officers in Chongqing and Nanjing, and in a kind of guilt-by-association, the American correspondents on the scene, were guilty of its loss. The infamous and now-discredited anti-American hearings of 1952, which McCarthy chaired, ruined the careers of many innocent men and women. One of them was an AP man who had covered the wartime activities of the Communist Eighth Route Army. Back in Washington he had a cultural job with the State Department, got summoned before the McCarthy committee on the grounds, as the China Lobby put it, that he must be guilty because of his year with the Red military. Half an hour after he appeared it soon became evident he was innocent and the committee sent him home. His innocence did not matter in the hysterical mood of the day. The mere fact that he had been brought before the committee destroyed him. His children were pelted with stones by their fellow students, they received late-night hate calls, and their lives were threatened. Finally, the State Department let him go and he had to begin another career all over again.

Having spent seven months with Mao and the Yan'an leadership, I wondered why the committee had not called me. It may have become more cautious after the bungled case of my predecessor. Or it may have been unwilling to bring me back from Paris where I then was ensconced.

What do I think about the performance of American correspondents in the 1945–49 period, the tempestuous time of the Marshall negotiations and the civil war? Looking back on a long reporting career, I think it remarkably good. Most of us, including John Hershey, Teddy White, Till Durdin, and myself were in China because we wanted to be. Fascination with its life, its history, and its people had drawn us to this poor and populous country. And because we loved it, we learned everything we could about it. I met many correspondents in forty years of foreign reporting, few as well informed or as dedicated as those covering China in the 1940s. They not only knew it, they lived it. China's problems were analyzed, discussed, chewed over and digested almost every day at meals, over drinks, and even while traveling. I sometimes yearned to talk about something else.

When we noted that the Nationalists were corrupt and in disarray and that the Communists were highly disciplined and incorruptible, these were not off-hand judgments but the result of firsthand knowledge, painstakingly gathered. When we wrote, after the Marshall negotiations broke down, that the Communists appeared likely to win, this was a logical extrapolation of what we knew. Our editors did not rebuke us for saying so. The U.S. embassy's knowledgeable political officers, Jack Service, John Davies, and other Chinese-speaking sons of missionaries, were not so lucky. Their reports, no more sensational than ours, aroused the ire of the mentally erratic ambassador, Patrick J. Hurley, who accused them of losing China, a charge taken up by Senator McCarthy. China, as someone astutely observed, was not ours to lose. But they were harried out of the State Department, their lives blasted. It was a classic case, all too familiar in a psychologically insecure America, of the messenger punished for the message.

By 1949 the question of who had won or lost China became purely academic for us. Over the next three decades, the burning question American reporters repeatedly asked was: When do we get back in?

From 1949 to 1979, Mao and his comrades struggled to make China over in the Marxist image. It was an epic struggle on a gigantic scale, a story of good intentions and failed endeavors, unspeakable oppression and bloodshed, and finally, despite all the difficulties, of change and progress. Barred from the mainland because the United States withheld diplomatic recognition of the new government, American correspondents reported these extraordinary events from listening posts in Hong Kong and Tokyo. They called themselves China Watchers and they were chief sources for many years of news from the China mainland. A brief account of what they saw and how they interpreted it appears in the pages that follow.

For six years, I followed the rapidly unfolding events of Chinese communism from assignments in the Middle East, London, and Paris. Though caught up in the news of those places—Israel's birth, Churchill's comeback, France's instability—I had time to do an occasional story analyzing from a distance what it all meant, or seemed to mean. I could no more purge China from my blood than I could stop breathing. I yearned to return.

In 1954 I left Paris on the long journey back, one which would take seventeen years and be realized in the most unexpected of company.

My first stop on this slowest of slow boats to China was Saigon where I reported the last days of the French Indochina empire. There I came almost face to face with the Chinese once more. They were in the hills around Dienbienphu, the flawed redoubt on the Laotian plain where the French had elected, fatally, to fight the last, critical battle of their war against Indochinese nationalism and communism. When the courageous defenders surrendered after fifty-five savage days of siege, I asked Gen. Henri Navarre, the French commander, why it had fallen.

"We did not anticipate that the Chinese would be able to bring in anti-aircraft guns," he said.

I wrote a friend that the United States should learn from the French debacle that it could not win a war fought against highly motivated, lightly armed, and mobile Nationalist/Communist forces operating from their own jungles and rice fields. He showed the letter to Senator John F. Kennedy who replied by enclosing two of his senate speeches which made the same point.

After the French withdrew and the Geneva Conference divided Vietnam into two halves at the 17th parallel, the period of calm and prosperity which followed made little news so I moved in 1956 to a new assignment as chief of the AP bureau in Hong Kong.

There I joined the small and exotic club of China Watchers.

Coverage of the first few years of the fledgling People's Republic by the Hong Kong–based China Watchers left a good deal to be desired. The Chinese complained, with considerable justification, that the reporting from the British Crown Colony was dismal at best. Much of the writing was speculative and many of the stories came from dubious or prejudiced sources. The Chinese easily could have remedied this situation by allowing Western correspondents to reestablish bureaus in Beijing. They were not in Hong Kong by choice but by necessity. Suggestions to this effect met with silence.

By the time I arrived in Hong Kong in 1956, things had improved thanks to the U.S. Consulate General and privately funded information agencies. Reporting by then had reached an extraordinary level of accuracy.

Though the United States continued to withhold recognition, it maintained a slender thread of contact with China through its ambassador in Warsaw and the Chinese ambassador, Wang Bingnan, whom I had known in Yan'an. It also spent millions of dollars on a staff of a hundred editors and translators busily engaged at the consulate-general in gathering every scrap of information it could lay its hands on through its agents on the mainland. It picked up copies of the Beijing *People's Daily*, the official organ of the Communist party, *Red Flag*, the party theoretical journal, and an assortment of magazines and provincial newspapers. We had access to these translations as well as those of an American intelligence agency which monitored Chinese broadcasts. We also did our own interviews of returning travelers.

The Xinhua (New China) News Agency, official voice of the government, had broadcast a daily news report since my days in Yan'an. With victory, it expanded its staff and its output, beaming its propaganda to many parts of the world. We picked it up in Hong Kong. Originality or liveliness were not its strong points. But deep down in a deadpan, pedestrian account of a party conference or an official speech, one could, with patience, pull out nuggets: the promotion or demotion of a party, government, or army leader, a change in policy or an until-then-unreported death. The greatest danger in reading Xinhua's monotonous prose was falling asleep, but for those able to stay awake, the rewards were great. Besides Xinhua and the consulate-general, China Watchers cultivated sources of their own, picked up what periodicals they could find and, above all, maintained a meticulous file. Knowing what had happened weeks or months before proved invaluable in checking out the clues one came cross. A good memory helped but a bulging file was essential. One also noted carefully where party leaders stood in relation to Mao during their appearances on the great gate of the Forbidden City in Beijing, or in what order their names were listed in Xinhua.

Two years after moving to Hong Kong, the AP China watching operation moved, at my suggestion, from Hong Kong to Tokyo. Japan had begun making economic overtures to the People's Republic, even though diplomatic relations did not exist, and more and more Japanese were flying from Tokyo to Beijing intent on doing business. Japanese journalists soon followed. As a result, Tokyo became an important vantage point from which to watch China. AP Hong Kong, under the able and knowledgeable Ronnie Wei, continued to report on China, giving AP member papers and broadcast media two sources of information on the unfolding drama there. In Tokyo, the hard-working Japanese staff pitched in to make the move a success. The star was the late George Inagaki, a personable reporter of Japanese-German parentage, and when the going got heavy, both Roy Essoyan, the Shanghai-educated chief of bureau, and Ed White, famous for his Vietnam war coverage, lent a hand.

China Watching proved to be an engrossing, riveting, and exhausting game. Anyone could play it if he had the time, the money, and the staying power. My years of covering China from a distance were fascinating, frustrating, and obsessive. One lived the story twenty-four hours a day; nothing else seemed important. I had to break away from time to time to help cover events in Japan or elsewhere in Asia, but to my mind these were interruptions to the main story—the China story. Editors also seemed to think it was. We were on the front pages day in and day out. Stories a month or more old, dug out of a Chinese newspaper or broadcast, made headlines back home. Given the passion Americans felt for China and the bravura performance Mao gave during its first three decades, it could hardly have been otherwise.

Though China watching had its moments of gratification, it was no substitute for the real thing. All of us hoped to return to the mainland to report on the scene, rather than second hand. My bags almost literally were always packed for twenty-two years in anticipation of the message which never came saying in effect, "All is forgiven, come to Beijing and start reporting as you once did on China and the Chinese." My hopes rose with each promising development in Sino-American relations only to be dashed when nothing came of it.

There was a time, in 1956, soon after I had arrived in Hong Kong, when it looked as though the dream would become reality. At the 1955 Bandung Conference of nonaligned nations Zhou Enlai announced a new policy of "peaceful coexistence." In effect, he said, China now was ready to establish relations with the United States and other Western nations. It was a bid to end the Cold War. As a gesture of goodwill, Zhou invited me and a handful of other Western correspondents to travel to Beijing. AP promptly named me its new Beijing chief of bureau and I went out shopping for office supplies.

Americans generally, and the media in particular, welcomed Zhou's initiative. But President Dwight Eisenhower's crusty secretary of state, John Foster Dulles, did not. A brilliant diplomat, he was inflexible in his dealings with international communism. Deeply religious, he summoned the United States to a crusade against what he called "monolithic, atheistic communism." I had met him a number of times during his periodic visits to Asia and was impressed by his grasp not only of the individual problems of each country but by his ability—a rare one—to remember and pronounce the names of their leaders. But communism, and Chinese communism in particular, was his blind spot. He reasoned that if he allowed us to go to Beijing, Mao and Zhou would interpret this as a willingness to improve relations with China. For no other apparent reason than his personal abhorrence of communism itself, he was not prepared to concede this. Consequently, he flatly refused to lift the restrictions which barred us from visiting the mainland. The penalty for violating them was five years in jail and a $10,000 fine.

American publishers and broadcast executives, eager to return to Beijing, kept up the pressure both on Dulles and Eisenhower. It became so great that "Old Iron Pants," as the media had begun to call Dulles, unexpectedly announced he had withdrawn his objections. Then he posed two conditions which he knew Beijing would reject: First, we must report all the nasty things going on in China, and second, China could not expect that the U.S. would reciprocally invite Chinese reporters to Washington.

The Chinese reacted precisely as we, and he, knew they would. They coldly withdrew the invitations.

What to do? Suddenly I recalled Mao's 1947 invitation, at the Yan'an airfield, to visit him in Beijing two years later. I sent off a telegram explaining that I had not been able to accept then but was ready to do so now. The reply was quick: Pick up your visa in Moscow or Ulan Bator.

Elated, I messaged AP's general manager in New York, Frank J. Starzel, saying that I was about to leave. It was a mistake. He cabled back proposing caution. He feared I would end up in jail if I did. I said I would gladly take that risk. No answer. At the end of two weeks, he suggested that I try to get one of our London-based English reporters in. When that failed, he urged me to see if my visa remained valid. I asked Beijing. Silence. The moment had passed.

It had passed not only for me but, more importantly, for the United States. Who can say what might have happened if someone less intransigent than Dulles had been secretary of state? Sino-American hostility could have ended in 1956 rather than in 1971, fifteen years later. Might this have averted war in Vietnam? We will never know. What is certain is that Eisenhower was presented with a dazzling opportunity to improve relations with China but, because of Dulles,

turned his back on it. Instead, he continued the palpably absurd myth
that the Nationalists on Taiwan represented all of China. No matter
how one felt about Beijing, it was undeniable that, well or badly, it
ruled the 800 million people of China.

Our activities in Hong Kong and Tokyo did not go unobserved by
Beijing. With enough material one could probably write a chapter
entitled "The China Watchers Watched."

Eric Chou, one of the editors of the Communist *Dagong bao* told me
one day that his bosses on the mainland took a more than passing
interest in our activities. He was eminently qualified to say so. A
handsome, smiling, pipe-smoking man much given to tweeds, he had
been with the paper when it was a left-leaning liberal organ, considered the most reliable in China. This was before 1949 on the mainland
and many of us had known him then. He and his wife Josephine were
popular with the foreign press corps in Hong Kong. Despite the
change in the paper's ownership, he continued to socialize with us.
Fluent in English, he was unusually intelligent and witty and did not
hesitate to discuss, in general terms, developments in the People's
Republic.

One day in 1952, the paper's publisher ordered him to take the
train to Beijing for a routine consultation of a few weeks. He did not
return until 1957. He told me later, in confidence, of his harrowing
experiences. Thrust into solitary confinement in a cell equipped with
a bucket for toilet and so small he could barely stand erect, he underwent the first of long, relentless and seemingly endless interrogations
about the foreign newsmen he had known. He had to set down the
story of his life and encounters a hundred, maybe a thousand, times
only to be told to do it again. He felt like Alice going through the
looking glass. The comfortable, normal world he had known suddenly
had become turned inside out. His jailers shouted abuse at him and
accused him of lying when they found the slightest deviation in his
"confessions." He insisted in vain he had nothing to confess. All his
contacts, he said, had been perfectly innocent. He was asked to tell
everything he knew about the U.S. consulate-general and to describe
its "spying" activities on the mainland. He was unable to do so. He
thought of "K" in Kafka's novel, *The Trial*, facing persecutors he did
not know and charged with he knew not what crime.

All this might have been understandable—if not defensible—if he
had been caught up in the anti-Rightist campaign of 1956–57. But the
puzzling thing was that this took place a full four years earlier. The
paranoia which was to infect the Chinese leadership for the next fourteen years had already begun to work its poison.

Suddenly, after years of anxiety and harassment, he was told he
could go back to Hong Kong but that his assignment would include

spying on the same foreign newsmen who had been the source of his long and pointless brainwashing. He was given an expense account and instructed to join the Hong Kong Foreign Correspondents Club. After we had met a number of times, he guardedly told me the story of his ordeal.

Eric was still under interrogation when the U.S. press corps in Hong Kong got its invitation to visit Beijing. He said he was glad to see that I, and most of his other American friends, were on the foreign ministry's approved list for entry to the mainland. Whatever he had said had not been that damaging.

In a way, Eric was one of the lucky ones. He was not told, but he may well have been given his freedom because of the new wave of cordiality to the American press. Beijing was notorious for turning the charm off or on, like a water faucet, when it suited its purposes. In 1956 charm gushed out all over us. The Communists could not have been nicer. They needed Eric in Hong Kong to show their shining new face. He resented his role as informer but decided that he would enjoy himself in the process. When the United States refused to let us return to China, the charm faucet suddenly went dry. Eric's usefulness presumably had ended but he continued to be friendly and available to us. His good luck was that he escaped the fate of hundreds of thousands of innocent "bourgeois right wingers." It is possible that after so long a trial Eric's superiors decided he either was not guilty or that he had genuinely repented whatever crimes he had committed.

While waiting for Dulles to give us the go-ahead signal which never came, I brushed up my Chinese with Eric's wife Josephine. A pleasant, well-educated woman of great warmth, she did part-time teaching in addition to working with the Institute of Oriental Studies at the University of Hong Kong. Sentence no. 22 in one of my lessons was: "Ni quguo Yingguo ma?" which translated means "Have you been to England?" I thought of it later when one day, many months later, Eric slipped out of Hong Kong and flew to England and freedom. There he wrote a book called *A Man Must Choose* (Longmans, 1963), which told what he had gone through.

The book, subtitled, "The Dilemma of a Chinese Patriot," summed up the anguish of the Chinese intellectuals of that day. Watching an anniversary parade in Beijing during his painful experience, the tears had come to his eyes and he felt a surge of nationalist pride as a half million of the faithful, eyes shining, filed through Tiananmen Square. A liberal, like many of his compatriots, he shared the Communist vision of a new China freed from imperialism, poverty, diseases, injustice, and corruption. Had he been a convinced Communist, he would have closed his eyes to the price being paid in individual freedom to achieve these goals. Being a true liberal, in the best sense of the word, he put a high value on human rights. When he saw them daily out-raged, he had to dissent.

Historians often note an extraordinary thing about China. In its long, and brilliant, existence it has experienced many rebellions but only one revolution, that of 1949. During its period of imperial rule, one dynasty succeeded the other with almost predictable regularity. All, from the fifth century B.C., governed according to the ethics, poli-tics, and morals laid down by Confucius, the great Chinese sage. Even the barbarian Mongols and Manchus accepted his precepts of good government, becoming more Chinese than the Chinese.

One rebellion which might have turned into revolution, that of the Taipings between 1850 and 1864, came within an ace of overthrow-ing the Manchus. Led by a religious fanatic proclaiming himself the brother of Jesus Christ, he introduced a mixture of socialism, democ-racy, and Christianity to his many followers and undoubtedly would have applied them to the entire nation had he won. It was an irony of history that a foreigner, the British general Charles George "Chinese Gordon," working for the Manchus, defeated the Taiping and prevented their alien ideas from prevailing. By the time they surrendered 50 million Chinese had died.

A second chance came in 1911 with the ouster of the Manchus by the followers of Sun Yat-sen. But the democratic and socialist revolu-tion he envisaged foundered in the flames of a long civil war. Mao and his comrades were the first in a long line of rulers to apply an entirely new doctrine to government and society, that of the German philoso-pher Karl Marx and his Soviet disciple, V. I. Lenin. China watchers like me, based in Hong Kong and Tokyo, had the rare and heady ex-perience of chronicling the first thirty years of their attempt to make Marxism work, a tempestuous and bloody exercise which ultimately claimed more victims than had the Taiping uprising.

Mao and his comrades had promised to smash the state and build socialism on its ashes. They wasted no time trying to do so. By the time they had finished they had almost destroyed the country and themselves. One extraordinary event succeeded the other with such speed it was difficult to make head or tail of them from our Hong Kong and Tokyo listening posts.

Land reform came first followed, about the same time, by involve-ment in the Korean War. They had barely ended before hundreds of thousands of intellectuals were purged and the country embarked on the Great Leap Forward. Its failure led to economic collapse and fam-ine and shattered the Chinese Communist Party. In the final act of a Wagnerian-like drama, millions of Chinese were pilloried, humili-ated, tortured, and killed in the 1966–76 Great Proletarian Cultural Revolution.

Few countries have undergone such convulsions in so short a time. One of the reasons was that the Yan'an comrades were long on theory but short on practice. Remaking so large and populous a country demanded the skills of thousands of administrators. Even if they had existed, there were no blueprints for the seminal changes the victors envisaged. Also, they had spent twenty-eight years fighting for the chance to turn China from a capitalist to a socialist economy and they were in a hurry. They considered, in the light of the distance they had traveled, that their work had just begun. Their objective was a daunting one: the abolition of classes in a country where the gulf between rich and poor had always been abysmally deep.

It did not surprise me that they gave Mao first chance at recreating China. I remembered how he had stood head and shoulders above the others in Yan'an and the respect, bordering on awe, he commanded. I had the impression then that few of them knew much about Marxism except Mao. They deferred to him even though most of his knowledge came from books. Such is the power of the written word that almost none dared to challenge his interpretation of what the German philosopher-economist had said. Marx was all things to all men; one could find in his writings anything to support a position one took, no matter how contradictory. Marxism was, after all, like a religion. Pragmatists, such as Liu Shaoqi and Deng Xiaoping, interpreted him freely, daring to bring him up to date and apply his ideas to the modern world. Whether he believed it or not, Mao spoke for the fundamentalists, insisting that every word was gospel truth. I thought while in Yan'an that he tossed around words and phrases such as "class struggle," "running dogs of imperialists," and "class enemy" a little too freely. But given the deference most Chinese accorded teachers, it was not astonishing the lesser-read comrades bowed to Mao the teacher. It would not be long before they referred to Marxism as Maoism plus Leninism, inferring that Mao, like Lenin, had created his own national brand of socialism.

Mao correctly saw that he had to begin changing society with the peasants, 90 percent of the population. During my travels around the country in the 1940s I was shocked to see how poor they were, burdened with debt and taxes, living little better than animals. Many told me they had to surrender most of their crop to absentee landlords or the tax collector. They were little more than poorly paid farm laborers. Mao seized the land from the landlords and gave it to them, a move which created an upsurge in agricultural production and gave the new government a solid financial base on which to build.

The land reform was a success except for the way it was carried out. Instead of doing it peacefully, Mao turned it into a purge of the landlord and "rich" peasant class. In thousands of well-orchestrated "speak bitterness" mass meetings, they were paraded before the peasants, beaten, humiliated, denied even elementary justice, then led out to the execution grounds.

Mao, familiar with the thinking of the peasants, knew that hatred, not love, ruled their relations to the landlords. But if land reform was a sound foundation for the rebirth of China, it seemed to me that hatred was not. During the civil war Mao won many supporters through a policy of forgiveness. In victory his infatuation with class struggle blinded him to the need to seek national reconciliation. As we have seen, he loved to manipulate words, Marxist words. "Class struggle" were his favorites. Brandishing them, he disposed of his enemies and rivals and brought China to the edge of disaster.

It is hard to say, even now, why the People's Republic risked its very existence to enter the Korean War (1950–53) only months after it had begun the Herculean job of converting feudal China to socialism. It threw "volunteers" under Peng Dehuai into the conflict after United Nation forces had pushed the North Korean Communists uncomfortably close to China's Yalu River border. Beijing apparently took Gen. Douglas MacArthur, the American UN commander, seriously when he defied Harry Truman and threatened to cross the river in "hot pursuit" of the fleeing enemy. Mao should have waited and listened to the doughty Truman himself. When he unceremoniously sacked his popular but arrogant commander, it became abundantly apparent that the United States had no intention of invading Manchuria, as Mao feared. The war put U.S.-China relations in the deep freeze for two decades and did nothing to improve Beijing's ties with Moscow, which had egged Mao into going into the conflict in the first place. The Russians infuriated Mao by refusing to help pay for the "volunteer" army and, adding insult to default, proposed to take command of the Chinese naval forces.

The war proved a drain on China's meager resources when they had little to spare. A prudent leader would have given the country a breathing space. Not Mao. He stunned the happy peasants by grabbing back their land and herding them into thousands of rural cooperatives. Having alienated the countryside, he now struck at the best-educated segment of the population, the intellectuals, the people he needed most for the industrial revolution he had in mind.

He announced that they were to be given freedom of speech under a new policy called "let a hundred flowers bloom, a hundred schools of thought contend." He asked for their criticisms. The response, voluble, heartfelt, and bitterly critical of the Communist party, alarmed him. Deciding that he had got poisonous weeds rather than orchids, he cracked down not only on the intelligentsia but on anyone with the smallest past ties to the Kuomintang or the United States. A number of my old, pre-1949 friends were among the hundreds of thousands of victims.

Mao despised intellectuals because he thought them unreliable and mercurial. He called them the "stinking ninth category of society." And he also still rankled at the memory of the cold shoulder they had given him when he was an assistant in the Peking University library.

Mao's explanation was that he was strengthening the country for its next big campaign, the Great Leap Forward. Its aim: industrializing China in fifteen years.

Mao believed China's burgeoning population was an asset not a liability. He proposed to march out of the Middle Ages and into the twentieth century on the backs of the Chinese millions, an idea which might have worked in an earlier era when technology did not exist. He did, in fact, accomplish a good deal using manpower alone. Dams, roads, irrigation projects, and airports sprang up where none had been before. More sophisticated undertakings had to be shelved: he had purged the architects, engineers, and scientists they required.

The Great Leap was one of the many mass-action campaigns which marked Mao's stewardship in the first decade of the People's Republic. His ability to whip up millions of his fellow countrymen into a frenzy of action was nothing short of remarkable. Usually regarded as emotionless and inscrutable, the Chinese in fact were highly impressionable and open to new ideas. They wanted to improve their standard of living, to join the Western industrial powers as an equal. They did not need to be coerced or struggled against to throw themselves whole-heartedly into the Great Leap program. All the reports we received indicated that the nation had been caught up in a wave of enthusiasm awesome in its size. Though they clearly were exhausted, everyone seemed to take pride in what he or she was doing. The desire for success was contagious. The disappointment was immense when all their efforts failed. It was not their fault. False production figures from the provinces, incompetence at the administrative levels and three bad harvests were the villains.

At its peak, when all appeared to be going well, the party was united in praising the mass response. If Mao had succeeded in this massive popular crusade his place in history would have been assured. But when the Great Leap stumbled, then fell, the search for a scapegoat began. At first, Liu and Deng withheld their fire, hesitant to attack the still powerdul Chairman. Peng Dehuai, the gentle bulldog whose Yan'an cave was bright with flowers, took the offensive. Honest, outspoken, and independent, he was one of the few who had challenged Mao in the past and survived. Now, while the others thrashed around trying to avoid a confrontation, he dared, like the child in the fable, to say that the emperor had no clothes.

Mao, furious, had enough clout to have him fired from his job as defence minister, this despite the fact his Korean service had made him a hero second only to Zhu De. Mao put the mousy little Lin Biao, the military genius I had met in Harbin, in his place.

It was Mao's last hurrah, at least for a while. His treatment of Deng prodded the pragmatists into action. Confronted with an economy in shambles, with millions dying of starvation, they put Mao on the shelf, where he remained for seven years. Liu took over as chief of state and the pragmatists seized power in the party where Mao, still chairman in name, withdrew into the shadows.

The issue the new rulers raised was not that Mao had failed—they knew the meaning of failure—but that he had bypassed an important stage in the march toward communism: a long period of limited democracy and controlled capitalism. Mao himself told me in Yan'an that it was vital. Without it, he said, there would be no wealth to redistribute.

Peng had raised the banner of inner party revolt (he was arrested during the Cultural Revolution and died, still under a cloud, in 1974) and the party split down the middle not over the ultimate goal, communism/socialism (everyone agreed on that), but on the road to take to get there.

The pragmatists accused Mao of wanting to leap into communism overnight using the 27,000 self-sufficient rural communes he created as the launching pads. This, they felt, was heresy. Mao, the poet and romanticist, wanted to realize communism in his lifetime. This was understandable after so much struggle and pain. His critics felt the same way but they lived in the real world, not that of dreams. They did not particularly like to delay the day of socialist triumph but believed it was still a long way off.

One is prompted to ask: Why didn't the opposing factions sit down and work out their differences? The answer is that fundamentalists and free thinkers everywhere find it next to impossible to reconcile their opposing views. Marxism is close to religion. It has its dogma. Mao was wrong when he said that "power grows out of the barrel of a gun." He knew that power came from ideas not bullets. He and his fellow revolutionaries used guns to come to power but never would have made it if their economic philosophy had not appealed to the long-exploited Chinese masses. The Great Leap was an idea gone wrong. It left China broken and disillusioned. Something else had to be tried to win back the people's confidence.

Given their chance to rule, the pragmatists dug in with a will. Despite the fact that the economy had been further crippled by the withdrawal of Soviet technicians helping to build large industrial projects, they persevered. Mao had made the mistake of giving priority to heavy industry rather than agriculture. They reversed this policy and fed the peasants new hope by alloting them more private plots on which to grow their crops. It was not private ownership but it nevertheless gave the economy a boost. By 1964, the pragmatists had staged a remarkable comeback, marked by the explosion that year of the first Chinese atomic bomb. Nikita Krushchev, Mao's arch rival and sharpest critic, stepped down almost the same time but relations, already badly strained, did not improve with his immediate successors.

Mao, repentant, indicated he was content to remain in the background thinking long thoughts and planning for the future. He might have stayed there if it had not been for Jiang Qing and Lin Biao. They put their heads together to figure out some way to restore the Chairman to power. The result was the Great Proletarian Cultural Revolution which began in 1966 and lasted, in one form or another, until Mao's death in 1976.

The motives of the three principals were diverse. Mao understandbly welcomed the possibility of putting his theories in practice once again. Jiang Qing saw the opportunity of winning respectabilty by championing Mao. Denied membership in the Long March club, this would be her Long March. Besides, she wanted her place as First Lady, usurped by Liu's American-educated wife, Wang Guangmei, restored to her. Lin masked his motives behind a torrent of Maoist flattery. His hidden agenda would emerge dramatically five years later.

The Cultural Revolution was neither cultural nor a revolution. Mao, clever at this sort of thing, persuaded his enemies that all he wanted was a Big Debate over the course of Chinese culture. Mistakenly, they humored him. Beginning on university campuses it soon expanded into something bigger, and more sinister. It became apparent that Mao was playing for keeps. Stormy seas lay ahead.

As both sides lined up, the big question was what Zhou Enlai would do. Though Mao commanded national respect, Zhou was China's best-loved leader. He was torn by conflicting loyalties. His logic told him that the pragmatists were right. But since the Long March he had had a warm, father-son relationship with the elder Mao. By common consent, he became the Cultural Revolution's arbiter, the man in the middle. He tried, unsuccessfully, to keep the debate civilized and, desperately, to contain the damage both sides were doing to the country's economy, morale, and sanity.

Analyzing what was happening, I noted that the pragmatists held all the big cards—the army, the government, the mass organs, and a majority in the party. Mao had only his immense national prestige.

When Jiang Qing enrolled the nation's young to defend her husband, that tipped the balance. Most of them were innocent of political knowledge. But they had the passion, imagination and cruelty of youth. Exempted from classes, and dubbed Red Guards, they roamed the country destroying old art, ancient religious shrines, and even old people because they were told anything old was bad. It coincided with their own childish thinking.

They were encouraged to parade Mao's opponents through the

streets dressed in dunce caps; it was generational revenge, their own experience turned upside down. At hysterical mass rallies they denounced their victims for crimes whose details were supplied by Jiang Qing and Lin Biao. Party secrets, once zealously guarded, saw the light in thousands of Red Guard posters and communiques pasted up on city walls for all to see. Copied by agents of the Hong Kong consulate and Japanese reporters on the scene, they furnished China Watchers with news which filled columns and made headlines in America.

Mao, an old hand at party rough and tumble, took the offensive from the start. He accused Liu and Peng of introducing Western-style capitalism and betraying the Revolution. It was effective propaganda, diverting attention away from his own Great Leap disaster.

If it were not so tragic, the Cultural Revolution would have been farcical. The Red Guards graduated from such absurdities as making red the signal for "go" in stop lights, because it was the color of revolution, to organized mayhem and murder. The confusion, violence, and killing were reminiscent of the worst days of the French Revolution's period of terror.

We reported everything we could lay our hands on and it was frightening. But it took years to discover the real extent of the horror. No one dared speak while Mao was alive. They opened up after he died, Jiang Qing was arrested, and Deng loosened the constraints on free speech. I heard many stories in that time, including Han Su-yin's description of how students in her home city of Chongqing bludgeoned their teacher to death. The famous Belgian-Japanese author could have revealed more during the Cultural Revolution but had to remain silent, she told me, because her numerous Chinese family was threatened with reprisals if she did.

Perhaps the most disturbing report of all appeared as recently as 1993 when the Chinese author, Zheng Yi, wrote (in *A Part of History*) his own investigations and revealed that the killing of "class enemies" was a qualification for membership in the Communist party in some areas. In a gruesome incident, villagers dragged out the son of an executed 1940s landlord, disemboweled him and ate his heart, liver, gall bladder, and kidneys. The victim was only a child when his father was executed.

The Cultural purge was an orgy, presided over by Jiang Qing and Lin Biao, with Mao's tacit backing, which left millions dead, more millions impoverished and many others scarred for life. I shook my head more than once in wonder and disbelief as I wrote the story of a nation gone mad. Could these be the same kind, gentle, intelligent Chinese I had known and admired?

The change in Jiang Qing hit me the hardest. The demure Yan'an housewife had turned hard and vindictive. From a hundred rostrums, she harangued the crowds, eyes glaring behind rimless glasses, arms flailing as she took Liu, Deng, sometimes even Zhou, over the dialectical coals. She had her revenge on Liu (he died, neglected, in prison in 1969) and on his wife. Decked in a necklace of ping pong balls she was humiliated before a mass meeting which forced her to don the yellow silk dress she had worn when she met Indonesia's President Sukarno. It was grand guignol at its most revolting.

Mao appeared overwhelmed by the chaos he had created. Because of his increasing mental illness, he left much of the antipragmatist campaign to Jiang Qing. He protested mildly at the heavy-handed way she interpreted his ideas and the ferocity with which she punished her enemies. But by the time he became aware of her ambitions to succeed him, the damage had been done.

No sycophant could have been more abject than Lin Biao. He praised Mao to the skies, compared him to a demi-god, said men like him were born only once in ten thousand years. His own secret ambition to replace him was revealed in 1969 when the old man called on him and the army to rein in the now out-of-control Red Guards. After doing so he and his followers gained the upper hand in the ruling politburo. In fact, if not in name, he was China's No. 1 man.

Mao said nothing publicly but inside he was seething. Not until the archives are opened at some future time will we know the real story of what happened after that. The record is confused and confusing. When I visited Beijing in April 1971 with the U.S. ping pong team, the city was dotted with huge billboards showing him and a beaming Mao together. I posed for a photo in front of one of them. Five months later, the little civil war hero and Mao's designated successor—he had written this into the new party constitution—was dead.

The official account said he had been caught plotting to assassinate Mao and, fleeing to Moscow, died when his plane crashed in Outer Mongolia. I heard another version in 1972 during the official visit of Japan's Prime Minister Tanaka. It said Zhou had personally ordered Lin eliminated after he had been arrested in Beijing and confronted with his crimes. Many questions went unanswered. Why, if he already was Mao's acknowledged successor, did he have to kill him? Mao was old and ailing. Could he not wait? What can be said with certainty is that Lin had grown too big for his breeches, posed a definite threat to Mao's ascendancy, and had to be removed. How and when it was done remains obscure. The deed restored Mao to his old power and strengthened Jiang Qing's dominant position in the Cultural goings on.

Three of the top leaders I had known in Yan'an—Zhou Enlai, Zhu De, and Mao Zedong—died in 1976, the same year that a catastrophic earthquake snuffed out hundreds of thousands of lives north of Beijing. These events rang down the curtain on the Cultural Revolution and marked the end of the Mao era. (I reported at length on the deaths of Zhou and Mao from Paris, where I happened to be visiting. Some American papers gave a full page to the obituary I had written on Mao. But there were no expressions of sympathy. Zhou's passing evoked tributes from most world leaders, including Richard Nixon and Henry Kissinger.)

I wrote at the time that Mao's life had been a triumph and a disaster, the one following the other. Few humans had had it in their power to be so powerful a force for good. Instead, he chose to be the instrument of a strange, little-understood foreign doctrine which, badly interpreted and carried out, brought terror, confusion, and death to millions.

Basically, I said, Mao was an insecure man, at war with all the contradictory elements within himself. He had begun life with a burning wish to rescue China from exploitation, foreign imperialism, and poverty and had accomplished much. The darker side of his being prevented him from doing more. He was suspicious of his most intimate friends, intolerant of rivals, and resented criticism.

His vision of China was a soaring but hopelessly romantic one, based on a naive belief that the Chinese, inheritors of a brilliant civilization, could bring their impoverished and backward country into the industrial age alone, without foreign help. It was a fatal mistake which isolated China from the outside world for three decades and hampered its development.

I was glad that I had known this larger-than-life dreamer and founder of the People's Republic. But I felt no emotion at his passing. When a Chinese official told me that weeks before Mao's death he had asked about me and wondered what I was doing, I shuddered as though I had seen a ghost.

Zhou's death left me with a feeling of loss and sadness. He was, to me, the quintessential civilized man caught up in the dilemma of his time. Had he been born in an economically comfortable Western democracy, his elite family background and education would have guaranteed success in whatever field he chose, business, politics, or academe. Instead he came into a society torn by corruption, exploited by foreigners, and indescribably poor. He could have played the mandarin and ignored these problems. But the warmth of his nature impelled him to rebel against these unfair conditions. Though he did not quail at the cruelties and killing demanded of him as a revolutionary, he remembered that the aim of the revolution was to make a better society, not a brutal one, and sought to temper the worst passions of his contemporaries. If he had not acted as honest broker between Mao and the pragmatists the damage to China might well have been irreparable.

I had known Zhu De more intimately than any of the others, and talked to him more often. I felt regret that he had lived so many lives, ardently, only to be humiliated and rejected by Mao. One of the great military chieftains of his day, he lived to see Mao claim sole credit for creating the Red Army which they had jointly built. What must have hurt most, though, was that when he died—a few months before the overthrow of the Gang of Four—the just, humane, and prosperous society he had given his life to realize was gripped by chaos and ruled by men and women seemingly gone mad. He deserved better.

Marshal Ye Jiangying, the fearless wolf-slayer of my Yan'an days, led the operation which rounded up and imprisoned Jiang Qing and the remaining three members of her Gang of Four. By doing so he scotched their plan to seize power and continue the Cultural Revolution's reign of terror.

Besides its inner turmoil, China had more than its share of international crises during the 1949–79 China Watching period. From the beginning, it dealt almost entirely with nations within the Communist bloc. Its relations with the Western democracies were either cold or nonexistent.

In fact, in 1968, at the apogee of the Cultural Revolution violence, China had only one ambassador abroad, Huang Hua, my Yan'an interpreter-liaison chief. The others had been recalled either because of strained relations or for political reasons: their loyalty to Mao was in question.

During the thirty-year China Watching period five major U.S.-China crises became grist for our news mills.

The first, the 1946–56 French colonial war in Indochina, involved the two countries only indirectly. Each contributed money, materiel, and military expertise to the warring sides. Franklin D. Roosevelt wanted Indochina to have its independence. But Harry Truman supported the failed French attempt to recover their old colony. The fact that he had fought in France during World War II and liked the French may have influenced him. His decision aligned the United States with an imperialism on its last legs. In 1954 Dwight Eisenhower rejected a proposal to use nuclear weapons to tilt the balance toward the French. He sent Dulles to Geneva instead to arrange for the division of Vietnam into Communist and non-Communist halves at the 17th parallel. At that conference, Dulles famously refused to shake hands with Zhou Enlai.

The second crisis, the Korean War, ended in stalemate in 1953. It prompted both sides, as a matter of prudence, to keep in touch. Neither wanted misunderstandings to lead to a similar conflict.

China touched off the third crisis in 1958 with an attempt to seize the Nationalist-held islands of Quemoy and Matsu which lay only a few miles off the Communist mainland.

The Communists gave up after losing the air battle between Nationalist U.S.-made fighter jets and Soviet MiG aircraft flown by the Chinese. The islands, heavily fortified (I visited Quemoy afterward) were subjected to bombardment intermittently until 1979.

The second Vietnam War (1964–75) found Beijing supporting Ho Chi Minh's Communists and Washington backing first Ngo Dinh Diem and then a succession of military rulers. The United States poured troops and treasure into the conflict; the Chinese, unwilling to repeat the Korean War debacle, intervened only with aid and advice. For China the enemy not only was the United States but the Soviet Union which, while also avoiding direct participation, wooed the North Vietnamese. Our China Watching bureau in Tokyo monitored both North Vietnamese and Xinhua reports. Their versions often sharply differed. Vietnam ceased being a burning Sino-American issue after Nixon's 1972 China visit.

The final crisis, a political one, was fought out in the halls of the United Nations. The United States had long maintained the fiction that the Republic of China on Taiwan represented all China. Its successful efforts to keep Taipei in and Beijing out failed in 1971, six months after the ping pong trip. Nixon's effort to give both membership sank in the wave of post–ping pong, pre–Nixon visit euphoria. I was there when the historic vote took place. A few weeks earlier I had interviewed Huang Hua, then ambassador to Canada, in Ottawa. He was uncompromising in his insistence the seat must go to Beijing alone. I welcomed him when he took up the China post as its first permanent representative. His speeches reflected the intransigence of the Maoist hard line but even George Bush, who as UN ambassador fought to keep Taiwan in, conceded that Beijing's presence in the world body made it more competent to cope with international crises.

Despite the euphoria of the Nixon China visit, diplomatic recognition did not follow for another seven years. Watergate deflected Nixon's attention from the issue. Gerald Ford planned to do so if elected. He was not. His successor, Jimmy Carter, bit the bullet, ending thirty years of hostility but not entirely eliminating the love-hate relationship which, since the Tiananmen events, persists today.

Sino-Soviet relations traveled a bumpy road between 1949 and 1979. They were at their roughest in the Mao era, and particularly so during the Cultural Revolution. The quarrel was ideological but also governmental. Though they improved after Deng took over, Soviet involvement in Afghanistan and Cambodia, and the stationing of formidable forces on the Sino-Soviet borders, were sticking points which prevented fully normal relations. The continuing dispute between these two old Marxist rivals gave us much to write about.

China had long enjoyed a special relationship with the Vietnamese Communists, led by Ho Chi Minh. This turned to bitterness after the Russians gained the upper hand in 1975 and established military bases in the new Communist republic. Relations with Hanoi and Moscow descended to a new low.

Crisis in Cambodia followed. The Khmer Rouge, backed by Beijing, ousted its American-sponsored government and in a reign of terror executed a million of its citizens. When Vietnam, supported by Moscow, evicted the genocidal Khmers there was an international gasp of relief but only fury in Beijing, which regarded Cambodia as a client state.

Prince Norodom Sihanouk, Cambodia's onetime king, had reason to be disillusioned with China. In exchange for asylum after the Americans had kicked him out in 1970, it asked him to become the Khmer Rouge chief of state. The experience was a bitter one but he remained strangely loyal to his Chinese sponsors. Meeting him in Tokyo I asked him why.

"I'm penniless," he said. "I owe them everything I have, everything I eat and wear."

He was equally unhappy over the role Henry Kissinger had played in forcing him out of his onetime kingdom. During lunch in Beijing, Sihanouk told me Kissinger, then in town, would like to see him, to assure him he had done everything he could to support him in 1970.

The prince reacted with heavy sarcasm. Wouldn't it be delightful for their respective wives to exchange recipes on chocolate mousse, he asked rhetorically. As for Kissinger's role in the 1970 coup, well, he should go on the stage. He was a superb actor.

In 1979, during his American visit, Deng disturbed his hosts by threatening to attack Vietnam to relieve its military pressure on Cambodia. A few months later he did, and failed. China supplied the Khmer Rouge, which had gone underground, with arms until 1993. Bumbling and cold-blooded, China's Vietnam policy could only be described as unfortunate and self-defeating.

Though Beijing insisted it was an internal problem, the way the Maoists treated Tibet bedevilled China's relations with India and the United States and outraged human rights advocates.

During my years of China watching I thought often of my encounter with the Panchen Lama, the mischievous little boy forced by the demands of religion to abandon his normal life of play for the solemnities that hedge in a living god. In spite of their number and variety, the Chinese appeared to have had fewer problems with their nationalities than the Soviet Union. Tibet was different. Though it had been given nominal autonomy, Beijing attempted in a brutal way to Sinicize it, to people it with Chinese soldiers and settlers. The 1959 uprising, bloodily put down, drove the Dalai Lama into sanctuary in India and broke the back of Lamaism. Marx had said that religion was the opiate of the people, an opiate its faithful stubbornly refused, in China at least, to surrender. The Tibetan Buddhists were particularly tenacious of their beliefs and despite the slaughter which marked the repressions—a new wave was unleashed during the Cultural Revolution—they continued to resist incorporation into the Great Han—all China—society. I never saw the Panchen Lama again but met his spiritual brother, the Dalai Lama, at the Foreign Correspondents Club in Tokyo in 1972. A gentle god wearing steel-rimmed glasses, he spoke out powerfully for Tibetan independence and condemned the harsh Chinese measures against his religion. As befits a living Buddha, he exuded compassion, even then offered an olive branch to his Chinese oppressors. When I told him of my days in Kumbum with the Panchen Lama, he smiled and refused to condemn him even though the Maoists were using him for their political purposes. The Panchen had, for a time, been under house arrest for opposing Mao's campaign to eradicate Lamaism. The Dalai praised the Panchen for his courage.

My memories of Kum Bum monastery, in the foothills of Tibet, were vivid ones and I yearned to travel to Lhasa to see this land at the top of the world whose religion and rich culture so captivated Americans they had made it the subject of a best-selling book and movie and launched the first air strikes against Japan from the deck of an aircraft carrier appropriately named *The Shangri-la*. When Tibet opened up to correspondents in 1979, I asked to go. Because my blood pressure was high, the Chinese turned me down. I was chagrined and disappointed when two later applications were similarly rejected.

Wang Bingnan, my old friend from Yan'an, had traveled to Tibet and praised the way Mao was handling it. He must have been blind. This was a period not only of harshness but of Cultural Revolution insanity; Mao and Jiang Qing had decreed that the Tibetans give up their religion and speak only Chinese. In an excess of zeal they insisted that barley, the main food crop, be replaced with wheat. Starvation ensued. The United States took the lead in condemning these policies.

Wang went a step further and proposed that Tibet be taken as a model of how to deal with Taiwan. It was an idea which would not fly. When I reported it, there was a small flurry of interst but a larger adverse reaction. He quietly dropped the idea.

These then, in brief were the major stories which kept us running during thirty years of reporting on China from our Hong Kong and Tokyo listening posts. Recalling them hopefully will make clear what follows. We who devoted ourselves to this curious assignment were at once exhilirated and depressed by it. The abundance of material which came to our hands and eyes made it satisfying. But our enforced distance from the events we were describing was maddening.

6

China Rediscovered

I t took Richard Nixon, the almost professional Communist baiter, to recognize what his predecessors had not seen, that China's fear of Soviet intentions not only in Vietnam but along the long Sino-Soviet borders was promising ground for negotiation. He had long nursed the idea of restoring Sino-American relations to normal.

As early as 1968, before becoming president, he began gathering background and advice on China. On a visit to Tokyo, he invited me to the American embassy for a long talk with his aide, Ray Price, on the China situation. In 1969, I accompanied Secretary of State William Rogers on an Asian tour during which he made an unprecedented stop in Hong Kong. There he openly called on the Chinese to respond to the friendly American overtures of the past few months. These included relaxation of restrictions on purchases of goods made in China. There had been a time when a shirt, a set of underwear, or an ivory carving bought by an American tourist in Hong Kong and suspected to have been manufactured on the mainland could be seized by U.S. customs agents.

It was not astonishing that there was no positive Chinese reply in 1969. The Cultural Revolution had just wound down with the Ninth Party Congress which left Lin Biao and the Army in control. Mao once again was on the sidelines and Lin opposed rapprochement with Washington. By April 1971, there apparently had been an important shift in the political tides which restored Mao's freedom to act on matters of state policy. Presumably persuaded by Zhou Enlai, he responded at last with what has since been called "Ping Pong Diplomacy."

The champion Chinese table tennis team playing in the world tournament in Nagoya, Japan, invited a number of the competing teams to make a visit to China. The U.S. team was included, the first time Americans had officially been invited to the mainland since 1949. This was not a story for the sports pages but for page one. It was the Chinese reply to the wooing of the Nixon administration, a friendly gesture which suggested that Beijing was ready again to test the waters, to see whether it was possible to end twenty-two years of Sino-American hostility. The AP man covering the tournament was Peter Sum, a Chinese who had been my assistant in Beijing in 1947. He at once saw the importance of the invitation and telephoned our Tokyo bureau with a bulletin. The ball, as they say in the larger game of tennis, now was in the U.S. court.

The Americans accepted.

Why had China taken such an indirect way to approach the United States on such an important subject? The answer was simple. The visit would be a trial balloon to gauge official and popular American reaction. If, like Dulles, Nixon rebuffed them the Chinese would lose no face. After all, it was only table tennis, was it not?

I met the American players in a downtown Tokyo hotel as they made preparations for their historic trip and arranged with one of the officials to supply AP with news and photos during the ten-day visit.

As soon as the news broke, I went through the now familiar and frustrating motion of messaging Beijing for a visa. I expected the usual stony silence. Two days later, our night desk editor Phil Brown phoned me in Kamakura at midnight to say that a reply had come in. He congratulated me. It was favorable. I still did not believe him. There had been too many disappointments in the past. To convince me, he read it.

"Visa granted for the purpose of covering U.S. table tennis team visit to China. Please contact China Travel Service, Hong Kong, for necessary arrangements."

I spent a sleepless night telephoning our Hong Kong office and making preparations for my departure early the next morning. AP kept a tight lid of secrecy on the news fearing that others would also apply. I did not doubt that there would be many allowed to report on this important event. I later learned that only two other Americans, John Rich and Jack Reynolds of National Broadcasting Corporation (NBC), had been given the precious visas. Like me, they had kept it secret, arrived in the British colony on a separate plane.

In Hong Kong, exhausted from lack of sleep, I went at once to the China Travel Service, a bureaucratically plain office in Kowloon, and presented my passport. The gentleman in charge, a Mr. Lee, looked puzzled. He knew nothing about a visa. My heart sank. He promised to contact me at my hotel if anything developed. Four anxious hours later the phone rang. Beijing had called. It was alright.

Examining my passport at last, a frown came over Mr. Lee's face.

"This is serious," he said. "I'm not sure we can give you a visa with that in your passport." He pointed to the large Taiwan visa which obviously had been much used. "There is only one China, you know," he added, sniffing.

I volunteered to tear out the offending page.

He pursed his lips and clucked disapprovingly.

"Oh no," he said, "that would be mutilating the passport."

After so many years of denouncing the United States, it seemed curious that he should be concerned about the condition of its passports. I insisted in vain that I would take the responsibility. He turned on his heel and disappeared into a back room for consultations while I reflected gloomily on the vagaries of fate. Had I waited a bit in Tokyo, I could, like Rich and Reynolds, have been issued a new passport at the embassy. Was it possible that after all those years of waiting I now would be denied the chance to return to China because of bureaucratic niggling? My thoughts were colored black for gloom.

Ten minutes later Mr. Lee returned looking a bit more cheerful.

"People who wish to show their disapproval of that regime usually scratch out the visa with a pen," he said almost jovially.

"Have you got a pen?" I asked. He produced one and I scribbled over the visa.

He looked closely at my handiwork. "Down there," he said, pointing to the great seal. I applied the pen once more.

"And now—," he said, all business, "about your travel arrangements to Canton."

Rich and Reynolds, old friends, joined me on the train from Hong Kong to the border crossing at Lowu. They were accompanied by a Japanese cameraman and sound man. Trudging across the small rail bridge between the British colony and China there was another brief moment of anxiety. A rosy-cheeked border guard in People's Liberation Army uniform held up my passport and stared for what seemed an hour at my desecrated Taiwan visa. He ordered me to stop while he popped into the security office. Returning five minutes later, he handed back the passport and, looking mildly disappointed, waved me on.

The customs people smiled and said that, as an exception, they would not open our bags. Gathered together in a waiting room, we shook hands and exclaimed, almost as one: "We've made it!" Rich and I had as youths worked together in the same press building in Portland, Maine, where he was a reporter on the local newspaper and I was an agency man. Based in Tokyo, he had made a brief visit to Shanghai in 1945.

On the train from the border to Guangzhou we met Guo Tianhua, an open-faced, friendly youth dressed in neat blue, well-pressed trousers. Fluent in English and French, he was our interpreter throughout our ten-day visit. He told us about his daily life, his family, his spare-time activities, his hobbies, and his personal hopes. Anywhere else this would not have been particularly remarkable. Americans are accustomed to speak to strangers on impulse and reveal the most personal details of their lives. We were assured by an awed French diplomat in the same car that Mr. Guo's volubility was astonishing. In three years based in Beijing he had not, he said, encountered such frankness. It seemed to be a sign of the new Chinese friendliness.

A loudspeaker exhorted anyone willing to listen to practice the Communist virtues and honor Chairman Mao. The atmosphere in the dining car proved less didactic; forty Chinese and twenty foreign dishes tempted the traveler. We sampled several and found them above reproach.

Arriving in Guangzhou we were given a whirlwind tour of the hot, populous, and throbbing city. It included visits to a museum built like a pagoda, Sun Yat-sen's old headquarters, and the sites of the early revolutionary activity. The streets swarmed with people, some carrying heavy loads, all scantily dressed against the tropical heat. Like Chongqing, it resembled a busy anthill but the mood was more cheerful, more active, and more randomly purposeless. I looked in vain for a fat man or woman. There were none. Moving through the colorful confusion I sensed something missing. Where were the filth and the garbage, the beggars and the starving people? No large Chinese city I had known in the past was without one or all of these. Guangzhou was almost spotlessly clean. I thought for a moment that the city had been tidied up for our benefit, a Potemkin village with false frontiers. But this was not so. In their struggle to prevent the spread of disease, Communist health authorities had carried out campaigns in every big city against filth, flies, and rats.

Driven to the airport, we boarded a plane for Beijing which had been held for hours awaiting our arrival. We were the only passengers.

Circling Beijing airport and peering down at the immense North China plain my heart leaped up. More than any other city in China this seemed like home. Nearly a quarter century had passed since I had lived there but the thrill of returning, which I had experienced so often in the past, remained undiminished.

I knew there had been change, but I was not prepared for it so soon on landing. In 1947 the airport was small and the terminal building modest. In 1971, the runways were long but virtually empty of traffic. Beijing was not exactly an international air center. Chairman Mao, heroic-sized, plump and benign, beamed down at us from an immense painting as we walked toward the vast new terminal. In fact, he was everywhere during our ten-day visit, in paintings, busts, statues, lapel buttons, and on the covers of millions of vigorously waved little red books replete with his quotations.

The high-ceilinged interior of the terminal, cold and bleak, announced that we were in the capital of the People's Republic, the home of the proletarian emperor whose cherubic face we had just seen. It had been built to impress rather than please. Our footsteps echoed through the huge halls.

The avenue leading to the center of Beijing continued the imperial theme. Wide and straight most of the way, it was lined with stately poplars through which one caught glimpses of more stately rows of trees. Kublai Khan would have approved. Villages became a blur, like those in hazy old scrolls, as our official car hurtled over this imperial roadway, scattering chickens, grazing horse-drawn carts and people in its eager haste to deposit us at our hotel, the Xinqiao or New Bridge, in the old tree-lined Legation Quarter.

Large, square, and architecturally undistinguished, it had been built by the Soviet comrades in the 1950s and was an exact duplicate of another of their creations, the Friendship Hotel, at the edges of town. The imperial stairs were flanked by paintings, one of the chairman's birthplace, the other Yan'an and the Tang pagoda I had grown to know so well. A white plaster bust of Chairman Mao greeted us on the landing. The American team had arrived the day before.

In the next couple of days I explored the city, strolling along Chang An, the avenue of Perpetual Peace, and revisiting the Forbidden City, once so tranquil but now teeming with soldiers and civilians. In the old days, it had seemed like a seedy relic. Tidied up, festooned with portraits of the chairman, it now had the vibrancy and familiarity which large numbers of people lend to large spaces. Some of its many rooms had been converted into museums of painting or archaeology, all of them thronging with genuinely interested workers and peasants who, in an earlier time, would never have visited them.

From the Forbidden City's Gate of Heavenly Peace, China's emperors once handed down their edicts in a gilded wooden box shaped like the legendary phoenix. Steeped in the history of Old China, it was only logical that Mao should choose to inhabit one corner of the Forbidden City and that he also would hand down his edicts from the vermilion-colored gate. One of the first things he did was to create a square grandiose enough to hold the immense crowds gathered twice a year—May Day and the October 1 anniversary—to renew the faith and receive his new marching orders. It had to be large to impress not only the masses but the outside world. Their very numbers also served to reassure this passionate believer in the power of the masses from whom he had sprung.

A hundred acres of flagstone, the new square, called Tiananmen, dwarfed Red Square, its Moscow counterpart, and its arrogant rulers. Almost insignificantly small in my day, it now was the spiritual and political center of the People's Republic, a stage on which many political performances had been acted out in Mao's first years but which became progressively less important after 1971, the year not only of ping pong diplomacy but of disillusion and treason revealed.

Scaffolding covered the long, low crimson walls and the Hall of Supreme Harmony as the city prepared for the annual May Day ceremonies. It was the last of the great shows. Never again would millions of people jam into the square as they had done in one agitated week in 1966 to acclaim Mao as demi-god and his former comrades, now enemies, as the vilest of humans.

The square was flanked by two large buildings, the Historical and Revolutionary Museum, and the Great Hall of the People.

Completed in 1958 in ten feverish months, the Hall occupies 561,786 square feet. Its theater holds ten thousand and is the meeting place of the People's Congress. A dining room can satisfy the hunger of five thousand. Thirty of its big rooms represent each of the nation's provinces, including Taiwan. They are thickly carpeted and hung with paintings, many nonpolitical in theme. The principal salon is lit by six large chandeliers and enclosed by 15-foot-high silk screens. The impression is one of opulence.

A massive granite obelisk in the center of the square commemorates China's past and its modern day heroes beginning with those of the 1842 Opium War. Called the Martyrs' Monument, it celebrates the Taiping peasant rebellion of 1851, the overthrow of the Manchus in 1911, the demonstrations against the British and Japanese after World War I, the creation of the Red Army in 1927, the victories of Red guerrillas over the Japanese, and the final Communist triumph with the crossing of the Yangzi River in 1949. So varied are the origins of the People's Republic.

Purists complain loudly that these edifices, and Mao's tomb which arose later at the south end, are inferior in style to the older structures and do violence to the brilliant vistas and architectural balance of the ancient city. A point well taken, it is no consolation to know that most countries, particularly Germany, Japan, the Soviet Union and the United States also are studded with the architectural disasters of inept politicians.

With a population at that time of five million, it was soon apparent that this was not my sleepy city of musical pigeons and ricksha boys clop, clop, clopping through the unhurried streets. A new sound had been added, the ringing of a hundred thousand bicycle bells as their riders pedalled down Chang An, on rubber-tired wheels. It was a strangely compelling sound, impressive in the mass but individually useless in warning pedestrians or other bicyclists of imminent collisions, which were frequent. These trilling sounds were overlaid by the less pleasing squawks and honking of assorted trucks, buses, jeeps, and passenger cars, the latter few in number. Traffic policemen in white uniforms, white gloves, and impenetrable mirror glasses performed at the intersections like frenzied symphony conductors. Despite everything, the traffic flowed in a measured, dignified stream as befitted an imperial capital, not at all like the ebullient anarchy of the Guangzhou streets. Beijing is not a city of revolution; Guangzhou is.

A number of government ministries, the State Council, the Post and Telegraph, and several hotels lined Chang An Avenue. The old Beijing Hotel, whose barbershop I used to frequent in the 1940s, had doubled in size, a grandiose new wing set off by garish red pillars covered with dragons attesting to the sad fact that the Soviet architects who built it had the same romantic illusions about China that capitalists did.

In Dr. Bussiere's Beijing, life continued in the streets, the restaurants, and the parks as night gently succeeded day. It was a time for pleasure and relaxation, for dining with friends or attending the theater. But when night fell in 1971 Beijing, life wilted with it. Few people ventured into the dimly lit streets. Restaurants remained opened no later than 8 p.m. and the lights had, by then, gone out in the narrow hutungs. Our presence was a brief, bright interval in an otherwise grim scenario. The Cultural Revolution had paused to catch its breath, but it was only in mid-course. Fear, uncertainty, and distrust hung over the city like a pall at night belying the smiles and friendliness of the day.

I looked in vain for Dr. Bussiere's old compound on the Great Sweet Water Well lane. New buildings, including that of the *People's Daily,* and the ebb and flow of busy crowds on Wangfujing, the shopping street from which the lane depends, confused and misled me. The adventure of rediscovery would have to wait another eight years.

With some difficulty and a good deal of persistence, I found the old Peking Club. Across the street from the sinister-looking headquarters of the Communist Party city committee, it looked lonely and forlorn. Renamed the International Club, it had succumbed to the gray institutionality of the proletarian era, looked neither international nor like any club I had known. At the top of the stairs, which once echoed to the confident chatter of American, French, and British expatriates, stood a plaster bust of the chairman and a painting of him as a young man. I wandered into the empty salon which had been a brightly lit island of recreation and pleasure. The piano, around which I had spent many happy and liquid hours enthralled by the music of Richard Rodgers, Irving Berlin, and Noel Coward, existed only in the memory. A sign proclaimed, "Unite to Win Still Greater Victories—Mao Zedong." Two visiting Swedes played a quiet game in the deserted billiard room. The plaster had yellowed and cracked with age and neglect. In the library, copies of the *Peking Review* and the works of Mao had replaced Somerset Maugham.

The tennis courts were overgrown with grass, the swimming pool filled in.

Exhausted from this sad journey into the present—and the past—I sat down in the dining room and surveyed the lonely little cakes in a glass case before me. I selected one. It was sweet, with the taste of something old.

The U.S. team was not the only one invited to visit China. The British, Canadians, Nigerians, and Colombians at Nagoya also made the all-expense-paid trip, but it was everywhere apparent that despite their low international ranking the Americans were the stars, politically and personally.

If the State Department had chosen the team—it had not—it could not have obtained a much better cross-section of Americana. The officials were led by Graham Steenhoven, 59, a graying Chrysler executive who headed the 3,000-member U.S. Table Tennis Association, and included Rufford Harrison, 40, a DuPont chemist from Delaware, Tim Boggan, an assistant professor at Long Island University, team captain Jack Howard, 36, an IBM programmer, and George Buben of Detroit. The male players, besides Howard, were Glenn Cowan, a self-styled hippie from Santa Monica, Calif. whose flying hair, held back by a red headband, fascinated the spectators, Errol Resek, 29, an immigrant from the Dominican Republic working in a Manhattan bank, George Braithwaite, 36, a United Nations employee, the only black, and John Tannehill, 17, a freshman at Cincinnati University. Buben and Resek were accompanied by their wives.

The women players were Olga Soltesz, 17, of Orlando, Fla., Judy Bochenski, 15, of Eugene, Ore., and Connie Sweeris, 20, a tiny housewife from Grand Rapids, Mich.

Off the court, Cowan, dressed in flaring purple corduroy trousers, blue denim jacket, floppy suede hat and wearing a Mao badge, was the cynosure of thousands of Chinese eyes. Once described because of their uniform dress as conformist blue ants, the good, gray citizens of Beijing had never seen such sartorial splendor, were as astounded as though he had just landed from the moon.

As people-to-people diplomats the players were an odd assortment; their reactions to China ranged all the way from the careful observations of Steenhoven to the rapturous praise of the young Tannehill.

In fact, the experience was emotionally almost too much for Tannehill, a psychology major. After three days of sightseeing he came to the conclusion that Mao was "the greatest of all moral and intellectual leaders in the world today because he reaches most of the people. His philosophy is beautiful."

Much quoted in the capital's press, his failure to appear at the inaugural match mystified the audience. The game announcer explained he was ill in bed at the hotel and expressed the hope he would soon recover.

The illness was more diplomatic and political than real. Quite simply, the dazed young man had expressed a desire to leave the team and spend the rest of his life in the People's Republic. This alarmed the Chinese more than the Americans. They feared that his defection would cast a pall over the atmosphere of goodwill they had so carefully built up and endanger the process of Sino-American rapprochement. They thanked him for his warmth toward China but persuaded him it would be better if he came back some other time. From his "sick bed" afterwards, he told me—apparently convinced—"I wouldn't like to spend the rest of my life here, but I'd like to see more of it."

The story was one of the best kept secrets of our visit; officials persuaded the accompanying newsmen not to report it, noting that Tannehill was young and impressionable and that he had, in any case, changed his mind. It would have been news if he had, in fact, defected; he did not.

He had recovered sufficiently the next day to attend the grand reception by Zhou Enlai in the Great Hall of the People. Dressed in a high-collared gray Mao jacket, Zhou received the teams and the newsmen in the large red-carpeted reception room. Spying me in the crowd, he extended his hand and said, "Welcome to Beijing, Mr. Roderick. It has been a long time."

He looked around the luxuriously furnished room and said, "How does this compare with Yan'an?"

I smiled, remembering the caves, and said, "It is somewhat of an improvement."

Premier and visitors sat at small tables to sip hot tea served in covered mugs. After some preliminary small talk, Zhou then made a statement which clearly spelled out the name of the game Beijing was playing at the political level.

He began by asking the team to extend the regards of the Chinese people to the American people.

"In the past," he continued, "exchanges between the peoples of China and the United States were very numerous. They have been cut off for a long time.

"Now, with your acceptance of our invitation, you have opened a new page in the relations of the Chinese and American people. I am confident that this beginning again of our friendship will certainly meet with the majority support of our two peoples."

He paused and then asked the Americans: "Don't you agree with me?"

The Americans applauded.

The peoples of China and the United States, he went on, will "in the near future be able to have many contacts. I believe they will not be slow in coming."

Then, turning to me and referring to the future visits of American news people, he said: "Mr. Roderick, you opened the door!"

I thanked him and observed that the stationing of American correspondents in Beijing would contribute to deeper understanding between the United States and China.

Zhou said that many American correspondents wanted to come to China and that we three there were only the first. "They will come in batches," he said, not only from the United States but also from Britain and other countries.

The reception lasted ninety convivial, enthusiastic minutes, the atmosphere charged by the recognition of those taking part that Zhou was offering his hand, which John Foster Dulles had ignored, to a new generation of Americans. The meeting was the start of the thaw in the Cold War which had for so many years isolated China and the Western world from each other.

Cowan, getting into the upbeat mood, asked the 73-year-old premier what he thought of the hippie movement then enjoying popularity in the United States.

Instead of turning the question aside with a joke, the former mandarin-turned-revolutionary answered seriously, "I'm not very clear about it. What I have seen is only very superficial. But perhaps the youth of the world today are dissatisfied with their present situation and are seeking the truth."

He noted that he too had been a rebel in his youth but that because of China's backwardness, poverty, corruption, and exploitation by foreigners he and his friends had chosen violent revolution rather than token protests. Cowan seemed satisfied by the answer.

We had written about it and reported on it from a distance, but a visit to Qinghua (Tsinghua) University, China's largest and most prestigious technical school, supplied mute, and not so mute, evidence of the violence which had scarred the early years of the Cultural Revolution.

Shattered stone lions at its entrance attested to the physical brutality of those years. They had been smashed, with Mao's blessing, between 1966 and 1969 during the heyday of the Red Guards. Their targets were anything old—old ideas, old institutions, old ways of thinking, and the old system of education.

During these turbulent years the no-school bell rang throughout China while the young went on a rampage of destruction. Now, we were told, classes were being resumed and an effort made to bridge the yawning gap which four years without education had created in the lives of a generation of young Chinese. The university's enrollment in this year of recovery was 1,800 compared to its normal 20,000. The new students were workers, peasants, and soldiers whose principal qualification was an unquestioning faith in the thoughts of the Chairman. They were studying science, agriculture, and manufacturing in a three-year course leading straight to the factory, the commune, the tool shops, and the construction sites.

Swept aside with fine disdain were the less practical disciplines—philosophy, psychology, literature, the arts, music, and the field of education itself. Acting in the name of Chairman Mao, Lin Biao, Jiang Qing, and other leaders of the new order had succeeded in carving out the sound core of the cultural apple and leaving the rotten part intact. Now they were applying their half-baked ideas to education. In an excess of inspiration, one of their student disciples had turned in a blank paper during a test. It was his way of saying that examinations were useless. From there it was a short step to the elimination of college entrance exams themselves. So in 1971 all it took was a middle school diploma and the backing of one's peers in the farm, factory, or military unit to enter university. Textbooks went out the window. Practice replaced study and theory. The new professors were peasant heroes, factory bosses, and model workers. Eminent theoretical physicists, pure researchers, and other clearly non-useful types lined up sheepishly to tell us that they were learning earnestly from them, regretted their past errors in trying to instill knowledge for knowledge's sake in the brains of their students. It was hard to grasp that these were the people who had helped make the Chinese atom bomb possible, had made some highly acclaimed discoveries in their fields. What had become of the famous Chinese inquisitiveness, imagination, and love of exploration which had led to the discoveries of the compass, gun powder, porcelain making, and silk weaving? There could be no art for art's sake, Mao had said in his 1942 essay on literature. Now he was seeing how deadly dull such a world could be.

We went with the table tennis players to see one of the results of a technical education—an automobile manufacturing plant run by the students. It had turned out thirty or forty dump trucks in six months, all named "July 27, 1968," the date Mao's backers had physically taken over the campus from the followers of Liu Shaoqi. Specialists on the U.S. team said they were technically adequate.

In the computer department, a computer built by professors and students gave a musical version of "The East is Red," the Maoist anthem. The verdict: amusing but unsophisticated.

Stacks of red-bound quotations from the Chairman filled the library shelves. There were dust-covered textbooks in a variety of languages, more for show it seemed than for consultation. If a library is the heart of a university, Qinghua was heartless.

I wrote then:

"Gone are the days when the Chinese invented gunpowder for their amusement only to see it used against them by others.

"Gone too for an unpredictable time are the Chinese philosophers who over the centuries have enriched human thought.

"In today's China there is room for only one philosophy, that of Mao. The Communists insist that he combines all that is needed for Chinese life.

"Time will be the final judge."

Four days after their arrival in Beijing, the American team played a Chinese team before 18,000 cheering spectators in a match which I described as "an exquisite display of Chinese politeness."

I explained.

"Regarded as the premier nation in this swift moving game the Chinese could have fielded some powerful players against the visiting Americans and humiliated them. They did not."

This was not my opinion alone. It was that of Steenhoven.

"They played us in what they had billed as a friendly match and I believed their selection of the players and the match they played was unquestionably friendly since they provided entertainment to thousands of people rather than trying to destroy us with a quick victory."

The Chinese men's team won 5-3 and the women 5-4.

In faraway Washington, the vice president of the United States, Spiro T. Agnew, read this story with growing exasperation. He let it all out several days later during a Republican governors' conference in Williamsburg, Va. Calling in nine reporters at 12:30 a.m. he told them in a marathon meeting that the United States had taken a propaganda beating during the tour of the table tennis team. He singled out my story as an example. Master of the onomataepoetic catch phrase—"nattering nabobs of the press" was one of them—he took particular exception to my use of the word "exquisite." Agnew said he had expressed his opposition to any moves which might draw the United States closer to China at the expense of Taiwan.

At the State Department, spokesman Robert J. McCloskey emphasized the administration's unhappiness over Agnew's remarks and quoted Secretary of State Rogers as being "eminently satisfied" with the upbeat in Sino-American relations.

He also indicated that he disagreed with Agnew over my reporting. McCloskey called it "excellent" and said "the government and the people have benefitted."

Agnew, later driven out of office after being convicted of influence peddling, obviously had not been consulted on the opening to China. Still vice president in February 1972, he had not forgotten the pain of reading how exquisitely the Chinese had behaved. Appearing before publishers of the Copley Press in Borrego Springs, Calif., where I was delivering a series of China lectures, he specifically barred me from being present at his speech. Cruel is the revenge of the truly great.

The visit of the U.S. team prodded Rewi Alley into a bit of poetry. A New Zealander, he had come to China in the 1920s to rescue children orphaned by the endless civil strife and later organized schools to teach Chinese rural youths mechanical and technical skills. By keeping the food plain and the housing spartan, he had no difficulty persuading the students to return to their villages where they were needed. Chinese in that day thought work beneath the dignity of educated men and women.

A square, white-haired man, quietly serious but not devoid of humor, he adopted a number of Chinese children, one of whom I met in Yan'an where he was an organizer of cooperatives.

Alley predicted that the ping pong balls then flying in Beijing would prove stronger than the U.S. bombs being dropped on Vietnam.

He and George Hatem believed deeply in the rightness of the Chinese Revolution. They had never wavered between Moscow and Beijing as Anna Louise Strong had done. When I saw them they had been scarred by the violence and irrationality of the cultural purge but were outwardly cheerful. I had met Alley three years before at a Tokyo antinuclear rally where he leapt to his feet to boisterously denounce the Russians in the stilted, dogmatic language of international communism. Already white-haired and carrying himself with dignity, he seemed shockingly out of place, like a truant schoolboy. Afterwards he looked deeply embarrassed at his obviously command performance.

I made it a point at most of my meetings with Chinese officials to ask whether Liu Shaoqi was alive. They assured me he was. Were they lying deliberately or were they ignorant of the truth? It came out only five years later that he had died—judicially murdered—in prison in 1969.

On the eve of our departure for Shanghai, ping pong team and journalists were exposed to an opera called "Taking Tiger Mountain by Storm." A heavy-handed propaganda piece, it had been created under the critical eye of Jiang Qing. More melodrama than drama, the villains were baser than base, the heroes and heroines of a saccharine sweetness and nobility. The music, drawing on Western themes, was unoriginal. The performers, heavily rouged, were attractive, highly competent, and well disciplined. But like Rewi Alley they seemed embarrassed by it all.

A towering figure of Mao in white plaster raised an imperious right arm in the Summer Palace's Pavilion of Virtue and Harmony. Had she lived to see it, the dowager empress, otherwise known as the Old Buddha, would not have been amused.

A strong-willed woman, she ruled China with an iron hand from the last decades of the nineteenth to the first decade of the twentieth century. The Summer Palace, which she restored after it was sacked twice by European troops, was her favorite hot weather retreat.

A practical woman, she also used it as a place of imprisonment for her liberal-minded heir, the unhappy Emperor Guangxu, after he attempted to introduce much-needed reforms in 1898.

She would have been appalled at the social and economic revolution introduced by Mao, a peasant's son. Guangxu would have approved.

Mao looked down benignly on the "Garden Where Peace is Cultivated" which she rebuilt with funds earmarked for modernization of the navy. Her concession to naval affairs was a marble boat as immovable as the empress' shrewd but limited mind.

Chicken wire covered the bronze dragons and cranes at the East Gate just as they had during my last visit twenty-four years before. But instead of the genteel tranquility of the place—the Nationalists spent little maintaining any of the nation's cultural treasures—there was a nervous purposefulness about the thousands of soldiers, students, peasants, clerks, and workers surging through the gardens around Kunming Lake and into the pavilions dotting Longevity Hill.

The Summer Palace, it was evident, was now more than a survivor from the imperial past. It was a living museum of the Communist Revolution, its exhibits presented with a dismaying lack of subtlety. Wherever one turned, Mao, now stern now jolly, intruded into the carefully laid out vistas of lake, hill, and pavilion. Plaster statues, statuettes, and heroic worker groups in clay gave this once delightful pleasure garden the morbid air of Madam Tussaud's waxworks museum.

In case one missed the visual message, blaring loudspeakers repeated it with a Peking opera on a revolutionary theme, personally approved by Jiang Qing herself. The impact was nerve-shattering to foreign ears, without apparent effect on those of the Chinese. Hardened by a lifetime of noise and years of Maoist propaganda, they enjoyed the palace's wonders serenely oblivious to the din. For Beijing's residents it is a favorite place of recreation, bathing and boating in summer and skating in winter.

Built in 1153 and called "The Garden of Golden Waters," the Summer Palace had survived wars, revolutions, and the whims of emperors and empresses. It also would survive Mao and enjoy a better, less garish day.

Despite the propaganda, much of its airy grace remained; Mao had

had the good sense to restore its neglected pavilions and covered walkways.

It seemed fitting that the first person we met on our strolls was a 78-year-old gentleman name T. S. Cai. Sitting next to the lake, his bright, old eyes lit up at the appearance of foreigners. He had once worked in a foreign firm and was attached to the British Expeditionary Force in France during World War I.

"There are no beggars now," he said in understandable English. "The differences between rich and poor are gone. We are closer together."

He nodded and we went on, pausing to admire the Empress Dowager's remarkable collection of clocks and watches and to speculate on the fact that, along with her unsinkable marble boat and these timepieces she had contributed something of value to China. So far, Mao had nothing culturally comparable to show for his reign. But old Mr. Tsai put his finger on another Mao contribution beside which the clocks and the boat, the palaces and the artificial lakes seemed mean and vain. On one thing, the old man was wrong: Beggars, more carefully concealed, still existed. But it was everywhere apparent that the living standards and the expectations of life of 700 million people had been raised higher than any emperor had ever been able to do.

China's first emperor, and possibly its greatest, was Qin Shi Huangdi. He united the warring kingdoms into one peaceful one in the third century B.C., established standards for weights and measures as well as the width of axle wheels—this last made it possible to build usable roads. His prime minister led a party called the Legalists, who stood for social reform very much in the same way that Mao did. They were China's first Communists. Like the first emperor, Mao united all China and carried out great public works. The First Emperor's greatest physical feat was to weld the scattered sections of the Great Wall into one. But in it, he buried alive thousands of dissident scholars and writers, burned the works of Confucius, and punished nonconformity.

After the Summer Palace, we trundled by bus the 26 miles to the wall. An occasional cherry tree brightened the dun landscape on the way. Small Mongolian ponies staggering under heavy loads turned the clock back centuries. China, like the Great Wall, was changeless. The mud-and-stone peasant huts, with their paper-covered windows and browsing domestic animals outside, could have graced the landscape of the First Emperor.

Snaking 2,300 miles over hill and valley like some giant dragon, the wall had been tidied up and repaired since I had last seen it in 1947. Much of the rubble had been cleared away, some repairs had been made, and clean restrooms installed nearby for weak-kidneyed tourists. Even Mao seemed to have been daunted by this earth-and-stone symbol of ancient imperial greatness. A single large painting, instead of the many which might have been put up, served as a modest reminder that a new master and a new philosophy now prevailed.

"If this had been in the United States," said Mrs. Resek, "it would have been a great tourist attraction and it would be mutilated and cheapened by discarded paper and garbage."

The American ping pong team and its journalistic camp followers flew to Shanghai from Beijing on the next leg of their China visit. The weather, fortunately, was clear. Officials of China's official airline, CAAC, explained that the planes did not fly when it rained or visibility was poor. The reason was simple: Most Chinese airports were innocent of the sophisticated guidance equipment needed for blind landings.

CAAC stood for General Administration of Civil Aviation of China, a bureaucratic mouthful. At the time, it was the only airline flying domestically. We rattled around in a four-engined Ilyushin turboprop normally seating eighty. It was obvious that we were getting VIP treatment.

A portrait of Chairman Mao looked down reassuringly from the front while one of his ever-ready quotations proclaimed: "The People who have triumphed in their own revolution should help those still struggling for liberation."

The apple-cheeked stewardesses, called *tongzhi* or comrade, were formless in gray pantaloon uniforms. One of them, armed with a fly-swatter, whisked it behind my ear, liberating a small fly forever. She subsequently appeared with a package of Tiananmen cigarettes, a glass of orange juice, a large slice of white bread, three kinds of cake, a meat dumpling, and a cup of tea.

Over the years, I have flown on CAAC too many times to want to remember; it now is quite undeniably not only the least glamorous but the worst airline on earth, bitterly criticized by the official press and ordinary Chinese. For years it ran without benefit of computers; tickets had to be picked up in person, after long waits, at the CAAC office. One never knew whether a flight might be over-booked or almost empty. Once aboard, the service was poor and the food, nearly inedible, consisted of an indigestible combination of Chinese and Western cuisine, rice and pork chops, bread and chocolate bars; one never knew what would be coming next. All this was incredible for an airline with one of the world's great cuisines at its disposal. To compensate for its inadequacies, it loaded down its hapless passengers with an assortment of small gifts, pocket combs, slippers, folding fans, and hard candy. Despite the establishment of a competing airline, neither service nor food seem to have appreciably improved.

"There's a smile on every face, a spring in every step," said Yu Zhongqing. I was a bit perplexed.

"Mark Twain," he said brightly. *"Tom Sawyer."*

Yu was 29, a member of the Communist party and one of the top interpreter-guides of China Travel Service. He and his assistant, Guo Tianhua, shepherded us along to Guangzhou. We met Guo first on the Guangzhou train.

Tall, slender to the point of emaciation and wearing glasses which gave him an owlish look, Yu's English was almost colloquial. He got that way from reading Mark Twain, O. Henry, Charles Dickens, and the *New York Times* during his days at the Beijing Foreign Languages Institute.

Like Yu, Guo also had graduated from the institute and mastered both English and French. As proof, he said,

"Bon jour, comment ca va?"

I replied in my own rusty French that everything went well.

Yu and Guo studied at a time when eighteenth- and nineteenth-century English and American authors were assigned as supplemental reading. In 1971, they had disappeared from the shelves, leaving the works of the Chairman, in a multitude of languages, the sole reference.

China Travel Service interpreters worked a six-day, forty-eight-hour week with considerable overtime thrown in, they said. If they had family far away, they got two to three weeks' annual vacation.

They were paid a salary of 60 yuan (about $30) a month but living expenses were low. A room cost 4 yuan a month and hospitalization was free.

Guo said he had campaigned against the chief of state, Liu Shaoqi, not because he disliked him personally but because, "I was against capitalist restoration." A sportsman keenly interested in ping pong, swimming, and volley ball, he yearned to be a party member like Yu. But he said it would take a good deal of study before he could.

Yu, the party man, felt it necessary to give us his views on the Russians, Nixon, and the Vietnam War. They were not strikingly original.

"We regard the Soviet Union as having degenerated into a capitalist state," he said, "Khrushchev is the arch-criminal responsible for this . . . but the Russian people are different. We make a distinction there."

I thought wanly of the persistent and unsuccessful efforts I had made twenty-five years before to get the Yan'an Communists to condemn the Soviet plunder of Manchuria. The wheel had come full circle.

Nixon, he said, was expanding the Vietnam War by using Asians to do the fighting, an apparent reference to the South Vietnamese.

He had his doubts about the American troop withdrawal.

"We'll wait and see," he said.

This said, he went back to saying how much he admired Mark

Twain.

Admiration was not a sentiment he wasted on me. By the time I crossed into Hong Kong two weeks after meeting him he wore a fixed look of worry.

An amateur photographer, he spent much of his time clucking disapprovingly at my ineptitude in that department. The first eight rolls I snapped turned out blank through a conspiracy of the Japanese camera manufacturer. Ten years earlier, when I had last done any photography, one wound the film clockwise. The one I had borrowed for the trip perversely went counterclockwise. How was I to know?

He may have been an expert cameraman but Yu did not have a clue on the subject of getting film developed. My New York office, eager to exploit this historic first trip to China, wanted photos of me and my two NBC colleagues. Yu obligingly snapped us but he said his obligation stopped there. I had to have the film developed and printed for radio transmission. Could we not go to a commercial photo studio? What about the Xinhua photo people? They had promised to be helpful. Perhaps the Foreign Ministry could do something.

To all these suggestions, Yu lugubriously shook his head. In desperation, I urged him to consult the little red book of Mao advice and come up with a solution.

That was walking on thin ice. There was an edge to his voice when he replied, "Now you're being sarcastic." I was.

At last, taking pity, he broke down and explained the reason for this curious impasse.

"China," he said, "is a vertical society, not horizontal. Orders go up and down, not sideways. The photo shop, Xinhua, and the Foreign Ministry are distinct from the Travel Service. It would be unthinkable to ask them to do something for us. They are in different compartments, doing different jobs."

I gave up, got a Japanese correspondent to take a photo of us with his instant Polaroid camera. New York was satisfied. It did not know how much I had suffered.

Suffering was an occupational disease with Yu. His recurrent refrain throughout our travels was, "Come along, come along, Mr. Roderick. We're all waiting for you."

He was a man in a hurry, clearly disapproving whenever I stopped to talk to someone or look at something intriguing along the way.

At the Lowu crossing into Hong Kong, we said our farewells. Guo said warmly, "Come back again." Yu did not echo this sentiment. He had had enough of large, laggard AP reporters.

Frank Starzel's fatal hesitation in letting me accept Mao's 1956 invitation to return to China gave me a subjectively low opinion of New York AP executives. A new general manager, Wes Gallagher, confirmed me in this attitude. Six AP men—three photographers and three reporters—accompanied Richard Nixon on his ground-breaking visit to Beijing in February 1972. Gallagher did not assign me to the climax of a story which had been part of my life for so long because, as he airily put it, "You've been." Rich and Reynolds were the stars of the NBC team. None of the reporters Gallagher selected was a China specialist. One was the White House correspondent, the able Frank Cormier, the second the resident AP humorist, Hugh Mulligan, and the third, the Tokyo chief of bureau, Henry Hartzenbusch. He had selected Henry, he said, because he wished him to negotiate for the opening of an AP bureau. Since I knew all the people with whom he wished to talk and he knew none, this seemed to me a dotty idea, particularly in the midst of a frenetically busy news event.

Gallagher told me of his decision in the midst of an AP board of directors meeting where a China TV documentary I had written and hosted, had just been shown and warmly endorsed. I was stunned.

I had nearly resigned from AP in 1956 and seriously considered doing so then. First, however, I asked my colleagues in New York, including the foreign editor, Nate Polowetsky, to persuade Gallagher to change his mind. All vehemently denounced the decision and warmly promised to speak to him. None, as far as I know, did. All feared Gallagher, a macho type with beetling eyebrows whose favorite expletive was "bullshit!"

During the Nixon visit I gave China lectures at a dozen or so universities and civic groups and watched its progress hourly on television. The lecture fees helped me smother my disappointment. But I knew I had missed a historic moment, the culmination of many years of China watching. The pain lasted a long time.

The visit was Nixon's finest hour. But in arranging it he bruised the feelings of the Japanese government which was kept in the dark until only a few hours before the public announcement of the forthcoming trip was made in July 1971. While welcoming the Nixon visit, the newspapers, the public, and the government described the unexpected move as the "Nixon *shokku.*" Prime Minister Eisaku Sato regarded it as a personal insult. It was hardly the way to treat an ally which had faithfully supported U.S. policy in recognizing the Republic of China on Taiwan and refusing to establish ties with Beijing. Sato lost "face" at this contemptuous treatment at the hands of Washington. Winner of the Nobel prize for peace, he sent an official letter to Zhou Enlai in November suggesting the possibility of diplomatic recognition and offering, like Nixon, to go to Beijing.

But it was too late. The Chinese resented Sato's past unfriendliness and were particularly upset when Japan voted against Beijing's admission to the United Nations. Zhou was quoted as saying, "To accept hypocrites is against Chinese principles." He added that China would not negotiate with Japan as long as Sato was premier.

That was enough for the ruling Liberal Democratic Party. Big business, which it represented, was hypnotized by the old dream of China as a vast marketplace. It believed Nixon's motives were commercial, that he wanted to give American interests a headstart in exploiting this vast, relatively untouched market. Since Sato stood in the way, he must go. In July 1972 he did and a dynamic, new leader, Kakuei Tanaka, pledged to make recognition his top priority.

A self-made man, Tanaka's origins would have satisfied the most exacting Marxist. Born poor, he worked his way up in the construction business, married the boss's daughter, entered politics and built up a large conservative following. He was so gung ho and exuded so much energy, the press soon labeled him "the computerized bulldozer."

The change in mood in Beijing toward Japan became immediately apparent. Xinhua and the official organs which had had a field day for years attacking Emperor Hirohito as a war criminal and denouncing the Japanese as militarists, suddenly abandoned that line and began to write of Japan in a more conciliatory tone.

On September 25, 1972, slightly more than two months after his election and seven months after the Nixon visit, Tanaka went to Beijing. I was one of two American newsmen allowed to accompany him.

The airport reception was, like Nixon's, subdued and brief. There was the usual honor guard review and the military band played the "Kimigayo," the Japanese national anthem. The flags of the two countries flapped on the same flagposts which had earlier held the American and Chinese emblems.

At a glittering state banquet in a huge cream-and-white dining room, 600 Japanese and Chinese sat down to a Peking duck dinner while a military band played "Sakura" (Cherry Blossoms), a traditional Japanese folk song. Before dinner the 50-member Japanese delegation posed for a group photo with Zhou and Tanaka. In his speech, Tanaka expressed Japan's regret and repentance for past aggression against China but stopped short of an outright apology because of the right wing of his party which remained critical of reconciliation with China and wished to continue relations with Taiwan.

"It is regrettable," Tanaka said, "that for several decades in the past the relations between Japan and China had unfortunate experiences. During that time our country gave great troubles to the Chinese people, for which I once again make profound self-examination."

Japanese officials told me later that the phrase *fukai hansei no nen,* or "profound self-examination," represented a traditional form of Japanese apology, conveying deep feelings of self-reflection over a half century of military aggression which left China broken and exhausted.

Zhou in his toast pointedly said: "The past not forgotten is a guide for the future. The Chinese people make a strict distinction between the very few militarists and the broad masses of the Japanese people."

Although Tanaka proposed the health of Mao, Zhou did not toast the emperor. It might have seemed strange to do so in view of the attacks on him only a few months before. (Deng Xiaoping harbored no such antagonism. A decade later, on a Tokyo visit he was formally received by Hirohito.)

Like Nixon, Tanaka had an audience with Mao. As usual the old man's attention span seemed unusually brief. He talked about one thing then switched to another almost in mid-paragraph. He embarked on reminiscences of his childhood and recalled how severe his father had been with him. Then, almost in the same breath, he observed that Japan seemed to have problems with elections. When Tanaka said campaigning was hard work, Mao commiserated.

It was a replay of the Nixon visit, from beginning to end, with one exception. It wound up with Japanese recognition of China and a break with Taiwan. In a way, Nixon had done the Japanese a favor. The shock of his secret decision to go to Beijing galvanized Tokyo into an uncharacteristically independent step in foreign relations, one for which it did not seek American assent. Washington could only say it warmly approved. But it was galling for the future American liaison chiefs to be placed below the salt at official functions while the Japanese ambassador sat close to the Chinese host.

Diplomatic recognition by the United States still was far off, but the two countries did not stand still after the Nixon visit. They opened liaison offices in each of their capitals to deal with continuing problems.

David K. Bruce, a veteran diplomat, became the first liaison chief. We had a mutual friend, Col. Joy Dow, of Maine. I wrote him asking that he do his best to persuade the Chinese that relations would be furthered by the presence of an American correspondent in Beijing. He replied that he certainly would try. If he did he failed.

Nixon's hope of establishing diplomatic relations with Beijing went up in smoke when he was accused of master-minding a politically suicidal small-time burglary of the Democratic Party's offices in Washington's Watergate apartments.

His successor, Gerald Ford, picked up rapprochement with Moscow where Nixon had left off. This infuriated old Bear-baiter Mao and the mood turned from sunny to sour.

Though the underlying malaise persisted, Americans and Chinese increasingly began to visit each other. The Associated Press and

United Press International vied for the honor of entertaining the first visiting Xinhua delegation. The *New York Times, Wall Street Journal,* and various other newspapers and magazines joined in the welcome. The Chinese were given the full treatment, from Texas to the space center in Florida. They marveled at it all, particularly the stock exchange in New York. Exhausted by the gruelling pace, the Xinhua director, a former Paris-based diplomat with an unquenchable thirst for cognac, issued an ultimatum. His eyes circled with fatigue, he announced that there would be no more travel until longer rest periods were thrown in.

AP dragooned me into service to help entertain the Beijing visitors, several of them my friends. We whizzed around town in two automobiles stopping at most of the famous sights, including the seedy ones in the Bowery and in Greenwich Village. The visitors nodded and took notes. For years they had been writing about the downtrodden American masses, the poverty, and the crime. Their stories, for the first time, began reflecting the reality.

At night, the Chinese news people dined in capitalist splendor, once as guests of the *Wall Street Journal* on the top floor of the Twin Towers and again, with AP, at the 21 Club. There was not a chopstick in sight at either of them. The Chinese apparently did not mind. They tackled juicy steaks and consumed quantities of wine and whiskey with the best of us. All the publishers of New York newspapers attended these affairs. During one I introduced them to a middle-aged Xinhua lady editor who, it turned out, had thirty years earlier edited my dispatches in Yan'an for publication in the information newspaper circulated to the party leadership. I had never met her before.

In 1974 Ford named George Bush Beijing liaison chief, an interesting choice in view of his earlier position as ambassador to the UN where he had led the fight against Beijing's admission. The Chinese press at that time had characterized the U.S. attempt to block Beijing's entry as having "lifted a rock to drop on its own feet." It said a "gloomy faced" Bush tried a last-ditch procedural maneuver to save the day but was ruled out of order. Actually, after the American UN defeat, Bush, having done his duty, joined in welcoming the Chinese delegation. The U.S. would have liked to keep both Beijing and Taiwan in the world body and this was the maneuver the Chinese press referred to. It was no coincidence, however, that Secretary of State Henry Kissinger was in Beijing talking to Zhou when the vote was taken.

I met Bush in Japan enroute to his Beijing post. As in Bruce's case we had a mutual friend in Colonel Dow. He wrote Bush immediately after his appointment urging him to see me. Never prone to understatement, the colonel described me as one of the world's leading China experts. When Bush arrived in Tokyo he telephoned me from the U.S. embassy and asked if he could come to Kamakura for a talk. I agreed with pleasure. The following day he made the forty-mile trip in the embassy's stretch limousine accompanied by his wife Barbara and Ambassador James Hodgson and his wife. The road to my hilltop Japanese farmhouse is narrow and winding. It took half an hour and the help of the security agent aboard to negotiate it.

My adopted son, Yoshihiro Takishita, and AP's Tokyo bureau chief, Roy Essoyan, who had spent his early years in Shanghai, and his wife, took part in the conversation which lasted two hours and a half. I recalled my Yan'an days, described the Communist leaders as I had known them then and subsequently and gave an assessment of the situation in 1974. The man who fourteen years later was to become president of the United States proved to be a good listener and showed an eagerness to learn all he could about his new job and the people he would be dealing with. His questions were frequent and intelligent. His manner was easy and relaxed, far less intense than Nixon's whom I had met earlier in Tokyo. Bush had spent much of his childhood in Maine where he had known Colonel Dow and we had this in common.

When he left, he thanked me warmly and promised that he would do everything he could to convince the Chinese they should allow at least one or two American correspondents to report on a regular basis from Beijing. Again the time was not right.

In 1975 Zhou Enlai was dying, Mao was rapidly losing control, the anti-American elements in China were getting stronger, and Jiang Qing was at her most unpredictable. It did not seem the best of all times for a second presidential visit. But Gerald Ford faced a tough election fight in 1976 and believed a visit to Beijing would help his popularity rating. He ordered Kissinger to make the arrangements.

Kissinger knew it was not the time. But orders were orders. He made a reluctant Mao promise in writing he would receive Ford, reluctant because Ford had met with Soviet leader Leonid Brezhnev in Vladivostok to advance the detente Mao detested. The Vietnam War had at last ended but in a way which lowered American prestige. The panic-stricken Americans picked up and ran, leaving many of their Vietnamese friends behind. It did nothing to raise Washington's stature in Mao's eyes.

There were almost as many newsmen and newswomen on the Ford visit as there had been with Nixon three years earlier. This time, I was one of them, sharing AP coverage with White House correspondent Frank Cormier.

Ford, his wife, Betty, daughter Susan, and Kissinger were given a correct but warm welcome at Beijing airport with Deng Xiaoping replacing the dying Zhou Enlai to meet them. The weather was crisp and cold and the hazy sky flecked with clouds.

At the state dinner that night there were the usual toasts and the band played American favorites like "Yellow Rose of Texas" but there was an edge to Deng's voice when he spoke. The Soviet Union, he said, "is the country which most zealously preaches peace and is the most dangerous source of war." The Americans, proud of their success in detente, were flabbergasted.

Ford replied that both China and the United States had a mutual interest in detente. Mao sent Jiang Qing to a picture-taking session before the banquet as a goodwill gesture. Dressed in a simple black blouse and matching trousers, she looked somewhat bemused. Beside the president was old Marshall Zhu De, 89, long in the doghouse but looking cheerful. Jiang Qing nodded at me and Zhu De warmly shook my hand, his eyes lighting up at old memories, Zhou's wife joined Betty for tea.

Keeping his promise to Kissinger, Mao received Ford in the Forbidden City and talked for nearly two hours, nearly twice as long as the historic Nixon interview. It did not add up to much. The chairman by now was what a British reporter called "gaga" as a result of two small strokes. With Deng listening he repeated the vice premier's warning that no one but the Russians benefitted from detente.

No final communiqué was issued. There really was nothing to say. Ford had made a five-day visit to China, had been given the red carpet, demonstrated his unexpected skill with chopsticks, had been criticized for nursing hopes of detente with the Soviet Union, and had replied that the United States would persist anyway. He refused to make any concessions on Taiwan so diplomatic recognition, and an exchange of journalists, remained as remote as ever.

All these problems were on Mao's enfeebled mind when he met Ford. Yet he had gone out of his way to be friendly to his visitors, treating them like erring children. They may have been fools, he undoubtedly reasoned, but they were his fools. He had no intention of reversing himself and cozying up to Moscow. Ford emphasized the positive. In a farewell banquet, at which California wine was served, Ford said his visit "confirmed that although our relations are not yet normalized, they are good: They will be gradually improved because we both believe that a strengthening of our ties benefits our two people." That was an affirmation Mao wanted to hear.

Perhaps most significant was the way the Chinese said farewell to George Bush as he left a few days later to take up his new job as director of the Central Intelligence Agency. We chatted during the few occasions we had together during the visit and he observed that though life had been politically interesting, socially his time in Beijing had been a bore. Low man on the diplomatic totem pole, he ranked below the ambassador of the smallest country. There were few diversions and few visitors. He had failed to budge the Chinese from their stubborn refusal to let American newsmen take up permanent residence until after formal recognition. Both Deng and Foreign Minister Qiao Guanhua called on him for a farewell chat and gave him lunch, an unprecedented gesture for a departing diplomat.

Kissinger had hoped for more. He did not say exactly what. But his mood was one of exasperation. On the flight from Beijing to Jakarta, Ford's next stop, he used some names unsuitable for a family newspaper in describing the Chinese. His inability to deliver anything spectacular to a waiting American electorate perhaps made him reflect on the fact that his own diplomatic career was about to end.

Roderick and Mao Zedong, with interpreter, Yan'an, 1946.
Associated Press Photo

Mao and 6-year-old daughter by Jiang Qing, with Colonel Ivan Yeaton and Roderick on right, and another Dixon Mission officer on left, Yan'an, 1946. Associated Press Photo

Roderick and Liu Shaoqi, Yan'an, 1945. Associated Press Photo

Zhou Enlai, arriving Yan'an from Chongqing on January 27, 1946, was greeted by Zhu De and Mao at the airport (photo taken by Roderick). Associated Press Photo

Roderick greeted by Zhou Enlai at the Great Hall of the People, Beijing, April 12, 1971. Associated Press Photo

Roderick of AP and John Rich and Jack Reynolds of NBC crossed into Hong Kong from China after a ten-day tour, April 20, 1971. Associated Press Photo

Left to right, Liaison Chief George Bush (back to camera), Betty Ford, Barbara Bush, President Gerald Ford, and Roderick during Ford's visit to Beijing in 1975. White House Photo

Roderick, Beijing AP bureau chief, going to interview Deng Xiaoping in the Great Hall of the People, 1980. Associated Press Photo

7

Love, Change, and Mao's Dog

O n January 1, 1979, the United States and China at long last established formal diplomatic relations. Zhou Enlai, Zhu De, and Mao Zedong, the companions of my Yan'an days had died and Deng Xiaoping, twice purged during the Cultural Revolution, had returned to power. It was he, and Jimmy Carter in Washington, who had taken the plunge.

I was one of twenty-five American correspondents covering the ceremonies. Arriving December 29, we found ourselves up to the neck in breaking stories. The first was the unexpected arrival in Beijing of Prince Norodom Sihanouk, released by the Khmer Rouge after three years of house arrest in Phnom Penh.

In a marathon, six-hour press conference, he told us how the killing fields had run with blood, claiming twenty-three members of his own family. It was a story steeped in horror but it did not appear to have dampened the ardor of the man whose life had begun as a playboy and turned into a long, harrowing crusade to restore his country to independence. At the end of the conference, I reminded the prince that we had last met in Phnom Penh twenty years earlier. Pulling me toward him, he bussed me on both cheeks.

The second event was a meeting with Deng during which he extended the olive branch to Taiwan. He promised his compatriots there that if they but adopted the Red Star flag of Beijing they could continue as they were, with their own leaders, their own government, and their own economic system. He announced an end to the shelling of the offshore islands of Quemoy and Matsu and called for peace in the Taiwan Strait.

The recognition ceremonies were quiet but impressive. Leonard Woodcock, soon to become America's first ambassador to Beijing, was the host at the modest liaison office. In an unusual gesture, something Mao would not have done, Deng himself showed up for the occasion. After a brief speech, he drank a toast in California champagne with Woodcock. Then, spying me, he raised his glass and we drank, a moment caught for posterity by the UPI photographer. Asked by *Time* magazine for the photograph, UPI at first demurred on the ground that this was giving aid and comfort to the enemy. But, succumbing to an unannounced financial inducement, it relented. The picture headed *Time*'s press section, reporting that U.S. correspondents would soon be back full time in Beijing.

The date set was March, when the liaison offices in Beijing and Washington would be raised to embassy status.

Between 1945 and 1947 I had met and interviewed all the top Red leaders with the exception of Deng Xiaoping. Though I followed his career closely from the mid-1950s, when he first gained international prominence, it was not until the Sino-American recognition ceremonies in Beijing that we finally met. He knew that I had been in Yan'an thirty-four years earlier and said he regretted he had not met me then. He explained that he was away "on business" in North China. The business: organizing the Second Field Army with one-eyed General Liu Bocheng. It played a critical role in the later civil war.

We met a number of times after that and I saw him frequently during his later tour of the United States. There also were brief encounters during my eighteen-month stay in Beijing after reopening the AP bureau there. Our longest talk together was in 1980 when, as I prepared to leave Beijing, he gave me a two-and-a-half hour, exclusive interview, the only one accorded a resident correspondent.

Then 75 he showed little signs of his age, answered every question in detail, and paused occasionally to make a humorous aside.

In a time when many party and government people had switched to Western-style suits and necktie, he continued to wear the revolutionary high-collared jacket with five buttons down the middle and two large pockets on each side. His step was sure, his attitude lively, his face smooth, and his hair still black. Like most of his Long March generation, he suffered from chronic bronchitis and from time to time during our interview spat noisily and unerringly into a silver-plated spittoon at his feet.

We sat in overstuffed chairs with a small table containing cups of hot tea and cigarettes between us and an interpreter somewhat to the rear. He chain-smoked throughout.

"Everyone warns me against smoking cigarettes," he said. "But I find it difficult to overcome this bad habit. I can't accustom myself to cigars or a pipe. Anyway, my cigarettes are special. They have a long filter." He smiled.

He told me he had three daughters and two sons, one of them studying in the United States.

"Do you worry about them?" I asked.

"All of them are grown and most of them are studying science and technology in university. They look after their own affairs. I couldn't practice paternalism at home and preach democracy to the country, could I?" he replied.

Saying he felt fine and had no major ailments, he dwelt for a while on the need for the old to step aside for the next generation.

"People of my age should leave their posts open for younger and more robust people," he said.

As it turned out, like a Japanese shogun operating behind the imperial facade, he continued to pull the strings. The one job he did keep, that of chairman of the Military Affairs Commission, had always connoted power in Red China.

More than a year had passed since the establishment of Sino-American diplomatic ties and I asked him to comment on the state of the relationship.

He was angry over the statement of a party member, a Qinghua University professor, that it was a tactical one, suggesting it could be broken off whenever it suited either side.

"He went haywire," Deng said. "He was absolutely wrong. It was a major strategic decision. Mao Zedong and Zhou Enlai made the original decision and we are carrying it out. It is not a short-term one."

I asked him about his two purges during the Cultural Revolution, noting that when the U.S. ping pong team came to Beijing in 1971 he was "somewhere in the suburbs," his own phrase.

He laughed. "I was not in the suburbs but doing physical labor, pretty much as I pleased, a few hours a day in Jiangxi Province. I could even refuse to work if I wished.

"Generally speaking, I was treated rather well."

During his second purge he was under house arrest in Beijing, he said, not in the South as some rumors had it. He carefully avoided all outside contact.

"The time was rather short, a year or so," he recalled. "Since I lived in my own house, I had to be more careful. Of course, the Gang of Four wanted me to see Marx at an early date."

In both cases, he said, things had not been so bad. And each time, he was, unlike Liu Shaoqi, under Mao's protection, shielded from the aimless cruelty of the Red Guards.

Turning to the economy he said:

"We will always be a Third World country, never a superpower. By the end of the twenty-first century we may be powerful and rather rich, but not so rich or powerful. We are big but poor and never will bully, exploit, or enslave other countries. If we do, the dunce hat of social imperialism should be placed on our head, just as we now put it on the Russians."

Did he worry that some of the thousands of Chinese students studying abroad might wish to overthrow socialism and put democracy in its place?

"That is possible," he conceded. "But they will be only a very small minority. It also is possible some of our students will betray their country. But they will be minority cases. The benefits of learning are big. Even my own son, now studying in America, may be willing to betray his country. I don't worry about it. And anyway, it won't matter. He is one of many."

The depth of his hatred for Jiang Qing, Mao's widow, came through during our talk.

What he resented more than anything else was the fact that she had not made the Long March, knew next to nothing about Marxism yet dared to attack him and Liu Shaoqi. He could take it from Mao because they were intimately bound by the ties of revolution and shared dangers which Jiang Qing had not known.

Speaking of her and her co-prisoners, Deng said:

"They had committed extremely grave crimes in violation of law, bringing great disaster on China and damage to the whole country. They have killed untold numbers, not with their own hands, but as a result of their policies."

He added: "Their crimes are so atrocious, they could be condemned with eyes closed."

He paused a moment, obviously agitated, and exclaimed: "Towering crimes! Those two words say it all." In most Western democracies these obviously prejudiced assertions from the head of state would have produced a judicial ruling that the defendants could not, under the circumstances, have a fair trial. The case would have been thrown out. But this was China, not the United States or Great Britain. Chinese justice was not yet blind or fair.

The Beiping of the 1940s enchanted me. The Beijing of the 1971 ping pong visit depressed me but, though it had lost its graceful way of life, it seemed ecologically liveable. The Beijing of 1979 was an animal of a different color, gray and miasmic. One of the most beautiful cities in the world had become almost uninhabitable as smoke from soft coal used in factories and homes deposited a layer of soot on window sills, turned laundry a tell-tale gray, and coated the lungs with a life-threatening goo which brought on wheezing, hacking coughs and endemic bronchitis. It was far worse than the yellow smogs I had known in the London of 1949–51. Official tests revealed that Beijing's polluted air was six times as bad as anywhere else.

"Look at that!" cried a visiting U.S. congressman, pointing at the smoky haze which obscured the sun at midday. "They want to industrialize but they can't cope with what little they've already got."

The man-made pollution of winter would be followed, I was told, by choking yellow dust storms in the spring from the North China plain. Already, the skin cracked and bled in the spark-producing dryness. I did not look forward to a long stay in the city I once loved.

The American correspondents were put up in the Minzu (Nationalities) Hotel, an old building on Chang An Avenue, west of Tiananmen. In two previous stays I found the food, service, and atmosphere good. The high-ceilinged rooms, however, were either too hot or too cold. Tinkering with the radiators produced no happy mean. There were cockroaches in the bathroom, but they seemed comfortable and non-belligerent so were spared.

Deng won the masses in 1978 by introducing freedoms of speech, assembly, and press. "Democracy Wall," a blank wall on Chang An Avenue on which blossomed hundreds of posters on as many subjects, symbolized the new openness. When we arrived for the recognition ceremonies at the beginning of 1979, it was a tourist "must," something to see in the New China which Deng seemed to be forging. It carried rent notices, long dissertations on life and love, and requests from the lovelorn for dates. An enterprising New York photographer pasted up a "I Love NY" sticker which got international attention. There was some political commentary, but nothing inflammatory. We made it a point to check the wall each day to see what new word from the "masses" it would carry. The mood was upbeat and the crowds milling around it large.

We raced around seeing and doing as much as we could in the two weeks at our disposal. The Beijing we saw seemed to have burst into life like an ebullient spring after a particularly deadening winter. For thirty years, China had been a cultural desert, its writers, artists, playwrights, musicians, ballet dancers, and movie directors straitjacketed by Mao's 1942 decree that there should be no art for art's sake, that all culture should serve the state and the proletariat. Jiang Qing carried this idea to a ridiculous extreme. Under her stern dictatorship, art became propaganda rather than a creative force. She called Beethoven "decadent" and banned his works, created ballets and plays set to "revolutionary" piano music which glorified Mao, castigated the capitalist enemy and portrayed the masses as heroes and heroines triumphant. She rewrote the Peking operas Mao loved so that they became little more than slogans sung in high-pitched voices.

All this had disappeared, with Jiang Qing, from the Beijing of early 1979. New plays, some with no more weighty a message than love thwarted, or love triumphant, others recalling the bitter days of Maoism and the Cultural Revolution, drew packed houses.

A new crop of novelists, and others who had been banned, produced works of striking realism which pictured society as it was rather than as Jiang Qing wished it to be.

Musicians who had buried their instruments during the Cultural Revolution to escape punishment for playing Western music, dug them up and joined the newly revived symphony orchestras and chamber music groups. One famous pianist whose fingers had been deliberately broken during that infamous period survived to play again.

A succession of famous symphony orchestras, ballet companies, and soloists poured into China from many countries to enrich an impoverished musical scene. They performed to overflow audiences in primitive halls for virtually nothing. Admission was less than a dollar a seat.

In February 1979, I accompanied the Boston Symphony Orchestra, conducted by its Manchurian-born, Japanese director, Seiji Ozawa, on a widely acclaimed nationwide tour. They not only played superb music but gave master classes for Chinese conductors and musicians. The combined Beijing Central Philharmonic and Boston Symphony Orchestras performed "The Stars and Stripes Forever" before 18,000 people at the climax of the tour in Beijing.

The more popular art of the cinema, long dead, also had its resurrection. For the first time in decades, ordinary Chinese now could see Western films, among them such oldies as Charlie Chaplin's "The Gold Rush" and "City Lights." Julie Andrews in "The Sound of Music" won Chinese hearts which had never known of her existence before.

The new liberalism embraced the press, television, and radio as well. For the first time since the late 1950s, Chinese newspapers reported accurately statistics on crime, disasters, and government performance. All these had been suppressed on the flimsy ground that to reveal anything on these subjects would give aid and comfort to China's enemies.

The newspapers also were allowed to criticize the way the bureaucracy operated and, on occasion, it poured sack cloth and ashes on its own dismal record of past concealment and deception, something few Western papers do even now.

Television, which had begun a slow development after Deng took over, now broke into a run with hours of programming in color. The live news it carried from many countries, and the documentaries it ran, opened the eyes of Chinese long sealed off from contact with the outside world. Radio followed its lead.

Finally, Deng threw the doors open to student exchanges with thousands of Chinese going abroad to study and other thousands of foreign youths flocking to China to see it for themselves.

Wang Bingnan, my old Yan'an friend, the former ambassador to Sino-American talks in Warsaw, gave me lunch in the Sichuan restaurant not far from my hotel. This was one of the other surprises of Beijing. Once the residence of Yuan Shikai's concubine, it had been renovated. Its graceful series of courtyards connected by moongates and its private rooms, held up by green and red painted timbers, made it the most attractive place to dine in Beijing. While we sampled the mouth-tingling, spicy morsels of Sichuan we could not help reflecting on the irony of it all. Yuan was the imperial commander who had aided in the overthrow of the Manchus, exacted the presidency of the new republic as his price, then plotted to become emperor himself only to die when it was within his grasp. Did he ever dream that Americans and Communists would one day sit down in his house and talk about the old days in Yan'an? Amused, we raised a glass to his concubine, whoever she might have been.

Not all Beijing's restaurants were so inviting. One of them I patronized, if that is the word, faced the avenue and looked relentlessly run down. Inside, the customers lined up, armed with their own enamel bowls, to serve themselves. The main dining room, heated by a pot-bellied stove, looked as though a gustatory battle had been fought within its four walls. Bones, flesh, and rice from a score of satisfying meals littered the tables and the slippery floor. The customers chewed mindlessly. Whenever their teeth encountered an obstacle they spat it out. Occasionally they rinsed their mouths with tea and ejected it in a stream the same way. I had dined in Beijing in the old days when rats ran across the floor. But this was too much. A friend assured me the fare was delicious. I decided not to try.

Besides Wang, I had a reunion with another old friend, Dr. George Hatem, the American doctor I had met in Yan'an in 1945. He had gained fame in the field of preventive medicine and epidemiology. Carefully steering clear of the quarrels of the Cultural Revolution, he continued in favor throughout the more than thirty years since I had last seen him. He was one of those selfless Americans who, like the Christian missionaries, devoted themselves to the eradication of poverty and disease. His skills, like those of my landlord, Dr. Bussiere, were used impartially without political conditions.

There were other Americans in Beijing then who seemed less admirable. They were the hangers-on of the Chinese Revolution, Johnny-come-latelys impelled by ideology, or sensed injustice, to live out their lives in China. This was their privilege and I respected their choice. But their behavior during the Cultural Revolution did not do them credit. Instead of remaining aloof as Ma Haide had done, they threw themselves into the fray. Again this may have been defensible. Everyone also was doing it and they were under pressure to choose sides. That they chose to oppose and attack Zhou Enlai seemed to me not only foolhardy but seriously lacking in good judgment. Their leader, aligned with the Gang of Four against Zhou, wrote a fawning article in praise of the premier after the Gang was overthrown. It was not an enviable performance.

During his meeting with the American ping pong players in 1971, Zhou Enlai had expressed a wish to visit the United States. He was never able to do so. In February 1979, Deng Xiaoping announced that he would. AP's new general manager, Keith Fuller, asked me to accompany him.

The Deng tour of America resembled, in the enthusiasm which it generated, the historic first visit of Japanese samurai to the United States in 1860. Americans from Jimmy Carter down to the lowest cowboy in Texas turned out to welcome him. Newspapers in Washington, Atlanta, Houston, and Seattle, which he visited, emblazoned their best wishes, in Chinese, on their front pages. He toured a Ford factory and met Henry Ford III, donned a ten-gallon hat and rode a stagecoach, to the delight of photographers, in Houston, and visited the Boeing aircraft factory in Seattle. He was witty, charming, and entertaining. Two hundred American and foreign reporters in two chartered planes tagged along reporting his every word and gesture. It was hard to believe that he was the representative of a country which Dulles had denounced as evil and godless. More astonishing was the peppery, little vice premier's references to Vietnam. It had attacked Cambodia with the pretext—some said justification—of ousting the rapacious Pol Pot and his Khmer Rouge. Worried over a renewal of warfare in an area where it had suffered so much, the United States tried to dissuade Deng from retaliating. It was less than four years after it had acknowledged defeat there. But it did no good. Soon after his return, the Chinese attacked the northern borders of Vietnam in an unsuccessful maneuver to lessen the military pressure on the Khmer Rouge. The Vietnamese were in Cambodia for at least a decade. And many observers, including Americans, pondering the barbarity of the Khmer Rouge, were secretly glad they were.

AP and UPI were the first American news organizations permitted to set up shop in the Chinese capital. Other journalists followed at six-month intervals, first the major newspapers and news magazines, and finally the three big radio-television networks.

In March 1979, I packed my bags, said good-bye to my adopted son, took one last look at the old Japanese minka farmhouse he had built for me in Kamakura, and flew to Beijing to reopen the AP Beijing bureau after an absence of three decades.

Alone among the newly arriving correspondents this was for me a homecoming. They were about to live in Beijing for the first time, but this would be my second long stay since 1947 when I had first known and loved it. I was 65 and glad that I had not resigned, as I had twice wanted to do, from AP. For the next eighteen months I worked harder, encountered more bureaucratic frustrations, and slept fewer hours than at any other time in my long AP career. But though I often fell into bed at 5 a.m., after wrestling all night with a rickety communications system which balked stubbornly at transmitting my stories, and though getting news at the beginning was like pulling teeth, I look back on those days now with satisfaction and pleasure. A powerful incentive kept all of us on our toes, the knowledge that what we wrote would make headlines in the next day's newspapers. It is all a reporter needs.

It helped too to discover that in China, at least, I was well known. This was because of *Reference News* (*Cankao ziliao*), an unusual Chinese newspaper meant to be read by party officials and cadres. The papers publicly available in China were heavily censored, at least until Deng began allowing greater press freedom. Anyone reading them would get a lopsided view of the world and of China. *Reference News* with a circulation of 8 million, was designed to give the decision-makers the real truth, or as close as one could come to it. Each day, it carried dozens of reprints of articles and editorials from the leading American and European newspapers and magazines. Even radio and television broadcasts were reported. Much of what *Reference News* printed was highly critical of China, the party, or the government. It did not matter. That was what it was created to report.

I learned from Chinese friends that during my long absence from China *Reference News* reprinted hundreds of my dispatches. Mine, it seemed, was a familiar byline. The stories, they said, often were accompanied by a note on my 1945–47 stay in Yan'an.

In Guangzhou one day, I found the plane to Beijing fully booked. The lady clerk, glancing at my passport, asked whether I was "Luo-de-li of the Associated Press." I confessed I was. She gave me a ticket.

On another occasion in Beijing, I urgently needed to get into the Museum of Chinese History. The doors were about to close.

"I'm Luo-de-li of the Associated Press," I said hopefully.

The guard stared at me blankly.

"But he's *the* Luo-de-li," said a young lieutenant to him. The guard let me in.

UPI's Robert "Buster" Crabbe and I moved into the Beijing Hotel for two weeks and then I was given an apartment in a compound housing foreign diplomats and journalists. I turned two of its four bedrooms into an office and settled down to the business of rediscovering Beijing.

The first thing I found was that love was blossoming again after years of official blight.

The people of Beijing were celebrating it in posters, plays, newspapers, radio, and magazine articles. Young lovers were walking hand in hand down Beijing's Avenue of Eternal Peace. For years Maoist puritanism had frowned on such displays.

In hotels and restaurants, waiters stopped dead before television sets when Gina Lollobrigida, cleavage exposed, did a sensuous if slightly dated dance with Anthony Quinn, the Hunchback of Notre

Dame, grimacing under the whip. It was the first Western movie to be shown in the Chinese capital in twelve years.

New plays with the message of love had begun to appear on the Beijing stage. One, sympathetically portraying homosexuality, played to standing room audiences. Only a few years earlier homosexuals faced long prison sentences, even death.

A serialized story of conventional love, adapted for radio, had in a short time attracted an audience of millions. Beijing Radio, which broadcast it, was swamped with approving letters. A postal worker wrote that as a child he thought love was noble only to be told by the Communist party that it was vulgar. The radio drama, he said, showed him what real love could be.

Mao and his widow, Jiang Qing, were accused in *China Reconstructs,* an official magazine, of giving love a bad name.

"One way of dividing young people, crippling their mental growth and setting them against each other is to forbid any discussion of love and marriage, an inseparable part of their lives," it wrote.

"Young people could not talk of it," it continued, "authors could not mention it. All love was labelled sensual, vulgar, cheap and obscene. Newspapers, magazines, radio, stage and cinema were not allowed to touch it."

A wall poster I came across demanded the "liberation of sex" and criticized the government policy of delayed marriage and delayed love which it called "a destroyer of young hearts and bodies."

One of the chilling aspects of Mao's program had been its reiterated emphasis on the power of hatred. He ordered the young to hate imperialism, the bourgeoisie, capitalism, even to hate one's friends, sweethearts, or parents if they showed any sign of turning against socialism. Deng took the opposite tack. He advocated tolerance for nonbelievers and endorsed individualism as a weapon against the conformity of the Mao years. He knew that even restricted economic reforms had to be built on a foundation of individual human rights. Freedom to love was part of the bigger package of freedoms which covered the press, speech, and assembly. It was a chip in a high-stake game.

On subsequent visits to widely separated parts of the country, I found the same openness and willingness to discuss love, marriage, and other highly personal subjects which would have been verboten during the Mao era.

In Chengdu, capital of Sichuan Province, in the far west, I encountered the new mood in "The Teahouse of the Surging Waves," long famous for its zest, lively talk, and gossip.

Short on decor, but long on atmosphere, its patrons—retired old gentlemen, young clerks, hayseeds from the country—came not only to drink tea poured from steaming copper kettles, but to see and be seen, a universal weakness.

Conversation lobbed back and forth like a ping pong ball from sex to politics, the high cost of living to the fortunes of the local soccer team.

What set the "Surging Waves" apart from others was its unhurriedness. Patrons lingered for hours over their jasmine brew, safe in the knowledge they could drink as much as they wished for 15 fen, about 8 cents. In other teahouses the price was 9 fen but dawdlers got cold stares and slow service.

After 5 p.m. the "Surging Waves" changed complexion. It became a theater for strolling players, singers, acrobats, and comedians. The tea drinkers were hard critics; some of the best artists in China did their first turns in teahouses.

"We come here to relax and catch up with the news," said Yang Zhonggui, 23, indicating his friend Peng Zhu, 21. Both bank employees, slender, open-faced, and dressed in blue cotton trousers and shirts, neither hesitated to talk with a foreigner—a red-nosed one at that. I asked them for a start what they thought about premarital sex. It was still officially banned as were early marriages.

"Sex before marriage is not a Chinese tradition," said Yang, who planned to marry two years later.

"But what do you do in the meantime?" I asked, remembering St. Paul's injunction it is better to marry than to burn.

"My fiancee and I study English together," he said. "Sometimes we stroll in the park. We are in love and ours is a love marriage, not an arranged one. We can wait."

I thought of the Japanese and how they would have replied to this kind of questioning with embarrassed titters. And of American young people, who would not have waited.

"Sex," said Yang, "is taught in the schools here from the first year of junior middle school." Americans then were still debating whether to teach it at any level.

"Love and sex were regarded as bad words only a few years ago," he continued. "That was when the Gang of Four was in charge."

Yang and his friend said the big news in Chengdu was that consumer goods like radios and black-and-white television sets were on the market. They had one of each and hoped to get a refrigerator and a washing machine next.

"We learn a good deal about foreign life from TV," said Yang.

His favorite American writers, he said, were Walt Whitman and Mark Twain.

The white-aproned tea pourer nodded so vigorously he almost scalded me. I left to a smattering of applause from the tea drinkers, most of whom had never seen a foreigner at such close range.

Sichuan at that time had undergone the worst floods in thirty years.

They killed 1,358 people and did about $1.5 billion damage. What impressed me were the stories of heroism which came out of them.

An anonymous army of thousands of volunteers rescued 400,000 people stranded by the rising waters. Six hundred people drifted down one river for distances of 50 to 100 kilometers, clinging to tree branches, perched on house roofs, anything that could float.

Three girls and five boys were trapped in a submerged house in Willow Tree Village. The only two able to swim wrenched timbers from the house and tied the others to them. Pushing and shouting encouragement, they guided them through 25 kilometers of raging currents to safety.

I relate this because it demonstrates the toughness and persistence of the Sichuanese, cradle of many famous reformers, among them Deng Xiaoping.

Harbin, my next stop, in northwest China had changed, but not necessarily for the better since the two weeks I had spent there with Lin Biao in 1946. An industrial boom which sent clouds of thick black smoke from hundreds of factories polluted the air. The more than a million inhabitants ran around like wound-up toys, in a hurry to get somewhere. But there was a general air of cheerfulness underneath these retrograde signs of progress. The people, many from Shandong, were taller than most Chinese and humor matched their size.

It was impossible to find Lin Biao's old headquarters where I had stayed. He was a nonperson and no one remembered where it had been. The old Russian yacht club, brightly painted, swarmed with Chinese boys and girls. There was not a single Russian in sight. It had been converted into a recreation center.

From its wharf hundreds of holiday-makers embarked on steamers and small boats which plied their way through shoals of swimmers to a newly created amusement park on an island in the Sungari River. Dotted with pavilions, zoos, restaurants, and carnival rides, it was the nearest thing to Disneyland I had seen in China.

After a day there, I visited an immense dance hall that night to see a new phenomenon: singles night. Its aim, as elsewhere, was to bring couples together with marriage in view. Dating was a particular problem in Harbin because many of its young people came from different parts of China and had little chance to meet singles partners outside their work places.

When I arrived, 100 girls and 70 boys were dancing to the strains of two big bands playing American tunes and a new, Deng-era dance number called "the collective." It looked like an American square dance and encouraged mixing.

Ice Cream and soft drinks were on sale, but no alcohol.

"We put ads in the newspapers and distributed invitations to various units," said Li Ganshan, the dance director, a pleasant, bespectacled woman of 39 dressed in a smartly tailored pants suit. "Five couples have become engaged so far, in three months. That's not much. But they are so terribly shy."

Mai Hua, 30, petite and bright-eyed, is one of the engaged girls. Whatever she may be, she is not shy. A teacher in a department store kindergarten, she knew what she wanted and seemed to have gotten it in Huang Tianhua, also 30, in charge of deliveries for cooking gas. Quiet, bashful, he let her do most of the talking except to say, at one point, "it was love at first sight."

Dressed in a plaid blue skirt and white blouse, Mai Hua said: "We both enjoy music and singing, and, of course, dancing. We dated after the first dance, in June. Since then, on our days off, we go to the theater, to the workers' club, or just stroll along the river embankment. It's not easy, but we have been able to steal some precious moments together.

The guitars twanged and the trumpets blared. Two boys, looking self-conscious, glided by holding each other at arm's length.

When will Mai Hua and Huang get married? I asked.

"We don't know yet," said Mai Hua with a little toss of her head. "I want to test him first."

You could tell by her tone of voice, half joking, half serious, that she meant it.

She said she would bring to the marriage a quite considerable dowry, comparatively speaking. She lived with her parents and had a tape recorder, a small electric organ, a radio, a bicycle, and a black-and-white TV.

"I have nothing," said Huang. "A camera . . ."

His voice trailed off.

She earns 43 yuan basic salary and 10 yuan in allowances each month. He got 45.20 yuan and 20 yuan allowances. Each had managed to save 700 yuan, at the then dollar rate, about $320.

They differed on one thing: He wanted her to live with his parents but although she was fond of them preferred to have an apartment of their own.

Through his company he would get a one-bedroom flat with toilet, kitchen, shower, and small sitting room for 2 yuan a month, less than a dollar. (These pre-inflation rates explain why some Chinese, despite the new freedoms, are nostalgic for the old days of a planned economy.)

Her father, a middle school principal, was tortured and demoted by the Red Guards during the Cultural Revolution. His experience, repeated hundreds of thousands of times, had soured the younger generation on politics.

"We are not interested in political problems," said Mai Hua. "Young people have to struggle to build their own lives through the new modernization plan. The Cultural Revolution taught us a bitter lesson."

The queue formed for the "collective." The music, waltz-like, struck up and the couples gravely went through their paces, bowing and criss-crossing.

"I wish we had had singles dances before," said a 28-year-old railway worker married a year ago who, with his wife, were chaperons.

"We met at our work place. I repair rail cars and she is in the office. But it was difficult. Friends joke and gossip if you start dating. This way is better."

Strolling down the broad Avenue of Heavenly Peace and then browsing through the courtyards and palaces of the Forbidden City I encountered thousands of Chinese. They were very much the same as I had known them in 1971 during the ping pong visit, except for one thing. They no longer wore Mao badges. These shiny metal likenesses of the Great Helmsman had become in the Deng era, collectors' items.

Gone too were the ubiquitous little red books of Mao's quotations brandished in the bad old days of the Cultural Revolution like Maoist credentials.

Few of the artifacts of that era remained. The Summer Palace had been cleared of Mao statues, busts, and banners and the loudspeakers had fallen silent, to everyone's relief. Mao portraits also disappeared from public buildings, hotels, railway stations, walls, and cultural sites. A few were in the expected places, such as the gate to the Forbidden City, the Historical Museum, and Beijing's main rail station. These exceptions proved the rule.

All this was part of the downplaying of the Mao myth. In his lifetime, he insisted on being the leader, even though many of his comrades-in-arms had worked as hard, suffered as much, and were as nationally popular as he. Pilloried during the Cultural Revolution, some of them harried to death, they now were being given their due.

Liu Shaoqi, Mao's No. 1 foe, was the most famous. I was astonished to see him reappear, ten years after his death, in an exhibition celebrating the history of the Chinese Communist Party in the years of struggle and bloodshed preceding victory. This was a news story and I hurried back to the office to file it. A nonperson since his 1967 purge, he was shown in photographs, a painting, and an account of the party's achievements. The vast retrospective filled forty rooms in the Historical Museum, which drew immense crowds in October.

Staged only a few yards from Mao's mausoleum in Tiananmen Square, it appeared to include almost everyone Mao had hated, including Lin Biao. The curator of the exhibition said it represented the new realism and honesty in the official approach to history. But with honors recently bestowed on Liu's widow, favorable publicity for his daughter and an oblique reference to him by the party's No. 2 man, Ye Jianying, it appeared to be—and was—the prelude to Liu's rehabilitation.

Another interesting aspect of the exhibition was the absence of Mao's widow, Jiang Qing. The curators explained rather weakly that she had not gained prominence until after 1949, the final year covered by the show. She was Mao's wife; what other credentials did they need?

One of the most romantic of Mao's victims, He Long, also had been rehabilitated and was the subject of a play staged in Beijing. I knew him in Yan'an, had a long interview with him during which he strode up and down the room, striking his riding boots with a whip. He looked like an oriental Clark Gable and had all his dash and charm. Born to a poor family in Mao's Hunan Province, he stabbed a government official to death during a big famine, escaped and created a Peasants' Army of several thousand men which robbed the rich and helped the poor, earning him the name Red Bandit.

Rewarded after 1949 with the somewhat humdrum job of Sports Minister, he was denounced in 1967 as a "counterrevolutionary revisionist element," which meant he resisted Mao and leaned toward Moscow. Broken physically and mentally, he died in disgrace.

Zhu De now was being identified as cofounder of the Red Army and he was the subject of poems and stories on his life. Ye Jianying, 81, had returned to public attention in another way. A composition based on one of his poems was played by the Beijing Central Philharmonic Orchestra.

Zhou Enlai, reviled by Jiang Qing in his last years, was portrayed in a song-and-dance revue at the Capital Theater.

Among those rehabilitated was Peng Dehuai, the blunt, forthright former defense minister and hero of the Korean War who alone had dared challenge Mao. The official story of his torture and death at the hands of the Red Guards appeared two years later in *Memoirs of a Chinese Marshal*, put out by the Peking Foreign Languages Publishing House. It said, in part:

Peng Dehuai's refusal to admit any crime infuriated his interrogators. They kicked him until his ribs were fractured and lungs injured. Beatings sent him unconscious to the floor.

He fought to the last. It is said that the noise he made banging on the table and shouting at his investigators shook the house.

"I fear nothing, you can shoot me!" he roared. "Your days are numbered. The more you interrogate the firmer I'll become."

Peng Dehuai was interrogated until he was bedridden. He was deprived of the right to sit, to rise up, to drink water, to go to the toilet or to turn over in bed. By the time he died on November 19, 1974, he had gone through over 130 interrogations.

The redoubtable Madame Wang was the nearest thing to a dictator in Beijing. Strong men paled when she knocked on their door.

This rosy-cheeked proletarian was the czarina of Zhijiayuan, the cluster of apartment buildings housing a thousand journalists and diplomats, which had become my home.

She listened with glacial indifference to my cries of anguish after I had pleaded in vain for permission to hire someone to paint the walls, install an air conditioner, or replace the ancient kitchen gas stove with a new one.

Madame Wang knew that all my lamentations were in vain, that there was no one else I could turn to. Her battalion of plumbers, painters, electricians, plasterers, carpenters, and mechanics belonged to the Bureau of Diplomatic Services of which she was the good and faithful, if immovable, servant. They were the only ones allowed to work in this foreign ghetto and two others like it which accounted for most of the three thousand *waiguoren* (foreigners) in Beijing.

The inhabitants of these ghettoes were the spoiled darlings of the People's Republic living in an island of luxury and comfort sharply in contrast to the gray poverty around them. High walls and permanent guards "protected" them from nebulous threats from the outside and made it possible for Big Brother to keep an eye on them.

The diplomatic services people not only attended to the general housekeeping but were prepared to supply, at short notice, some of the extras which made life bearable. These included waiters and waitresses for cocktail parties, interpreters, office managers, cooks, drivers, telex operators, and messengers. For 25 yuan, or about $25, they would produce uniformed professionals to lay out the "small chow," mix the dry martinis, serve a full- course dinner, and wash up afterward, leaving the apartment as spotless as they had found it.

I was lucky. My cook specialized in Western cuisine. This was a rarity much prized. The restaurants of Beijing were famous for their Chinese cooking. Almost none, including the newly opened Maxim's, had anything spectacular to offer in the way of Western food. Invitations to the AP dinner table were much sought after. My successor, unaware of the jewel I had acquired, insisted after my departure on getting Chinese noodles daily. The cook, his professional pride wounded, quit in disgust.

I think it can safely be said that I have never been a good, much less a great, cook. The kitchen, old fashioned and tiny, discouraged me. Padding sleepy-eyed into it the first night in search of a glass of orange juice, I encountered a further deterrent. When the light went on, what I took to be the black wall dissolved into a horde of madly fleeing cockroaches! No amount of washing, scrubbing, or lethal temptations discouraged them. They refused to abandon their cozy refuge. Presumably of the hardy Siberian variety, they probably were brought in two decades earlier by the Soviet builders.

The arrival of my assistant, Victoria Graham, from New York, posed a new problem for Madam Wang. Where to put her? After a few weeks in the Beijing Hotel, she found her a small but comfortable apartment on the seventh floor of my building. It had one drawback. The windows were barred, giving the interior the look of a well-furnished jail for women. The problem was that she could not escape to the adjoining roof should there be a fire or earthquake. Madam Wang was flint-like in her refusal to remove them.

"Why not?" I asked. She refused to reply.

"Then how about doing something to make it possible to open them in case of emergency?

Stony silence

I pleaded, I joked, I cajoled. I appealed to her on the ground of health. Vicky could take the sun on the roof if the bars were removed. She would not budge. The mangled and charred body of Vicky Graham rose before my eyes. I pictured the horrid scene in lurid colors. Madam Wang allowed herself a wintry smile and, like a lady jailer, her keys clanking in the ring on her belt, left. The bars, I believe, are still there.

A fortyish matron of otherwise pleasant mien, Madam Wang was at her stoniest in the case of the new kitchen gas stove. I had bought it in Hong Kong, along with a refrigerator, the air conditioners, living room furniture, and an eight-piece dining room set of Chinese design. I had been warned that no ordinary gas stove would work in Beijing because of the nature of the gas which tended to eat away the gas rings. Bearing this in mind, I bought a handsome stove especially adjusted for use in Beijing. When it arrived, I unhooked the beaten up old stove, the only furnishing in the apartment when I arrived, and had it carted to the cellar. Then I hooked up the new creation.

Within hours Madam Wang, keys still clanking, was on the scene.

"What," she asked in her perfect English, "is going on here?"

"It's a new stove," I said nervously, not knowing what to expect.

"Then where," she persisted frostily," is the old one?"

"In the cellar," I replied.

"You are perhaps not aware," she said in the tone of voice that suggested I was perfectly aware, "that that stove is a permanent fixture of this apartment. It is not to be removed under any circumstances."

What, I asked her, about my new stove which I had brought at great expense from Hong Kong.

"If you insist on keeping it," she said, "We will have to charge you one hundred U.S. dollars a month for the old one."

I gasped in astonishment.

"One hundred dollars!" I exclaimed. "What on earth for?"

"Storage," she said. "We will have to keep it in storage until you move out when we will return it to the kitchen from which it came."

The new cook, at this point, arrived on the scene. I explained the situation, pointed to the shiny new stove and told him it was his to create great dishes by. He lit the gas. It poured out in a modest but efficient blue flame.

"*Buhao!*" he exclaimed. "No good!"

"What do you mean?" I asked, incredulous.

"The flame is hotter on the old one. Besides I'm used to that kind of stove. Please bring it back."

Defeated, I bowed to Madam Wang and she left, triumphant.

Next day, I showed the sparkling new stove to Crabbe.

"It's yours," I said, for the purchase price plus shipping costs. I hate to give it up but my cook prefers the old one."

He took it.

Whoever said "you can't go home again" has my undiluted sympathy. A Dragon Lady in the Textile Ministry said I could not.

Having failed on previous visits to find my 1947 residence at 16A Datianshuijing, the Lane of the Great Sweet Water Well, I made several other tries in 1979. It was not so much the place as the mood which lured me. Over the years I had seen, in my mind's eye, old Dr. Bussiere, pink-cheeked, mustache twirling upward, as he presided with gallic bonhomie over the little compound, a cell in the sleepy body of Beijing where I had spent so many languid days, and nights. I dreamt that somehow it had still survived, an oasis in a proletarian desert.

I thought back to the splendid table he set and the cobwebby wines which came from his cellar. What had happened, I wondered, to the Panchen Lama's wisdom tooth? Thirty years later, of course, the good doctor was gone, living in a heaven of crisply chilled muscadet and spice-scented bouillabaise.

Old men—and I was old by then—are plagued by a disease called nostalgia which agitates the synapses of the brain but produces drowsiness in others. Nostalgia drove me to persist even though the once-muddy lane eluded me. It had been easy in the old days when the main shopping street from which it depended was named Morrison Street. But now there were the additions to the Beijing Hotel and the new building of the *People's Daily* to confound my already imperfect sense of direction.

One day, thanks to the sensitive eyes and nose of my office manager, the dignified Mr. Gu, we found it. Mud no longer made walking in the lane hazardous: asphalt brought it resolutely up to date. There it was, on my left, the massive red double door (it looked smaller now) through which I had passed so many times. A number scrawled in white chalk revealed that it had been changed from 16A to 24.

Before knocking, I looked across the lane at the gate of the house once occupied by my old friend Jim Burke, the only man I knew able successfully to move from photographer to writer. It was in his house that Reynolds Packard said farewell with a single gulp which emptied his silver gift flask of gin. And there, next door, was the house of Plaut, the German antique collector from whom I had obtained my old Tang dynasty official.

The door of my old home swung open to reveal a rosy-cheeked girl, her hair in twin braids. Amused and possibly intrigued by this large foreigner in search of his Chinese roots, she led us in and introduced her handsome fiance, a fourth-year aeronautics student with whom she shared her room and life.

A wall ran through the middle of the courtyard, destroying the illusion of size which I had remembered and the lone tree, which had survived, understandably had grown larger. Children played under its shade.

The doctor's office and living quarters, once so comfortable in an over-stuffed French way, were clean but spartan, wooden chairs, tables, and desks of a depressingly utilitarian style having replaced the sofas, the antimacassars, the elegant Ming chairs and side tables. The glass cabinet in which had reposed his Chinese curios and the tooth of the sainted Panchen Lama was no more. A feeling of coldness in mid-summer was accentuated by the bare floor, innocent of its rich carpeting. Only the ceiling, with its fretwork, testified to a more opulent time.

Four iron beds from which the enamel had begun to peel, flowered wash basins, and a cement floor had turned my snug, little apartment into a barracks. A white porcelain bust of Chairman Mao, smiling benignly, stood in the spot once ruled by my austere, elegantly dignified Tang official.

Visits to other haunts of the past had prepared me for the disappointments of going home. But my reception at the hands of the dozen or so occupants had been so pleasant and so natural, I resolved to come back one day with a bottle or two of wine and a picnic lunch for a longer visit. They enthusiastically agreed.

Aware that Communist bureaucracy can be as bureaucratic as any other, I approached the idea cautiously. The Foreign Affairs Office of the Beijing municipal government thought it would be a splendid thing, a new rung in the ladder of Sino-American friendship. But the final authority, it said, must come from the Textile Ministry, which ran the place.

We put it to them in writing. After several days of study, the answer came back. Sorry, no.

Unwilling to go down to defeat, I asked Mr. Gu to phone the responsible official. It turned out to be a woman. Since she refused to give her name, I must be content to identify her as the Dragon Lady.

"You will not revisit the housing site at 24 Tatianshuijing for which we are responsible," she said haughtily.

I asked Mr. Gu to explain that it was an innocent request, only a picnic to get to know the people now living in my old house.

"*Buxing,*" she said adamantly. "No way."

"But why?" I persisted.

No answer.

Mr. Gu, usually the soul of coolness, began to get excited. A dark flush crept over his face. His voice rose. He shouted. She shouted back. The exchange lasted for several minutes. I did not ask him what was said: I prefer not to know.

The Dragon Lady would not budge. There would be no picnic within her jurisdiction.

Dr. Bussiere will understand, I hope, that I did everything I could. In China, you cannot really go home again.

All was far from being wine and roses in the Beijing of 1979. When I had arrived at the start of the year an ugly event intruded into the euphoria induced by Sino-American recognition and Deng's economic and political reforms. This was a daily demonstration on Chang An Avenue, in front of the prime minister's office, of a ragamuffin collection of men and women from the rural areas, some in bandages, others brandishing crutches, as they cried out for justice.

Rejects of the system, they were nonpersons, unattached to any of the work units or official organizations which are the life-lines of existence in China. For some reason or another, either criminal or political, they had been cut off from these sources of housing, food, and employment. Now, facing starvation, they demanded the right to become once more part of a society which had rejected them.

The government, embarrassed by the public display of this flotsam and jetsam of an imperfect system, hustled them off to a more remote corner of the capital, away from the eyes of the foreign visitors they wished to convince that all was for the best in this best of Marxist worlds. Graphic photographs of these wretched humans and continuing coverage by AP and other news organizations of their plight kept their cause alive until, one day, they were moved out of town. No one knew what happened to them after that.

A month after I reopened the permanent AP bureau in the Chinese capital, a new source of unquiet surfaced around Democracy Wall. For months it had been a tourist showplace, the gossipy and amusing forum for a newly liberated population, a wall newspaper for all to read. Then quite suddenly, its character changed. Political activists, some of them leftovers from the Cultural Revolution, turned it into a vehicle for their dissatisfactions with the government, the Communist Party, and the socialist system. Their leader, a handsome,

29-year-old veteran and zoo technician named Wei Jingsheng, edited
a dissident magazine called *Tansuo* (Explorations). When it was suppressed and some of the activists arrested, it went underground,
resurfacing five months later with a bold challenge to Deng.

"So long as dirt still exists on this piece of land, so long as servants run roughshod over masters in society, and so long as our
throats have not been cut, we shall by no means stop crying out," Wei
wrote defiantly.

Deng cracked down when the wall posters began attacking him by
name. Arrested, Wei was sentenced in a one-day trial to fifteen years
in prison. No reporters, other than those of the official Xinhua News
Agency, were permitted to cover the trial. AP picked up additional
details by interviewing some of the few spectators present.

In his later interview with me, Deng defended the severity of the
sentence. The crime, he said, was so grave that Wei could regard himself as lucky it was not longer.

Those who believed in Deng's human rights decrees and his establishment of a nominally fair system of criminal justice hoped the trial
would prove a model for the future. They were bitterly disappointed.
No witnesses were called for the defense, Wei was not permitted coun-
sel nor could he cross-examine the witnesses against him. In any
event it was monstrous, it seemed to many Chinese, that anyone should
be punished so savagely for expressing a political opinion. The trial
resembled one of those conducted in the cultural purge where even
defense attorneys were arrested for defending their clients.

Two things explained Deng's overreaction. The first was the fear,
groundless or not, that the Wei activists were seeking to purge him
as the Red Guards had done twice before. The second was his deep
attachment to socialism, a philosophy to which he had devoted his
life and fortune. Any threat to supplant it with democracy in any form
pushed the danger button in his makeup. In this he was like Mikhail
Gorbachev in the Soviet Union. He was willing to reform the system
but would fight to the death against abolishing it.

The pro-democracy demonstrators of 1989, a decade later, failed
because they were unable to recognize that this little man with the
mischievous grin could be rational when it came to remaking China
but totally irrational when his lifelong political beliefs were challenged.

Deng could have escaped humiliation and punishment had he re-
canted his pragmatic beliefs during the Cultural Revolution. But he
refused. In his hatred of those who tried to make him do so, he was
ready to set aside all the rules of fair play and justice. In the closing
weeks of 1980, he did that in the trial of his old and despised antago-
nist, Mao's widow, Jiang Qing, and her friends and accomplices.

In a lifetime of acting, first on the stage, then in the movies, and finally as wife of the most powerful man in Communist China, Jiang Qing rose to her greatest dramatic heights during her December 1980 trial for an assortment of "crimes" committed during the Cultural Revolution.

There were nine codefendants, including the three other members of the Gang of Four accused, in a lengthy indictment, of committing "counterrevolutionary crimes" and doing "enormous damage to the state."

Often compared to the beautiful but cruel Empress Wu of the Tang dynasty and the Manchu Empress Dowager, Jiang Qing carried herself more like an empress than a criminal. The men cringed and fawned, their spirits broken, but Mao's 67-year-old widow walked into the court head high, shoulders thrown back, eyes defiantly sweeping the ranks of her accusers.

Confined to a cage, as were the others, she made the telling point that in all matters her late, great husband approved. By insisting on this she tried—and nearly succeeded—in turning it into a trial of Mao himself, something none of the judges dared do.

"I was Chairman Mao's dog," she cried in her high-pitched voice. "Whomever he told me to bite I bit."

The indictment accused her of hounding 35,000 of her enemies to their death and shattering the lives of half a million others. It said she isolated Mao in his old age and plotted to seize power even while he was dying.

Breathing fire at one moment, silent at others, she acted like the accuser rather than the accused. Those trying her, she said cuttingly, should be in the dock beside her; they had committed all the crimes imputed to her alone. It looked, as the trial ground on, as though she would not be allowed to talk in her own defense. But she insisted and the judges sat back, stunned at her counterattack.

Dressed in a dark pants suit, wearing glasses, she looked more like a severe school teacher than the glamour girl she had always wished to be. On several occasions she indulged in hysterical outbursts and had to be frog-marched from the room. She held center stage throughout. The others, only bit players, readily admitted everything and eagerly testified against her, thinking that they would be treated leniently. Jiang Qing had nothing but scorn for their weak-kneed performance. She was determined to go out as she had entered—a star.

Open only to 600 hand-picked Chinese spectators, an eager public learned the details again, as in the Wei Jingsheng case, only through the Xinhua News Agency and brief television clips supplied to Chinese and foreign media by the equally official Beijing radio-television network. By the time the verdict was announced a month later, there had been forty-two sessions of the court, forty-nine witnesses had testified, and 873 pieces of evidence had been examined. In a 14,000-word judgment—made by the party politburo dominated by Deng Xiaoping—Jiang Qing and the most intelligent of the gang, Zhang Chunqiao, got the death penalty, postponed for two years to see whether they would repent. The others received sentences varying from sixteen years to life.

The Beijing *People's Daily,* reporting the sentences, called the trial "a great victory for the socialist legal system" which would "help to restore the sanctity of law."

To many observers, including myself, there seemed little evidence to support this claim. Under the new 1979 legal code, defendants could call witnesses, cross-examine the state's witnesses, and present evidence on their own behalf. Nothing in the restricted reporting of the trial indicated Jiang Qing had been able to do any of these things.

Doubts could have been dispelled by allowing foreign reporters or foreign judicial observers to attend. If, as the *People's Daily* said, it had been a test of the new legal system, this could have been confirmed by release of the full transcript. It was not done.

What could not be denied was that the ten defendants got a better deal than did their many past victims. Trials then were a farce. Defense lawyers were themselves jailed for daring to defend the so obviously guilty. Soon there was no pretence and Jiang Qing's enemies quietly disappeared into nameless prisons, reeducation centers, or rural hard labor. Thousands died. No one had the courage to fight back.

When, in 1982, the time came to determine whether Jiang Qing had repented—if she had not she would be executed—the judges announced in a fuzzily worded statement that she had not "resisted reform in a flagrant way," even though she insisted as adamantly as ever that she was innocent. But no one wanted to find out what effect execution of the widow of the chairman would have on the masses. Her sentence was commuted to life.

Eight months after the reprieve, Lu Jian, spokesman for the Ministry of Justice, told me that she remained unrepentant.

"The facts are clear," he said. "She is one of the most difficult people to reform. Chairman Mao once said that a few counterrevolutionaries have brains of granite."

She had seen no one but unidentified members of her family during her three and a half years in the notorious Qincheng Prison outside Beijing.

"She is healthy. But she is old [70] so we don't make her do labor. She cleans her own room, can watch television, listen to the radio, has her own tape recorder," he said.

The other three members of the Gang of Four were in the same prison, he said, but isolated from each other. They too were exempted from manual labor.

"There is no special program for them. But they are told to reform themselves. Jiang Qing is treated better than other prisoners."

In the beginning, she wore prison garb, "but now she wears her own clothes. It is not true, as some Western reports say, that she has lost her hair. She eats quite good food, including pork and fish dishes. If she is sick, she is given medical treatment, just as other prisoners are."

One day in the hot summer of 1991, Jiang Qing, the girl who had risen from the grinding poverty of Shandong Province to become a Shanghai actress notorious for her scarlet love affairs, then as Mao's wife, the First Lady of Red China, decided to put an end, through hanging, to the comedy and tragedy which had been her life.

She was my age. Had she not broken her promise not to meddle in politics, she might be alive today.

In 1980 I left the Beijing AP operation to my talented and imaginative successor, Vicky Graham, and returned to Tokyo, my baggage piled high with so many books, mostly on China, the airline people charged me $800 overweight.

For the next four years I roamed Asia as an AP Special Correspondent, one of seven, covering whatever story caught my interest. I returned at least once a year, sometimes twice, to write a dozen or so stories each time on China, a country and a people that had to me been endlessly fascinating and, in its rapid drive to a market economy, continued to be.

When I retired, at the age of 70 in 1984, my interest in China and its fortunes continued in high gear. I wrote and lectured, and read everything I could lay my hands on which had the word "China" in it. I kept up contacts with Chinese friends, professors, students, travelers, to learn the truth about what was going on after Tiananmen.

I also had time to think back on my long years of involvement with China, to reflect on the role foreign reporters, be they travelers, missionaries, diplomats, or journalists, have played in shaping Western perceptions of it.

Marco Polo was the first Western reporter, if you stop to think about it, on China. Received courteously, with his father, in the court of Kublai Khan in the thirteenth century, he gave a glowing account of Chinese customs, culture, and civilization. But he was not the best and most accurate of reporters. He owed too much to the Chinese and wished too eagerly to keep their goodwill to be entirely dispassionate. The result was a great story, one of the most exciting ever told, but it did not tell us of the harsher realities, the poverty, the corruption, and the cruelty.

For centuries the West accepted his glowing version of what China was like. In the sixteenth century, Western missionaries, also beholden to the Chinese for tolerance and favors, reasserted this positive appraisal. So much so that Voltaire and the scholars of the French Enlightenment believed China to be the best-governed and wisest of nations, its subjects paragons of restraint living in perfect harmony with each other. It was, Voltaire said, a model Europe could imitate.

A savage and senseless civil war in the mid-nineteenth century which pitted an army of pseudo-Christian believers—its leader claimed to be a brother of Christ—against the Manchus disabused many foreigners of Voltaire's notion. Fifty million people died before this exercise in folly ended, revealing the Chinese to be just as frail, misguided, and badly governed as anyone else.

Things did not get any better in the twentieth century which opened with a rebellion of fanatics, called the Boxers, ostensibly against the Manchus. The shrewd and hard Empress Dowager soon directed it against the foreign imperialists who were then engaged in a feeding frenzy on China's prostrate body. It took a joint military expedition of Americans, Europeans, and Japanese to raise the siege of their embassies in Beijing. The experience left a bad taste in foreign mouths, a bitter one in those of the defeated Chinese who, forced to pay a huge indemnity, had to restore the rights and privileges the imperialists deemed theirs by divine favor.

American missionaries, largely Protestant, painted a glowing picture of China in the years before the Boxer uprising. They were, in a sense, the first American reporters. In slide-and-lecture shows across America they described the misery and the potential of the Chinese peasants among whom they lived. When the Chinese responded in a lukewarm way to their urging that they abandon Buddhism and Confucianism in favor of Christianity, and the Boxers attacked their missions, killing many, the mood changed. The Chinese were then seen as evil, scheming, filthy, and self-serving. By the 1930s, they were portrayed in the popular press, in books and movies, as inscrutable, emotionless, murderous. The United States closed its door to them in the early years of the century.

Despite this, a hidden reservoir of American affection for China and the Chinese remained. Two children of missionary parents tapped into that reservoir and once more changed the image.

One was Pearl Buck, author of a sensitive and popular novel called *The Good Earth,* on the patient and enduring peasant which created American sympathy for them and their impoverished country.

The other was Henry Luce, head of a publishing empire which included the widely circulated *Time* and *Life* magazines. He used them to create support for Chiang Kai-shek whom he described as leader of a gallant people struggling to survive the sledge-hammer pounding of the invading Japanese Imperial Army.

Through the articles his correspondents wrote, Americans gained a good deal of information about Chinese culture and the Kuomintang the Generalissimo led. But there was little about the Chinese Communists with whom he had been at war since the Shanghai Massacre of 1927. The Generalissimo threw a blockade around their capital at Yan'an, making it impossible for Western reporters to go there.

The Japanese, dropping their bombs on Pearl Harbor in 1941, inadvertently helped end Yan'an's isolation. Now a wartime American ally in the fight against Japan, China suddenly became a Big Story which had to be covered. The correspondents, pouring into Chongqing's press hostel, aggressively tackled aspects of China the smattering of prewar reporters had not had the facilities, or the inclination, to report. Their efforts were hampered by both Chinese and American censorship. (Jack Anderson, then a young war correspondent, told me he was drafted into the army, after the war had ended, because he defied the American military censor and sent out what he said was a purely political story.)

What the Americans and other foreign news people wanted, after they had reported exhaustively on the Nationalists, was a visit to a still-barricaded Yan'an. They got it after appealing to their publishers who, in turn, put pressure on the Roosevelt and Truman administrations.

After Truman announced the Marshall mission, Yan'an could no longer be hidden away from the foreign press. One of its conditions was that correspondents have free access to all of China included in the mediation effort.

Yet, because they were short-staffed and the day-to-day story in Yan'an could not rival the news coming out of Nationalist Nanjing, Shanghai, and Beiping, few Americans stayed more than two weeks there. When they visited, it was for two or three days only. As far as I can determine, only Jack Belden, besides myself, spent more than a month in the Communist areas. He wrote a perceptive book on his experience.

I have often wondered whether the American view of China might have been different if we had been allowed to report on the scene from 1949 to 1979.

The Chinese position was political, not realistic. It barred us because our governments had not yet recognized Beijing diplomatically. In doing so, it implied that we were the creatures of our government, as the Chinese press then was. They were wrong. The reporting they could have received from a Western press corps on the scene during the first thirty seminal years of their governance would have been as fair and even-handed, with rare exceptions, as they were during the long years of China Watching. Being there would certainly have added an extra dimension to our stories.

Having said this, one is led to ask whether the presence or absence of the press, particularly television, exerts an undue influence on an event which is unfolding. The answer is as nettling as the one might give to the Zen riddle about the tree alone in the forest. Does it make a noise when it falls?

The British historian, A. J. P. Taylor, reports that the greatest tank battle in history took place between Soviet and Nazi forces during World War II. But because it took place on D-Day in Europe, and there were no Western reporters present it did not become known until twenty years later. Similarly, he said, the U.S. submarine force had, in effect, won the war against Japan by sinking all of its shipping six months before the surrender. But because no American reporters were attached to the undersea service, no one knew it. Except the Japanese.

One of my friends, an American network correspondent, was assigned to Beijing in the first batch of reporters allowed to reopen permanent bureaus. For we print people, this was a choice assignment. Whatever we wrote, even if it repeated what our British, French, and German colleagues had already reported, got page one treatment. It was not so with the network people. The Chinese, for some obscure reason, would not let them have the full-time producers, sound and light people they needed to get the story out. They thus were reduced to radio spots or an occasional special project done with outside staff who had to get special visas. My friend, a China expert, treaded water during his three years in Beijing, his career retarded by the almost total invisibility that went with the post.

The Tiananmen demonstrations of May and June 1989 exemplified the power of television to shape the event it was covering. The big names of American TV, the anchormen whose shows were seen by millions of viewers each day, were on hand with their crews because of the state visit of Soviet President Mikhail Gorbachev and his wife, Raisa. They stayed on to photograph and report the mounting tide of excitement pouring over the square. Though the print press also was reporting these events in headlines, what the demonstrators saw was the television reportage, beamed back to China each day. That it affected them and many millions of other Chinese watching at home, even more deeply than it did the American television audience, seems undeniable. Its leaders, courageous and determined, were encouraged by these broadcasts to continue their street marches perhaps longer than they had originally intended. Watched on Chinese television the Tiananmen massacre touched off demonstrations in major cities all over the country.

Tibet is another example of the important role of words and pictures in shaping attitudes and policies.

When I interviewed the boy Panchen Lama in 1947 it was little known, a mysterious but seldom visited land at the top of the world. Though nominally independent, the British and Chinese fought for influence, pitting one faction of the lamas against the other. These maneuvers, sometimes bloody, went largely unnoticed in the West.

When the Tibetans rose in rebellion in 1959, there was no one there to report it. It was not until after the Ping Pong opening in 1971 that Western reporters got their first glimpse of it. Floyd Gibbons, a famous publicist and TV personality, was among the first to go. His book aroused increased interest in this remote and picturesque country.

Regular visits by the Beijing-based foreign press corps further opened it to the outside gaze. It soon became a prize tourist destination, earning valuable foreign exchange for the Beijing regime. But this new exposure had its risks for the government. Reporters sometimes were on the scene to record instances of brutal repression. Tourists armed with cameras did the same, exposing a policy Beijing would have preferred to keep hidden away in the closet.

And this leads us to another kind of reporter, the ubiquitous tourist. China depends more than most countries on the revenues which organized tourism brings in. One of the crippling side effects of the Tiananmen massacre was a 50 percent drop in tourism. The pain in hard currency loss was great.

Like the missionaries of old, the tourists help educate the people of America through their stories, repeated at a thousand family gatherings, and their snapshots all too readily available for anyone to see.

They are a guarantee that China, no matter how hard line it may be, will strive to keep the door, which Zhou said I had opened in 1971, from ever closing.

8

Epilogue

The journey which began for me at the age of 13 on a golf course in central Maine, where I stared in horror at the photos of the headless victims of the 1927 Shanghai Massacre, has come to an end. But I still see the antagonists and protagonists—Chiang Kai-shek, George Marshall, Mao Zedong, Zhu De, Zhou Enlai, Liu Shaoqi, Deng Xiaoping, and many others—so vividly they seem alarmingly alive.

You may well ask why, among the many people of all kinds I have known in a half-century of journalism, this should be so.

The answer is that my China experience was a rare one. How many persons are privileged to have been eyewitnesses, not only to a revolution, but to the first thirty-five years of the government and society it produced?

Revolutions usually are short, nasty, and brutish. The one in China began in 1911 with Sun Yat-sen and the overthrow of the Manchus, continued for a while under joint Kuomintang-Communist auspices then split in two, with the Generalissimo on one side and Mao on the other. The Shanghai Massacre photos record that break.

Unlike the Soviet struggle to seize power, which lasted only a few months, that of the Chinese Communists endured for twenty-two long years. Their story has an epic quality, combining courage, suffering, sacrifice, persistence, chicanery, deception, and brutality, which no other in this century can equal. It is, in fact, more saga than epic, a long, rambling tale of human endurance and, however misguided it may seem to others, unflagging faith.

I joined the Associated Press news agency at the age of 22 and was its faithful, if often critical, servant for forty-seven years. Its high standards of reporting—objectivity, accuracy, and speed—and its insistence on fairness, giving both sides of the story, commanded my loyalty despite its often niggardly approach to financial reward.

In my reporting on China, and elsewhere, I tried to stick to these principles, showing no public favoritism. But I remained human and thought my own thoughts.

My seven months in Yan'an with Mao and his comrades without question influenced my thinking. Their idealism and unflagging dedication to restoring China to the independence it had lost to foreign freebooters, plus their determination to cure China's many ills, appealed powerfully to me. On the other hand, their inflexible dogmatism and tight control of the people, press, and politics of North China turned me off. I believe I succeeded in keeping these conflicting emotions out of my reporting, but I could not help hoping that, victorious, Yan'an would create a brave, new world.

Mao's excesses dashed these hopes only to have them revived when Deng took over. I was not alone—all China and much of mankind joined me—in wishing him well. In his first ten years, he fulfilled the confidence they placed in him, beginning the dismantling of Mao's central command economy and replacing it with what became a flourishing free market. When he gave the press a freedom it had never enjoyed, freed the arts from the shackles Jiang Qing had forged, opened the door to foreign exchanges, and captivated us by wearing a ten-gallon cowboy hat in Texas, he seemed the answer to China's prayers.

But Deng's capitalist incentives created grave problems. Suddenly, after three decades of a predictable, unchanging life—gray but affordable—Deng ordered them to make the leap into the free market. Inflation, unemployment, rising prices, and widespread corruption followed. Some got rich but many others were impoverished.

The street demonstrations of 1989 initially were aimed at this unsettled situation. As week stretched into tempestuous week, and the klieg lights of world television shone on them, the student-led demonstrators came out for greater press freedom and political democracy. It was almost an afterthought, but from that point on they were not ordinary demonstrators but "pro-democracy" ones, a label which engaged the sympathy of millions in the watching West. Though they denied they wished to overthrow Deng's reforms and replace them with American-style democracy, the pro-democracy tag stuck. No government would allow a challenge to its authority to last so long. Had it been put down with tear gas and water hoses, it might have been just another violent episode, soon forgotten. Tanks and bullets turned it into a massacre of the innocents, a defeat for a vaguely understood democracy, vaguely demanded.

Why did Deng, knowing that his reforms were at risk, nonetheless order the tanks into the square? There are a number of explanations, none officially admitted. He had spent a lifetime fighting for his brand of socialism and had told me, and others, his reforms were meant to reinvigorate it, not replace it, with Western-style democracy. Democracy, to him, was a dirty word, a negation of all he believed in.

Perhaps he believed that the demonstrators would tire and go away. Instead, enjoying their international television fame, they picked up strength, were joined by hundreds of thousands of ordinary Chinese.

Carried away by enthusiasm, they forgot that Deng had twice been purged, his son crippled, by youthful Red Guards in the Cultural Revolution. When the demonstrators set fire to army trucks and hanged soldiers the night before the massacre, it did not take much to convince him that once again he faced the chaos (*luan*) of those Maoist days. He was old and probably frightened but determined not to be purged a third time.

The old guard survivors of the Long March were another factor. Deng, sweeping away the deadwood, aroused their anger in 1985 by putting them on the shelf because they opposed his reforms. Allied with the hard-line premier, Li Peng, they used the Tiananmen massacre to regain power and dismantle many of them. For a while it looked as though the clock had been turned back to the absolute dictatorship of the Party. In his mid-eighties, and craftier than his foes, Deng refused to admit defeat or step aside. His espousal of the Open Door internationally made the survival of his ideas, not those of the hardliners, desirable to his Western trade partners. Despite widespread criticism at home they lined up behind him. Armed with this support, he began chipping away at the restrictions Li Peng had imposed. The free market and some limited political reforms were restored. More subversive than guns, they thrive on individuality, competition, and personal freedom. Marxism, as we have known it, is the free market's enemy, democracy its natural state.

Deng has often been compared to Gorbachev. Each sought to bring his country out of feudalism into the twentieth century. Each hoped to save communism by borrowing the tools of the industrial democracies—limited capitalism and controlled democracy, the incentives of a free market and just enough individual freedom to keep the masses quiet.

Gorbachev failed because he introduced deep and far-reaching political reforms on a weak economic base. The hunger and confusion which followed doomed the Soviet Union which, unable to cope, broke up into separate states.

Deng shrewdly avoided these errors. The economic infrastructure he had put in place survived the internal shocks of inflation, unemployment and instability. An efficient rail system got food to the right places in time. Deplorable as it was to many, the harsh crackdown on the Tiananmen demonstrators proved to be a boon for Deng. It discouraged any thought of demonstrations or rebellion after the collapse of the Communist parties of the Soviet Union and Eastern Europe. Many Chinese may well have wished to shrug off their own socialist system but they dared not, in the wake of the brutality they had witnessed, do so.

Another factor was that democracy was a hope rather than a conviction for the Tiananmen students. It did not have the cherished place it had among Europeans, descendants of a tradition which went back to ancient Greece.

Few Chinese know what democracy is. In a long and splendid history, they have experienced nearly every kind of government, including a form of communism called Legalism in the reign of the first emperor, Qin Shihuangdi, in the third century B.C. The Kuomintang promised democracy after a period of tutelage had passed. The Communists made their bow to the idea with a National People's Congress. It was a rubber stamp for the Party, its members essentially appointed by it. Deng did hold multiparty elections at the city district and county level in 1980; it was a revival of something tried in 1954.

Family values, based on Confucianism, remain strong despite everything, my Chinese friends tell me. Even, or particularly, among high-ranking Communists, family interests often come first.

This does not mean that the People's Republic lacked a constitution or that it failed, in it, to spell out, elaborately, the human rights of its citizens. In some ways it was superior to those in Western countries. It not only guaranteed freedom of worship but freedom not to worship. The problem, as Shakespeare put it, was that it was more honored in the breach than the observance. Put another way, it was only words on paper, never invoked. Like their comrades in Moscow, the Chinese described themselves as democrats. They knew the enormous appeal democracy had for their people and third world countries. It was cynical play-acting which fooled no one.

In the post-Tiananmen recovery period, Deng's revived market reforms succeeded, perhaps all too well. They brought prosperity to coastal, rural, and southern China. A new god, money, replaced the old idols. The China of the 1990s, with its skyscrapers defacing Beijing, its expensive hotels, flashy automobiles, choking pollution, and spreading crime fulfilled, with a vengeance, the fear Mao expressed to me of the corrupting influence of the big cities. Yan'an was a forgotten symbol in this fast-growing new society.

It used to be that the West dreamt of supplying oil for the lamps of China. Now, in an ironic reversal, China supplied shoes and textiles, radios, and television sets for the once-hated barbarian/imperialist. Its trade surplus with the United States was second only to that of Japan.

The trouble with all this was that economic development proved uneven. And political reforms lagged far behind those of the market. China hobbled rather than walked, one leg shorter than the other.

More democracy, not less, might have restored the economic balance. But the Old Guard clung to its rigid ways, keeping a wary eye on intellectuals and making sure that everyone walked a politically correct line. In this situation, where making money was acceptable and political activity not, no one talked about the Communist party and its objectives any more. Suppressing dissent, it choked off any meaningful dialogue between the party and the people. It had become irrelevant.

This did not mean that the critics and the pro-democrats abandoned their beliefs. They merely went underground, mouthed the usual slogans in order to survive, kept their noses politically clean, and waited for the gerontocrats to die or retire. When they do, a younger generation, better educated, more international and more realistic than Deng's will take over.

But there is no guarantee that it will choose democracy as we know it. For more than forty years the Chinese were fed large dosages of political conformity which will be hard to shrug off. Individuality, competition, and confrontation—earmarks of Western democracy—grew somewhat in the post-Tiananmen period but largely in the free play of the market. Applying them to a political system where all these qualities have long been discouraged will not be easy.

The absence of the rule of law—criminal and commercial codes were introduced by Deng only in the 1980s and haltingly applied—adds to the complexity of the problem. To succeed, the justice system must be shaken up. Because it allows political dissidents to be sent to "reeducation camps" without trial, millions live in a Chinese gulag dedicated to breaking their independent spirit. There is no appeal and they may languish forgotten and mistreated for years in these throwbacks to barbarism. Democracy cannot be built on such a forbidding foundation.

Human rights, as Westerners know them, remain largely unprotected in a China brought up on centuries of arbitrary imperial justice and even more arbitrary socialist rule. When Americans speak about human rights they talk right past their Chinese Communist listeners who deny the existence of political prisoners and apply the law swiftly and harshly in criminal cases because that is the way it always has been done. In a China which wears its civilized past all too lightly punishment for dozens of crimes, many economic, is death with a bullet to the head.

I look back with affection at China and the Chinese. The men and women revolutionaries I knew, both Communist and Nationalist, were larger than life. They had known periods of greatness and, as the poet says, had supped on horrors. Yet as individuals they often were modest, polite, and civilized in their contacts with me.

This was true, as well, of the ordinary Chinese, in their hundreds, I met along the way. They were not, as Voltaire believed, paragons of virtue. They laughed and they cried, they stole and dissembled and murdered like other humans. But they carried themselves with so much dignity, looked one so fearlessly in the eye, and were capable of such devotion one could easily visualize them as living in some great era, such as the Tang, for example, rather than in twentieth-century China.

I loved them for all the good reasons, their food, imaginatively created out of poverty, their gossamer art, their civilized ways and yes, even the cacophony of their opera. I hated them, or at least some of them, for blundering in attempting to apply an alien philosophy which they little understood, called Marxism, to a country unprepared for it. They could have plumbed the Marxist depths and found those undiscovered nuggets which advocated a more reasonable society, greater democracy, and a deeper happiness than their formulas envisaged. They need not have gone so far in their search for a role model; Western democracy, imperfect as it was, had virtues they could have enhanced and built on.

Two cities, Yan'an and Beijing, are China for me. I often dream of them. During the long, anxious years of seemingly endless China watching, they were often in my thoughts, both waking and asleep.

In my mind's eye I see Yan'an, the city of ten thousand caves, through a mist, a distant, almost unattainable goal at the end of a long journey.

I walk though dense forests and encounter Mao as I emerge into the plain. But why Mao? I would prefer to meet Zhou or any of the others. But there he is, aloof, detached, and prophetic, leading me into a citadel with turrets and towers, drawbridges and moats.

At other times I see Yan'an, uninhabited, a city of gleaming tall buildings, paved highways, and silent commuter trains.

Neither one is the city I knew, at the edge of the Gobi Desert. But they keep getting mixed up, in my dreams, with the Yan'an I did know. The old Yan'an is a highly personal experience for me. It was there that I met the survivors of the Shanghai Massacre and the Long March, where I began my career as a foreign correspondent. In those days it was important, exciting, seminal. Now it is a relic of the past. I could not be persuaded to live there again.

There is no ambivalence in my dreams of Beijing. It is eternal and unchanged. My heart beats with elation as my plane touches down at the airport, the small, old one, not today's coldly functional affair. The fast drive into the city, speeding past a blur of trees and farmhouses, brings back memories. I get out of the car, stretch, and look around me. The vistas are breath-taking, the long avenues running north and south, east and west, the Temple of Heaven on one horizon, the less visible Temple of Earth on the other. I stroll down Chang An, the avenue of Perpetual Peace, into Tiananmen Square and through the great gate leading to the Forbidden City. Why do I notice that the bronze phoenixes in front of the Throne Hall are covered in chicken-wire? Dreams are full of contradictions.

I am alone, but I hear the voices of old friends, long dead.

Then my steps take me down the muddy lane called the Great Sweet Water Well and I find myself before the lacquered red gate of 16A, where I lived in 1947. I enter and am bathed in the warm, cherubic smile of my old landlord, Dr. Bussiere. We pause to admire the Panchen Lama's wisdom tooth in its glass cabinet, pat Johnny's head as he leaps all over us, and sit down to yet another Chinese meal, enlivened by the golden wines of the doctor's cellar. We talk of nothings while the crickets chirp in their cages, the pigeons wheel through the night air making distant music, and the noodle vendors and scissor sharpeners cry out their wares. I retire to my comfortable, blue apartment and go to sleep under the gaze of my three-color glaze Tang official. Then I awake to find the blue gone and Chairman Mao's white plaster bust frowning down at me. I switch him off and go back to sleep.

The doctor leaves on his rounds and I am alone, in the shaded courtyard, leisurely reading a book while sipping jasmine tea. I look up and think to myself with a sigh that I have, at last, come home again.

Acknowledgments

Any book is the product not of one mind but many. This one is no exception. Without the input of many people it would not have seen the light.

I owe a debt to Prof. D. W. K. Kwok of the University of Hawaii for reading the manuscript and steering me to Anthony Cheung of Imprint Publications, who has patiently cooperated in its creation above and beyond a publisher's duty.

If the book makes sense and is relatively free of mistakes and bloopers, I owe this to my editor, Frank Gibney of Encyclopaedia Britannica, an old and valued friend.

Hijino Shigeki, former publisher of the Encyclopaedia Britannica Japan Yearbook and of Newsweek Japan, now Director of Publications, TBS-Britannica, was quite literally in at the creation, encouraging me when I most needed it. Raymond Chao, an old friend of my China and Hong Kong days, dug up valuable material which I have used in the manuscript.

I am grateful to my former AP boss, Roy Essoyan; my sharp-eyed onetime editor, Edwin Quigley White; and Bruce Dunning, CBS chief in Tokyo, a former Beijing correspondent, for reading the manuscript and making valuable suggestions. Another friend, Prof. William Zanella of Hawaii Pacific University, a China historian, followed the manuscript through to the end and gave informed advice.

Norm Goldstein, Special Projects editor of AP in New York, inspired me to begin the project and I give him my special thanks. Finally, I would not have undertaken it without the support and gentle prodding of my adopted son, Yoshihiro Takishita, an unofficial China watcher, to whom I have dedicated this memoir.

The views expressed are mine but who would be vain enough to insist that they were not influenced, in one way or another, by all of the above? I wouldn't.